Cash-in-Hand Work

Cash-in-Hand Work

The Underground Sector and
The Hidden Economy of Favours

Colin C. Williams
University of Leicester

First published 2004 by
PALGRAVE MACMILLAN
Houndmills, Basingstoke, Hampshire RG21 6XS and
175 Fifth Avenue, New York, N.Y. 10010
Companies and representatives throughout the world

PALGRAVE MACMILLAN is the global academic imprint of the Palgrave
Macmillan division of St. Martin's Press, LLC and of Palgrave Macmillan Ltd.
Macmillan® is a registered trademark in the United States, United Kingdom
and other countries. Palgrave is a registered trademark in the European
Union and other countries.

ISBN 1–4039–2172–5 hardback

This book is printed on paper suitable for recycling and made from fully
managed and sustained forest sources.

A catalogue record for this book is available from the British Library.

Library of Congress Cataloging-in-Publication Data
Williams, Colin C., 1961–
     Cash-in-hand work: the underground sector and the hidden economy
        of favours / Colin C. Williams.
        p. cm.
     Includes bibliographical references and index.
     ISBN 1–4039–2172–5 (cloth)
        1. Informal sector (Economics) – Evaluation. 2. Cash transactions.
     3. Social exchange. 4. Social capital (Sociology) 5. Informal sector
     (Economics) – Government policy. I. Title: The underground sector
     and the hidden economy of favours. II. Title: Hidden economy
     of favours. III. Title.

HD2340.8.W55 2004
330—dc22   2004046491

10 9 8 7 6 5 4 3 2 1
13 12 11 10 09 08 07 06 05 04

Printed and bound in Great Britain by
Antony Rowe Ltd, Chippenham and Eastbourne

This book is dedicated to Jan and Toby

Contents

List of Tables   viii

Acknowledgements   x

1 Introduction   1

Part I Examining Cash-in-hand Work:
Theory and Methods   13
  2 Theorising Cash-in-hand Work   15
  3 Methodologies for Measuring Cash-in-hand Work   40

Part II Socio-spatial Variations in the Nature
of Cash-in-hand Work   63
  4 Employment Status and Cash-in-hand Work   65
  5 Gender Variations in Cash-in-hand Work   84
  6 Geographical Variations in Cash-in-hand Work   106

Part III Evaluating the Implications of
the Policy Options   131
  7 Deterring Cash-in-hand Work   133
  8 A *Laissez-Faire* Approach   161
  9 Harnessing Cash-in-hand Work   177
 10 Conclusions   198

References   207
Index   230

List of Tables

1.1 Adjectives and nouns used to denote cash-in-hand work 3
2.1 Character of suppliers of cash-in-hand work in
English localities 28
2.2 Motives of purchasers of cash-in-hand work in
English localities 29
2.3 Motives of suppliers of cash-in-hand work in
English localities 32
3.1 List of tasks investigated in the English Localities Survey 58
3.2 Overview of areas studied in the English Localities Survey 60
4.1 Proportion of cash-in-hand work conducted by the
employed and non-employed in England 70
4.2 Wage rates for cash-in-hand work in Quebec region:
by employment status, 1993 and 1985 75
4.3 Mean wage rate for cash-in-hand work in England:
by employment status of individuals and households 75
4.4 Types of cash-in-hand work of the registered unemployed
and employed in English areas: by nature of customer 76
4.5 Reasons for engaging in cash-in-hand work in English
localities: by employment status 78
4.6 Motives of employers when using unemployed and
employed cash-in-hand workers 80
5.1 Cash-in-hand wage rates in three regions of Canada:
by gender, 1993 87
5.2 Relationship between gender divisions of cash-in-hand
work and unpaid domestic work in England: by task 90
5.3 Average hourly wage rates in second-jobs, Germany 95
5.4 Motives of suppliers of cash-in-hand work in English
localities: by gender 97
5.5 Motives of purchasers of cash-in-hand work in English
localities: by gender 99
6.1 Estimates of the magnitude of cash-in-hand work obtained
through indirect methods 108
6.2 Percentage of everyday tasks undertaken using
cash-in-hand work in England: by locality-type 111
6.3 Participation in cash-in-hand work in England: by area 112
6.4 Suppliers of cash-in-hand labour in lower- and higher-income English
neighbourhoods: by socio-economic status 113
6.5 Character of suppliers of cash-in-hand work in England:
by area-type 116
6.6 Motives for employing cash-in-hand workers in England:
by type of area 117
6.7 Motives of suppliers of cash-in-hand work in
English localities 123

6.8 Spatial variations in the extent of participation in formal and
     informal community involvement: by Index of Deprivation   125
6.9 Regional variations in the extent of formal and informal
     community involvement, in the United Kingdom   127
7.1 Benefit overpayments due to fraudulent failure to declare
     earnings   144
7.2 Labour force participation rates, 1960, 1973 and 1999   149
7.3 Expenditure on social protection as a percentage of GDP in
     European Union nations, 1993 and 1998   152
8.1 The polarisation of employment between households,
     OECD Nations, 1983–94   172
9.1 The 12 steps to formalisation of cash-in-hand work of Street (UK) 186

Acknowledgements

This book reports the findings of five separate but inter-related research projects conducted over the past five years. The English Localities Survey reported in this book that examines cash-in-hand work in deprived and affluent English urban and rural localities is the cumulative result of three grants. The Joseph Rowntree Foundation funded the study of urban lower-income neighbourhoods as part of its programme of research and innovative development projects, which it hopes will be of value to policy makers and practitioners. The facts presented and views expressed in this book, however, are those of the author and not necessarily those of the Foundation. The author would also like to thank Jan Windebank who co-authored the final report on this project as well as Stephen Hughes who provided the research assistance to bring this study to fruition.

The data set on higher-income urban neighbourhoods, meanwhile, was funded in part by the European Commission's DG12 under its Targeted Socio-Economic Research (TSER) programme. This evidence was collected as part of a project entitled 'Inclusion through Participation' (INPART). In this regard, the author would like to thank Rik van Berkel who managed the six-nation project team as well as the other European partners. In particular, I would like to thank my UK colleagues, namely Maurice Roche and Jo Cooke, without whom this data could not have been collected.

The third data set on rural localities arose out of a project funded by The Countryside Agency. I would like to take this opportunity to thank them for funding this project on mutual aid in rural areas as well as to display my gratitude to Richard White and Theresa Aldridge for their energetic and enthusiastic research assistance.

Many of the ideas on cash-in-hand work developed in this book were first tried and tested in the context of a twelve-nation project funded by the European Commission's Targeted Socio-Economic Research programme entitled 'Comparative Social Inclusion Policy and Citizenship in Europe: towards a new social model'. The regular and enjoyable meetings with the partners from other European Union nations enabled me to forge my ideas in a way that would not otherwise have been possible. In this regard, I would like to thank the following people in particular for their inputs: Claire Ainesley, Rik van Berkel, Soledad Garcia, Henning Hansen, Pedro Hespanha, Iver Hornemann-Møller, Angelika Kofler, Jens Lind, Enzo Mingione, Maurice Roche, David Smith, Ben Valkenburg, Jacques Vilrokx and Enid Wistrich. Although they will doubtless take issue with many of the ideas in this book, their interventions and inputs have played a large part in helping me develop the ideas conveyed herein.

The fifth and final source of funding that has fuelled the ideas expressed here was the Economic and Social Research Council (ESRC) grant 'Evaluating Local Exchange and Trading Schemes as a tool for combating social exclusion' (R000237208). This was carried out in collaboration with Theresa Aldridge, Roger Lee, Andrew Leyshon, Nigel Thrift and Jane Tooke. I would like to take this opportunity to thank all of my co-partners in this project as well as the respondents who gave their time freely and committed far more to this project than could have been expected.

This book was completed during a period of study leave from the University of Leicester, for which I am very grateful to the University. As always, however, the normal disclaimers apply.

1
Introduction

How many readers of this book can claim that they have never had some involvement with the 'cash-in-hand' economy? Sometimes engagement with this sphere is blatantly evident to all concerned, such as when self-employed builders, plumbers and electricians offer customers lower fees for cash or when employees of formal businesses tender cheaper deals if they do the job personally in the evening or at the weekend. At other times, however, contact with this sphere is less direct and obvious. When customers pick fruit and vegetables from the shelves of a grocery store, how many stop to consider whether the 'gang-masters' who organise the agricultural labour have employed illegal immigrants or welfare recipients on a 'cash-in-hand' basis? And how many when purchasing an item of clothing from a designer shop pause to think about whether it was produced in an underground 'sweatshop' using child labour? Closer to home, how many of us even contemplate that we might be partaking in the cash-in-hand sphere when an acquaintance is rewarded with 'a drink' (i.e. cash) for providing us with a particular piece of merchandise or some service?

Given these diverse and multifarious channels through which cash-in-hand work permeates our daily lives, sometimes in an obvious manner and sometimes less so, the aim of this book is to gather together the available evidence in order to sketch a portrait of cash-in-hand work in contemporary advanced economies. The outcome will be that a number of myths are challenged concerning what it is, who is doing it, where and why. Put succinctly, the widely held view that permeates discourses on cash-in-hand work in both academe and beyond is that such work is a low-paid and exploitative form of employment conducted mostly by marginalised populations for the purpose of economic gain with few, if any, positive features. Based on this reading, the argument has been that such work must be deterred using ever more stringent regulations and punitive measures so as to increase the rate of detection and change the cost-benefit ratio for those considering engagement in such activity. By unpacking each and every one of the assumptions inherent in this dominant discourse and subjecting them to critical scrutiny, this book will reveal that such a characterisation of cash-in-hand work and resulting policy approach is hopelessly out of touch with the nature of cash-in-hand work in contemporary society and is in dire need of a radical overhaul.

To move towards a more accurate portrayal of such work and appropriate policy response, this book provides a fresh empirically grounded and theoretically informed reading of cash-in-hand work in terms of what it is, who does it, where it takes place and why people do it, as well as what needs to be done about it. In this introductory chapter, and in order to set the scene for what follows, therefore, my intention is first of all to define what is meant by cash-in-hand work and then to outline the arguments of this book.

Defining cash-in-hand work

Throughout this volume, the term 'cash-in-hand work' refers to the paid production and sale of goods and services that are unregistered by, or hidden from, the state for tax, social security and/or labour law purposes but which are legal in all other respects (European Commission, 1998; Feige, 1990; Marcelli *et al.*, 1999; Portes, 1994; Thomas, 1992; Williams and Windebank, 1998). Cash-in-hand work is thus composed of three types of activity: evasion of both direct (i.e. income tax) and indirect (e.g. VAT, excise duties) taxes; benefit fraud where the officially unemployed are working whilst claiming benefit; and avoidance of labour legislation, such as employers' insurance contributions, minimum wage agreements or certain safety and other standards in the workplace, such as through hiring labour off-the-books or subcontracting work to small firms and the self-employed asked to work for below-minimum wages.

This definition of the scope of cash-in-hand work is the standard one used throughout the social sciences and on which there is widespread consensus. On the one hand, it excludes unpaid informal work, including the production of goods and services for a family's own consumption or as an unpaid favour for friends, neighbours or one's community. On the other hand, it explicitly denotes that the only criminality about cash-in-hand work is the fact that the production and sale of the goods and services are not registered for tax, social security or labour law purposes (e.g. Feige, 1990; Portes, 1994; Thomas, 1992). Criminal activities where the goods and services themselves are illegal are not included (e.g. drug trafficking). In other words, cash-in-hand work covers only activities where the means do not comply with regulations but the ends (goods and services) are legitimate (Staudt, 1998).

Although there exists a strong consensus throughout the academic literature with regard to the type of activity that is involved when such work is being discussed (e.g. Feige, 1990; Leonard, 1998a,b; Pahl, 1984; Portes, 1994; Thomas, 1992; Williams and Windebank, 1998), there is no such consensus when it comes to denoting such work. Throughout the literature, a multitude of different adjectives and nouns are used (see Table 1.1). In Europe, for example, the most common adjective until recently was 'black'. Indeed, this has been the most popular adjective employed in the United Kingdom and the Netherlands and the second most favoured name in France (following 'subterranean'), Germany (behind 'shadow') and Italy (after 'submerged'). In North America, in contrast, 'black' has been seldom adopted. Instead, 'underground' is the standard adjective used and 'hidden' the next most popular (see Thomas, 1992).

During the past decade or so, however, Europe has followed North America in discarding the use of 'black'. Although still widely used in everyday discourse to refer to this type of work, its popularity in academic and policy-making circles has quickly waned as it has become recognised that to name this type of activity the 'black' economy and to contrast it to the legal 'white' economy is heavily imbued with racial

Table 1.1 Adjectives and nouns used to denote cash-in-hand work

Adjectives

Black	Cash-in-hand	Clandestine	Concealed
Dual	Everyday	Ghetto	Grey
Hidden	Invisible	Irregular	Marginal
Moonlight	Non-observed	Non-official	Occult
Off-the-books	Other	Parallel	Peripheral
Precarious	Second	Shadow	Submerged
Subterranean	Twilight	Underground	Unexposed
Unobserved	Unofficial	Unorganised	Unrecorded
Unregulated	Untaxed	Underwater	

Nouns

Activity	Economic activity	Economy	Employment
Sector	Work		

Source: Author's survey.

overtones that are far from acceptable. In this book, in consequence, and despite having occasionally used 'black' in the past to define such work (e.g. Williams and Windebank, 1995a), another adjective must be found.

As will be seen later, many of the adjectives listed in Table 1.1 are highly inappropriate as descriptions of this type of work. Although some cash-in-hand work is 'irregular' or 'precarious' for example, not all such activity is of this type. Some engage in regular or stable work even though it is unregistered by, or hidden from, the state. Neither is 'unorganised' or 'unregulated' an accurate description for reasons stated below and which will be returned to throughout this book. Adjectives such as 'shadow', 'subterranean', 'invisible', 'hidden', 'unobserved', 'underground' and 'twilight', meanwhile, all suggest that such activity somehow exists in the hidden interstices of contemporary society. We reject this metaphor because although mostly hidden from the state for certain limited administrative purposes, this activity is frequently very visible in the communities in which it occurs (see, e.g., Harding and Jenkins, 1989; Leonard, 1994; MacDonald, 1994).

One prominent adjective that remains, therefore, once these others have been rejected, is 'informal'. Indeed, this is the most popular adjective used to describe all forms of paid and unpaid work existing outside employment. It is also perhaps, as will be shown as the argument of this book unfolds, one of the most accurate adjectives that could be used to portray how the social relations in at least a large segment of this realm of economic life differ from the more 'formal' social relations in which official employment is embedded. A major problem with using this adjective, however, is that it cannot be combined with any of the available nouns without conjuring up false pictures of what is being discussed. When united with nouns such as 'economy', 'sector', 'work' or 'activity', the vast majority of academic commentators assume that the subject matter includes not only cash-in-hand work but also unpaid forms of work. One possibility, nevertheless, is to use the adjective 'informal' and attach it to the noun 'employment' since employment denotes a relationship where one's labour is recompensed by a wage or fee, in other words, paid. Indeed, in the fairly recent past, I have used this option of 'informal employment' to denote what is being discussed (e.g. Williams and Windebank, 1998).

In this book, however, this terminology is rejected. By attaching the adjective 'informal' to the noun 'employment', the strong intimation is that cash-in-hand work takes place under market-like relations akin to those found in formal employment. One of the key arguments in this book, however, will be that although some cash-in-hand work is akin to formal employment in terms of the work relations and motives within which it is conducted, the majority is embedded in work relations, and undertaken for reasons, more akin to unpaid reciprocal exchange. To use the noun 'employment' is thus deliberately avoided here since it attaches to such work a set of relations and motives that it is my explicit intention to contest throughout this book.

In consequence, and by a process of elimination, one of the few principal adjectives remaining that is commonly used in everyday language to refer to such work is 'cash-in-hand'. Although it is now recognised that 'cash-in-hand' is not always an entirely accurate adjective since cheques are sometimes used to recompense such work, this name is here adopted if only because it is perhaps the only instantly recognised term used in everyday discourse that remains and as such, most people understand what is being referred to when this adjective is used.

Having decided on this adjective, the next issue is to make a decision on the noun that will be employed. Here, and despite the popularity of the noun 'economy' (e.g. Ahn and Rica, 1997; Atkins, 1999; Bajada, 2002; Benton, 1990; Caridi and Passerini, 2001; Crnkovic-Pozaic, 1999; International Labour Office, 2002), this is not used. To call this set of economic activities an 'economy' is to suggest that there exist 'dual' or 'separate' economies in society when it has become increasingly apparent that activities are all part of one economy (Cappechi, 1989; Harding and Jenkins, 1989; Thomas, 1992). As Gershuny (1985, p. 129) asserts, 'the informal economy ... is of course not a separate economy at all but an integral part of the system by which work, paid and unpaid, satisfies human needs'. To speak of an 'economy' of cash-in-hand activity, therefore, is to imply that such work enjoys a degree of autonomy from the other spheres of economic activity that is misleading. As this book argues throughout, an intimate inter-dependent relationship exists between cash-in-hand work and not only its formal counterpart but also unpaid reciprocal exchange. For this reason, activity conducted on a cash-in-hand basis is not referred to as an 'economy' in this book.

Neither is it called a 'sector' (e.g. Biggs *et al.*, 1988; Felt and Sinclair, 1992; Ferman *et al.*, 1978; Husband and Jerrard, 2001; Lagos, 1995; Thomas, 1992). The problem here is that sectors in common parlance and in the Standard Industrial Classification (SIC) index, are defined by the good that they produce or the nature of the service offered. Cash-in-hand work, nevertheless, cannot and is not defined in such a way. It is not constituted by a particular set of tasks or activities but crosscuts all sectors (see International Labour Office, 2002). Put another way, the fact that production is unregistered by, or hidden from, the state for tax, social security and/or labour law purposes is not an inherent property of a specific set of goods and services (e.g. home-working, window-cleaning). All goods and services can be produced and distributed either formally or informally. As such, even if the production and sale of some goods and services are more likely to be conducted on this basis than others, cash-in-hand work does not refer to a particular set of activities.

For these reasons, the notion that activities conducted on a cash-in-hand basis form an economy or a sector are here rejected. As the subtitle of this book clearly portrays, nevertheless, these terms have been both used in that I refer to the underground 'sector' and the hidden 'economy' of favours. I hope, therefore, that readers will forgive the journalistic licence that I have taken in this regard. Despite rejecting on theoretical grounds the use of such nouns, they have been nonetheless employed in the subtitle of this book if only for the purpose of bringing this book to the attention of those conducting bibliographic searches to find literature on this subject. Let me be clear, however, that this is the only reason for using these nouns that are still in common circulation with regard to this activity. There is absolutely no intention behind their usage to suggest that these subspheres of cash-in-hand work constitute in any way separate 'economies' or 'sectors'.

Here, therefore, the nouns remaining that can be combined with the adjective of 'cash-in-hand' are 'activity', 'economic activity' and 'work'. Throughout this book, any of these nouns could be used. They are all accurate. Tasks conducted on a cash-in-hand basis are a form of 'work' or 'economic activity', rather than leisure, in that a 'third party' definition applies to any activities conducted in this manner. That is, these tasks could be all undertaken on a paid basis by somebody else and as such, are forms of work rather than leisure activities. Indeed, for precisely this reason that tasks conducted on this basis are essentially 'economic' activities or forms of 'work', the noun 'activity' is seldom employed since it does not sufficiently conjure up the essentially economic nature of this work. Just because tasks conducted on a cash-in-hand basis are 'economic' however, and as will be emphasised throughout this book, does not mean that they are always imbued with the profit motive. The fact that an activity could be given to a third party to conduct on a paid basis does not mean that the rationale underlying participation is making/saving money. In recent years, a swathe of literature has emerged with the 'cultural turn/s' across the social sciences that reveals how the relationship between monetised exchange and the profit motive is not hermetically sealed and that monetised exchange can be conducted for reasons other than making profit (e.g. Bourdieu, 2001; Carrier, 1997; Cornelieau, 2002; Crang, 1997; Crewe and Gregson, 1998; Kovell, 2002; Slater and Tonkiss, 2001). This book, as will be now shown, follows this recent development by re-reading the nature of this form of work that is so often seen to epitomise the worst excesses of the profit motive.

Argument of the book

What are the varieties of cash-in-hand work? Who undertakes these different forms of cash-in-hand work and why do they do it? Where is such work to be found? And what should government do? Throughout the advanced economies, this book argues, cash-in-hand work is in a state of flux. As monetised exchanges penetrate ever more deeply into every nook and cranny of our contemporary commodified societies, this book reveals that cash payments appear to have become more common in circumstances where previously they would have had no place. More particularly, when people conduct favours for friends, neighbours and kin, it has now become much more common for cash to change hands. The result of this broadening of the circumstances in which monetary exchange takes place, it will be asserted, is that the constitution of cash-in-hand work has started to change.

My argument is that cash-in-hand work is now composed of not only the 'underground sector' (forms of cash-in-hand work akin to formal employment conducted for profit-motivated purposes) but increasingly, a 'hidden economy of favours' where the work relations underpinning these monetised exchanges and the motives are more akin to those found in the sphere of unpaid mutual aid. This transformation in the forms of work conducted under the umbrella of cash-in-hand work that is resulting from the increased use of payments when favours are given or received between friends, neighbours and kin, it will be displayed, necessitates a fundamental rethinking of the anatomy of cash-in-hand work as well as how it is dealt with in policy.

To both situate this theoretical perspective in terms of previous literature on cash-in-hand work and to reveal how it extends existing standpoints, Part I reviews previous theories and methods that have been used to understand cash-in-hand work. Chapter 2 provides a review of the vast and rapidly growing literature on cash-in-hand work. This will show that until now, the principal focus of inquiry when studying such activity has been upon the magnitude of the underground sector and how this varies geographically and across socio-economic groups. Grounded in the 'marginality thesis' that views cash-in-hand work as concentrated amongst marginalised groups and areas, a narrow approach to enquiry has ensued with empirical investigations concentrating on whether or not cash-in-hand work is always distributed in this manner. Most studies in the advanced economies, it will be shown, find such work to be a means of accumulating advantage for more affluent groups and areas.

To break out of the shackles of this at best incremental approach to knowledge advancement, an exploration is undertaken of two so far seldom considered issues, namely the relations within which such work is conducted and the motives of purchasers and suppliers. Until now, it has been simply assumed that the relations and motives underpinning cash-in-hand work are exemplary of unbridled profit-motivated capitalist exchange. For adherents to the marginality thesis, such work is characterised as a low-paid form of work conducted under exploitative employment-like relations by some of the most marginalised groups in society (e.g. Castells and Portes, 1989; De Soto, 1989; International Labour Office, 2002; Lagos, 1995; Maldonado, 1995; Rosanvallon, 1980; Sassen, 1997). Although the recognition that affluent groups also conduct such work has led some to show that such work does not always have to be low paid or conducted under exploitative working conditions (e.g. Fortin *et al.*, 1996; Hellberger and Schwarze, 1986; Mattera, 1980; Renooy, 1990; Van Eck and Kazemeier, 1985), nobody has stopped to question whether cash-in-hand work is always conducted under work relations akin to employment or whether the motive of profit always prevails.

In Chapter 2, however, such a reading of cash-in-hand work as universally market-like and profit-driven will start to be questioned. Reviewing evidence from throughout the advanced economies, it will be shown that there is starting to emerge evidence that cash-in-hand work is not simply conducted under work relations akin to formal employment and heavily imbued with profit motivations on the part of both the purchaser and supplier. Instead, it will be revealed that although some cash-in-hand work is of course of this variety, there is also emerging more and more cash-in-hand work that is being undertaken under social relations more akin to mutual aid for friends, neighbours and kin in what some see as a 'moral economy' of favours. In the final section of Chapter 2, therefore, this re-reading of cash-in-hand work will be embedded in a body of literature not usually discussed in the same breath as cash-in-hand work, namely the research on social capital. The intention, in so doing, is to begin to reveal not only that there is a need to recognise the heterogeneity of cash-in-hand work if a fuller understanding is to be achieved but also how the literature on social capital must expand its scope to incorporate the 'hidden economy of favours' if the contemporary nature of social networks, trust and reciprocity is to be more comprehensively understood.

Having theorised cash-in-hand work to be composed of not only an underground sphere composed of work conducted under economic relations akin to formal employment but also a 'moral economy' of favours akin to mutual aid, Chapter 3 then sets about evaluating the validity of the various methods that have been so far used for assessing cash-in-hand work, ranging from the indirect monetary and non-monetary methods to the more direct survey methods. This will reveal that when it comes to understanding the heterogeneous nature of cash-in-hand work in contemporary society, the indirect approaches are of little use since they are not only underpinned by specific assumptions about the character of such work that are highly questionable but are themselves incapable of unpacking the variegated character of such work. This chapter thus concludes by reviewing the range of direct methods that have been used to investigate the character of cash-in-hand work and outlining the direct method used by the author to conduct a survey of the nature of cash-in-hand work in English localities, the results of which will be reported throughout this book to explain the contemporary anatomy of this type of work.

Having provided both a theorisation of the heterogeneity of cash-in-hand work as well as a method for studying it, Part II then turns its attention to providing a detailed analysis of the social and spatial variations in the nature of cash-in-hand work. Chapter 4 commences this review by examining how cash-in-hand work varies according to the employment status of the participant. This will reveal how the formally employed not only conduct more cash-in-hand work than the unemployed but also how the nature of cash-in-hand significantly differs between these two groups. It uncovers how cash-in-hand work is more market-like amongst the formally employed and non-market-like amongst the unemployed, and how a culture of paying for favours (rather than conducting them on an unpaid basis) is more prevalent amongst the unemployed than the employed.

Turning to the gender dimension, Chapter 5 then reveals that although women are usually more likely than men to engage in cash-in-hand work, there are again some significant differences in the nature of the cash-in-hand work that they conduct. This chapter will uncover that when men engage in cash-in-hand work, it is much more likely to be of the market-orientated variety. Women's cash-in-hand work, in contrast, is significantly more likely to be conducted for friends, neighbours and kin for rationales other than profit or, put another way, embedded in a social economy of favours. The implication is that just because women are often found to be poorly paid for their cash-in-hand work does not mean that women are more likely to engage in exploitative low-paid organised forms of informal employment in the underground sector. Instead, and although it does not seek to deny the fact that some women engage in exploitative low-paid work in the underground sector, the argument here is that their low pay is also due to their propensity to engage in the social economy of favours where market rates seldom apply.

Chapter 6 then addresses the issue of the geographical variations in the nature of cash-in-hand work. Until now, most of the cash-in-hand literature on spatial variations has concentrated on how its magnitude varies mostly on a cross-national level but also regionally and locally. Here, however, the focus will be upon identifying the geographical variations in the nature of cash-in-hand work. In the few instances where this has been previously touched upon, the intimation has been that cash-in-hand work in deprived areas is characterised by low-paid exploitative forms of 'organised' cash-in-hand work conducted for informal or formal businesses, whilst cash-in-hand work in affluent areas tends to be composed of more 'autonomous' better paid forms of cash-in-hand work conducted on a self-employed basis.

However, Chapter 6 will argue that such a reading of cash-in-hand work as being always embedded in market-like work relations akin to formal employment misrepresents not only the nature of cash-in-hand work but also the spatial heterogeneity of such work. Reporting primarily evidence from a large-scale survey of English localities, this chapter will reveal that although cash-in-hand work in affluent areas is more likely to be conducted under work relations akin to employment and motivated by economic gain, in deprived areas the majority is undertaken for and by close social relations for redistributive and social reasons. As such, it will be shown that there is a need to recognise the different meanings of cash-in-hand work in different geographical contexts.

Again, this will be asserted to have implications for understanding social capital. Until now, the assumption has been that deprived areas have lower levels of social capital. Given that this chapter reveals how the culture of doing favours in deprived areas is deeply engrained with payment and that the provision of favours on an unpaid basis is often seen as a last resort, it will be argued that the contours of social capital might be slightly more even than previously thought and importantly, argues that policy-making will need to much more fully take into account the culture of paying for favours in deprived neighbourhoods if it is to build social capital in a more effective manner than has so far been the case.

Taken together, therefore, the constituent chapters of Part II will reveal that to conceptualise cash-in-hand work as profit-motivated market-like exchange is to read such work through the lens of, and to reflect the meanings of cash-in-hand work for, the employed, men and those living in affluent areas. It does not resonate with the meaning of such work for the unemployed, women and people living in deprived areas. To break out of the shackles of such a narrow reading of cash-in-hand work, therefore, the argument will be that it is necessary to recognise not only the existence of both an underground sector and a hidden economy of favours but also for appropriate policy approaches to be developed when dealing with such work.

Having provided this empirically grounded theorisation of the heterogeneous nature of cash-in-hand work, Part III evaluates the implications of pursuing three possible policy options. These are the options of deterrence through increasing detection and punishment, laissez-faire and harnessing such work. Starting with the currently dominant policy approach that seeks to deter cash-in-hand work, Chapter 7 will argue that this is ultimately both impractical and undesirable. It is impractical because deterrence is an ineffective way of eradicating the underground sector and the hidden economy of favours is heavily embedded in everyday life. It is undesirable, meanwhile, because such paid mutual aid is one of the principal vehicles through which redistribution occurs and social capital is forged and cemented in contemporary societies, especially amongst deprived populations where cash for favours is part of the culture of exchange.

Second, therefore, a laissez-faire approach towards cash-in-hand work will be reviewed in Chapter 8. If this is pursued, however, it will be shown that not only would the underground sector persist, which possesses exploitative work conditions and defrauds the state of revenue that could be used for social cohesion purposes, but such an approach would also fail to help those currently excluded from the hidden economy of favours to gain access to such aid as an additional coping practice to meet their material and social needs.

In Chapter 9, therefore, a third policy option is introduced, namely 'harnessing' such work. Indeed, this is an approach that has started to gain in popularity in recent years as this sphere has begun to be seen not as an obstacle to modernisation but, rather, as a potential 'motor' for economic development (e.g. International Labour Office, 2002; Tabak,

2000). Until now, however, nearly all of this emergent literature that discusses the notion of 'cultivating' or 'harnessing' cash-in-hand work will be shown to have conceptualised such activity as something to be transformed into formal employment. Although the ideas propounded in Chapter 9 resonate with this emergent stream of thought, the realisation that cash-in-hand work is composed of not only an underground sector but also a hidden economy of favours that possesses very different characteristics and motives, will be here argued to necessitate some significant modifications to existing views on how to harness such work.

In this chapter, it will be argued that although it is appropriate to assert that both forms of cash-in-hand work need to be harnessed, what is meant by 'harnessed' needs to markedly vary according to the form of cash-in-hand work being discussed. In the realm of the underground sector, that is, 'harnessing' cash-in-hand work will need to refer to the transformation of such work into formal employment. So far as the hidden economy of favours is concerned, however, 'harnessing' cash-in-hand work must be seen in a very different light. Given the character of this type of cash-in-hand work, the meaning of 'harnessing' such work here will have to refer to the very different process of transferring paid mutual aid out of the illegal cash-in-hand realm into a sphere of legitimate paid mutual aid. How, in each case, this can be achieved is the subject matter of this chapter which details a number of policy initiatives that can be used for these twin purposes.

Finally, Chapter 10 synthesises the overall argument of the book so as to make the case for a distinction to be drawn between the underground sector and the hidden economy of favours when formulating policy to deal with cash-in-hand work in the advanced economies. Indeed, this concluding chapter will show that unless this is done, then those governments intent on eradicating what they view as profit-motivated informal employment will unintentionally destroy one of the chief means of cementing social capital in deprived populations. The book thus concludes with a call for 'joined up' thinking in relation to policies towards cash-in-hand work and developing social capital, and summarises the findings about how this could be achieved.

Part I

Examining Cash-in-hand Work: Theory and Methods

2
Theorising Cash-in-hand Work

Introduction

This chapter reviews the previous literature on cash-in-hand work so as to help the reader situate the theoretical framework developed here with regard to what has gone before and to identify how this book takes forward knowledge on cash-in-hand work. Analysing the past literature, it will be shown that until now, the principal focus of inquiry has been upon estimating the magnitude of the underground sector and how this varies either spatially or socially (e.g. Feige, 1990; Fortin *et al.*, 1996; Leonard, 1998; Renooy, 1990; Thomas, 1999; Williams and Windebank, 2000b, 2001a). Taking as the starting point the 'marginality thesis' that views cash-in-hand work to be concentrated amongst marginalised groups and areas (e.g. Castells and Portes, 1989; De Soto, 1989; Lagos, 1995; Maldonado, 1995; Rosanvallon, 1980), most studies will be shown to have done little more than attempt to either corroborate or falsify this thesis by analysing whether or not such work is concentrated amongst marginalised groups and/or areas (see Williams and Windebank, 1998).

Here, however, and to transcend this incremental approach to knowledge advancement, attention turns towards the relatively unexplored issues of the economic relations within which these monetised exchanges are embedded and the motives of the purchasers and suppliers of such work. In recent years, the cultural turn/s across the social sciences have resulted in a rethinking of whether monetised exchange is always embedded in profit-motivated behaviour (Crang, 1996; Crewe, 2000; Crewe and Gregson, 1998; Davies, 1992; Gudeman, 2001; Lee, 1996, 1997, 2000a,b; Thrift and Olds, 1996; Williams, 2002b, 2003d; Williams and Windebank, 2001c, 2003b; Zelizer, 1994), by which is here meant the desire to 'achieve maximum money gains' (Polanyi, 1944,

p. 68). The aim of this chapter is to further contribute to this emergent literature by analysing cash-in-hand work, a realm of activity that has often been considered the exemplar of unbridled profit-motivated capitalism.

In the vast majority of previous research, that is, cash-in-hand work has been widely assumed to be a type of exploitative low-paid employment heavily imbued with profit motivations on the part of both the consumer and supplier (e.g. Castells and Portes, 1989; De Soto, 1989; Matthews, 1983; Sassen, 1989). In this chapter, however, such a reading is put under the spotlight. By uncovering that such abstract universal hues oversimplify and obscure the heterogeneous contemporary meanings of cash-in-hand work, this chapter develops a less totalising conceptualisation of this sphere of work. Here, the economic discourse that portrays monetary exchange in general, and cash-in-hand work in particular, as universally market-like and profit-motivated is replaced with a more socially, culturally and geographically embedded appreciation of monetised exchange. It is revealed that although some cash-in-hand work is of this variety, such work is also often undertaken under economic relations more akin to mutual aid for friends, neighbours and kin for non-profit reasons. As such, cash-in-hand work is theorised to be composed of not only an 'underground economy' of market-like profit-motivated cash-in-hand work but also a 'hidden' or 'social' economy of favours conducted under economic relations and for purposes more akin to unpaid mutual aid.

Until now, this heterogeneity in cash-in-hand work has not been recognised. Identifying a hidden economy of favours grounded in social relations and motives more akin to unpaid mutual aid, however, means that new explanations are required for the growth of such work. At present, the dominant argument is that cash-in-hand work is not some leftover or 'a mere "lag" from traditional relationships of production' (Castells and Portes, 1989, p. 13) but is a new form of advanced capitalist exploitation that is a direct product of the neo-liberal project of deregulation taking hold (e.g. Amin, 1996; Castells and Portes, 1989; International Labour Office, 2002; Sassen, 1997; Ybarra, 1989). Here, nevertheless, this is seen as a necessary but insufficient explanation for understanding the totality of cash-in-hand work. Although this might explain the growth of the 'underground economy', it does not explain the advent of this 'hidden economy of favours'. To do this, it is here asserted to be necessary to consider how as monetised exchanges penetrate ever more deeply into every nook and cranny of our contemporary commodified societies, cash payments appear to have become more common in circumstances where previously they would have had no place. More particularly, when people conduct favours for friends, neighbours and kin, it has now become much more common for cash to change hands, not least in situations where the lack of trust would otherwise prevent such an economy of favours from existing. The argument that starts to be developed here, therefore, is that money appears to be acting as the lubricant for one-to-one favours.

This emergent view that mutual aid is composed not only of unpaid giving and receiving but also monetised exchanges conducted for non-profit reasons has important implications for understanding the nature of social capital that have not so far been considered. In the final section of this chapter, therefore, this rereading of the nature of cash-in-hand work will be embedded in the wider literature on social capital so as to show how this body of knowledge needs to further expand its scope to incorporate the 'hidden economy of favours' if it is to more fully understand the contemporary nature of social networks, trust and reciprocity. Indeed, the argument that starts to be developed is that by solely focusing upon unpaid reciprocity in contemporary society, this social capital literature might have underestimated the extent to which social capital persists in contemporary society and not recognised the way in which the nature of reciprocal exchange varies across populations. To conclude therefore, this chapter starts to develop a more rounded and dynamic understanding of the relationships between social networks, trust and the nature of reciprocal exchange in contemporary advanced economies. Before doing so however, it is first necessary to briefly review the subject matter covered by the vast bulk of the literature on cash-in-hand work, namely the issue of its variable magnitude.

Studies of the magnitude of cash-in-hand work

Studies of cash-in-hand work have addressed the issue of its magnitude in a number of ways. On the one hand, whether it is growing or declining has been investigated (e.g. Gadea and Serrano-Sanz, 2002). On the other hand, how its magnitude varies either on a cross-national basis, regionally or locally, by socio-economic group or by gender, has been considered. Here, each of these sets of literature is briefly reviewed.

On the issue of whether it is growing or declining over time, two contrasting perspectives exist, namely the 'modernisation thesis' that views cash-in-hand work to be in long-term decline and the 'globalisation thesis' that views it to be growing (see Pfau-Effinger, 2003). For adherents to the modernisation thesis, cash-in-hand work is seen as some kind of traditional outdated type of work contract that is in long-term terminal decline and will vanish with the pursuance of modernisation. Such a view of cash-in-hand work, however, has come under considerable criticism due to the recognition that in the contemporary era, it is growing rather than declining (see Castells and Portes, 1989; International Labour Office, 2002; Sassen, 1997; Williams, 2002a, 2003d; Williams and Windebank, 1999a,c).

Until now, for the majority of analysts critical of the modernisation thesis, the argument has been that it is the processes associated with economic globalisation that are causing an expansion of cash-in-hand work. In this economic reading, economic globalisation refers to a dangerous cocktail of deregulation and increasing global competition that produces an expansion of cash-in-hand work (e.g. Castells and Portes, 1989; International Labour Office, 2002; Sassen, 1997). This exploitative form of employment is thus seen to have emerged as a new facet of contemporary capitalism. Particularly prevalent in the USA (but not in Europe), this body of literature views such work to be especially prevalent in global cities and amongst immigrant/ethnic minority populations (e.g. Marie, 1999, 2000; Ross, 2001; Sassen, 1991, 1994a,b, 1996, 1997; Snyder, 2003; Sole, 1998; Waldinger and Lapp, 1993).

As will be shown throughout this book, however, the problem with the globalisation thesis is that it portrays the development of cash-in-hand work as taking place according to a universal logic. This is ultimately misleading. Such work takes on various forms in different contexts and is by no means solely a product of neoliberal economic globalisation. Besides such economic readings, more cultural accounts of monetised exchange are required in order to fully explain this heterogeneous sphere of work.

Measuring and explaining its changing size over time, however, is not the only focus when considering its magnitude. There is, in addition, a large volume of literature examining how its magnitude varies across populations. Economists have explored the cross-national variations in its size (e.g. Feige, 1990, 1999; Fortin *et al.*, 1996; Friedman *et al.*, 2000; International Labour Office, 2002; Ott, 1999; Schneider, 2000, 2001; Thomas, 1999), geographers have analysed the local and regional variations in its magnitude (e.g. Jensen *et al.*, 1995; Renooy, 1990; Williams and Windebank, 1998) and sociologists have sought to unpack how the level of such exchange varies across socio-economic groups (e.g. Leonard, 1994, 1998a; Pahl, 1984) or by gender (e.g. Cornelius, 1992; Fernandez-Kelly and Garcia, 1989; Hoyman, 1987; Leonard, 1994; McInnis-Dittrich, 1995).

At the very heart of nearly all such studies is a desire to evaluate whether or not the 'marginality thesis' holds true. This asserts that cash-in-hand work is concentrated amongst marginalised populations, whether these be poor nations, deprived localities and regions, lower-income socio-economic groups or women (e.g. Castells and Portes, 1989; De Soto, 1989; International Labour Office, 2002; Lagos, 1995; Maldonado, 1995; Rosanvallon, 1980). Taking this thesis as the starting point of their analyses, a Popperian-like mode of enquiry has tended to ensue. Most studies have done little more than to test whether or not this is the case.

Starting with the economists and their cross-national studies, a particular interest has been to consider whether this work is concentrated in poorer nations (e.g. Dallago, 1991; Feige, 1990; Feige and Ott, 1999; Pedersen, 1998; Schneider, 2001, Schneider and Enste, 2000). On the whole, their finding has been that although such work is more substantial in poorer nations, it is by no means confined to such countries. Rather, its presence and even growth is seen as ubiquitous (e.g. International Labour Office, 2002; Pedersen, 1998; Schneider, 2001). On the whole, therefore, these economistic cross-national comparative surveys have confirmed the marginality thesis that such work is concentrated in poorer nations, even if there is now widespread recognition that it is prevalent in every corner of the globe.

When its distribution amongst different socio-economic groups is considered, however, a very different conclusion has been reached. For the sociologists and sometimes economists and geographers considering this issue, the widespread conclusion has been that the marginality thesis does not hold (e.g. Fortin *et al.*, 1996; Pahl, 1984; Williams and Windebank, 1998). On this issue, therefore, there has started to be a significant change of opinion in the last two decades. As Chapter 4 will highlight, during the 1970s and 1980s in particular, and stretching into the 1990s, it was commonly held that cash-in-hand work was concentrated amongst deprived populations (e.g. Blair and Endres, 1994; Gutmann, 1978; Parker, 1982; Robson, 1988; Rosanvallon, 1980; Stauffer, 1995).

A multitude of studies of the socio-economic distribution of cash-in-hand work, however, have countered this popular conceptualisation concerning who engages in cash-in-hand work. The widespread finding throughout the advanced economies of direct surveys has been that cash-in-hand work chiefly benefits those already in employment. This has been found to be the case in France (Barthe, 1988, Cornuel and Duriez, 1985; Foudi *et al.*, 1982; Tievant, 1982), Germany (Glatzer and

Berger, 1988; Hellberger and Schwarze, 1987), Greece (Hadjimichalis and Vaiou, 1989), Italy (Cappechi, 1989; Mingione, 1991; Mingione and Morlicchio, 1993; Warren, 1994), the Netherlands (Koopmans, 1989; Van Eck and Kazemeier, 1985; Van Geuns *et al.*, 1987), Portugal (Lobo, 1990b), Spain (Ahn and Rica, 1997; Benton, 1990; Lobo, 1990a), the United Kingdom (Economist Intelligence Unit, 1982; Howe, 1990; Morris, 1994; Pahl, 1984; Warde, 1990; Williams and Windebank, 2001a, 2003a) and North America (Fortin *et al.*, 1996; Jensen *et al.*, 1995; Lemieux *et al.*, 1994; Lozano, 1989). On the whole, therefore, the marginality thesis has been largely refuted so far as the socio-economic distribution of such work is concerned.

It is similarly the case that although earlier studies often assumed that cash-in-hand work was concentrated in deprived regions and localities, such a view has become much less common recently. Earlier studies, for example, often asserted that such work was concentrated in lower-income areas such as deprived inner city localities (e.g. Blair and Endres, 1994; Elkin and McLaren, 1991; Haughton *et al.*, 1993; Robson, 1988) and poorer peripheral regions (e.g. Button, 1984; Hadjimichalis and Vaiou, 1989). The overwhelming finding of the detailed studies conducted over the past two decades, however, has been that this is not the case. Instead, lower-income areas have been found to conduct less cash-in-hand work than more affluent localities. This has been identified in the Netherlands (e.g. Van Geuns *et al.*, 1987), Britain (e.g. Bunker and Dewberry, 1984; Williams and Windebank, 2001a), France (e.g. Barthe, 1985; Cornuel and Duriez, 1985; Foudi *et al.*, 1982) and Italy (e.g. Mattera, 1980, 1985; Mingione, 1991; Mingione and Morlicchio, 1993).

It is also the case that the view in the marginality thesis about the gendering of cash-in-hand work has started to come under some pressure. The vast majority of studies have found that men do a greater proportion of such work than women (e.g. Fortin *et al.*, 1996; Lemieux *et al.*, 1994; MacDonald, 1994; McInnis-Dittrich, 1995; Mingione, 1991; Mogensen, 1985; Pahl, 1984; Renooy, 1990; Van Eck and Kazemeier, 1985; Vinay, 1987), although the relative gap is on the whole found to be quite small.

Previous studies on the heterogeneity of cash-in-hand work

In a bid to move beyond solely examinations of the volume of such activity, the last decade or so has witnessed the emergence of various studies that seek to distinguish between different types of cash-in-hand work. At the outset, however, it needs to be stated that this body of literature has not distinguished cash-in-hand work conducted under economic relations akin to formal employment and the hidden economy of favours characterised by relations akin to unpaid mutual aid. Instead, this literature still largely views all cash-in-hand work as conducted under relations akin to formal employment for profit-motivated purposes but has distinguished different types of market-like cash-in-hand work (Fortin *et al.*, 1996; Jensen *et al.*, 1995; Laguerre, 1994; Leonard, 1994; Mingione, 1991; Pahl, 1984; Renooy, 1990; Waldinger and Lapp, 1993).

Until now, the major way in which cash-in-hand work has been disaggregated is by distinguishing a continuum ranging from 'organised' types of cash-in-hand employment conducted by employees for a business that undertakes some or all of its activity informally at one end of the spectrum to more 'individual' or 'autonomous' forms of informality at the other (for a review, see Williams and Windebank, 1998). These latter 'autonomous' activities cover forms of cash-in-hand employment conducted by the self-employed concealing a proportion, or indeed all, of their earnings, as well as casual one-off jobs undertaken on a cash-in-hand basis, such as for a neighbour, friend or relative.

One outcome of identifying this continuum of types of market-like cash-in-hand work has been that not all cash-in-hand work is now viewed as low-paid, exploitative and undertaken by marginal groups. Besides forms of organised exploitative informal employment, such as in labour-intensive small firms with low levels of capitalisation, utilising old technology and producing cheap products and services for local markets and export, which involve on the whole marginal populations engaging in low-paid exploitative activity (e.g. Lin, 1995; Sassen, 1991), other forms of cash-in-hand work have been identified. There are organised forms of cash-in-hand work which are autonomous in orientation, in highly capitalised small firms which are modern and use high-technology equipment to produce higher-priced goods and services and whose informal employees are well-paid, employ higher skills and have more autonomy and control over their work, with relations between employers and employees based more upon co-operation than domination (Benton, 1990; Cappechi, 1989; Warren, 1994). There are also forms of individual cash-in-hand work that can be relatively well recompensed. Not all types of cash-in-hand work, therefore, are now seen as low paid and exploitative in character.

The result is that rather than view cash-in-hand work as an exploitative form of low-paid employment sitting at the bottom of a hierarchy of types of formal employment, it is now much more common for cash-in-hand work to be discussed as a heterogeneous labour market with a hierarchy of its own. In other words, just as there is a segmented formal labour market, a segmented informal labour market is also seen to exist. As Williams and Windebank (1998, p. 32–3) have put it,

> existing alongside the formal labour market is a heterogeneous informal labour market composed of very different groups of people engaged in widely varying types of informal employment for diverse and contrasting reasons and receiving varying rates of pay. This informal labour market, to adopt a simplistic dual labour market model, ranges from 'core' informal employment which is relatively well-paid, autonomous and non-routine and where the worker often benefits just as much from the work as the employer, to 'peripheral' informal employment which is poorly paid, exploitative and routine and where the employee does not benefit as much as the employer. Just as in the formal labour market, moreover, there exist those excluded from even the most exploitative peripheral informal employment.

Despite it becoming much more common in the literature on cash-in-hand work to distinguish between its 'organised' and 'autonomous' varieties (e.g. Leonard, 2000; Maloney, 1999), however, little attempt has so far been made to consider whether the economic relations within which these different forms of cash-in-hand work take place are always market-like and whether the motives of participants are universally profit-motivated.

The cultural turn and re-theorising of monetised exchange

The continuing dominance of this market-centred reading of cash-in-hand work is perhaps surprising when the broader shifts in social enquiry are considered with regard to monetary exchange. Across the social sciences, the cultural turn, by which is meant a growth of interest in culture and a turn away from economy (Ray and Sayer, 1999), has led to new topics being investigated as well as new explanations for established issues. One issue that has benefited from some fresh thinking in recent years is monetary exchange. Although it is now widely accepted that 'Monetary relations have penetrated every nook and cranny of the world and into almost every aspect of social, even private life' (Harvey,

1982, p. 373), cultural theorists have begun to ask whether this seemingly endless and deeper intrusion of monetary relations always and necessarily marches hand-in-hand with the profit-motive. Until now, the conceptualisation that the only type of monetary exchange is that which is profit-motivated has run deep in most economistic discourse of both the neoclassical and Marxian variety (Ciscel and Heath, 2001; Harvey, 1989; Sayer, 1997). The general non-anthropological view of exchange is that it is always rational and profit-motivated: it is essentially market-like and that is what is important about exchange (see Carruthers and Babb, 2000; Crang, 1996; Crewe and Gregson, 1998; Davies, 1992; Lee, 2000a; Zelizer, 1994). As Sayer (1997, p. 23) argues:

> The commodity may be valued by the user for its intrinsic use value, but to the seller it is unequivocally a means to an end, to the achievement of the external goal of making a profit, and if it is unlikely to make a profit it will not be offered for sale.

This reading of monetised exchange in economistic discourse is reinforced by a 'formalist' anthropological tradition that sees exchange mechanisms in advanced economies as less 'embedded' than those in pre-industrial societies. From this perspective, the idea is that there has been a separation of the 'economy' from 'culture', resulting in exchanges in western societies being 'thinner', less loaded with social meaning and less symbolic than traditional exchanges (see Mauss, 1966). Is it really the case, however, that the market has left no other nexus between people than naked self-interest and callous profit motivation? Or is such a perception a consequence of both how analysts look at exchange and where they look?

For those influenced by the 'cultural turn/s', the intention in unpacking the nature of monetary exchange has been to decentre the notion that the only type of monetary exchange is that which is profit-motivated and market-like (e.g. Byrne *et al.*, 1998; Carrier, 1997; Crang, 1997; Crewe and Gregson, 1998; Gibson-Graham, 1996; Gibson-Graham and Ruccio, 2001; Kovell, 2002). As Carrier (1997) puts it, 'the Market Idea' has played a central role in organising the modern West's conceptual and normative universe. Indeed, and as Jessop (2002) explains, this image of monetised exchange as always profit-motivated serves the interests of both neoliberals whose belief is that this must be met with open arms and radical theorists who believe that this requires fierce resistance. The result is the perpetuation of a crude reading of monetised exchange as always market-like and profit-motivated.

In recent years, however, there has been a concerted effort to transcend such abstract universal hues that view all monetary exchange as market-like and profit-motivated (e.g. Amin and Thrift, 2000; Crang, 1997; Crewe, 2000; Crewe and Gregson, 1998; Lee, 1997; Thrift and Olds, 1996). As Crewe and Gregson (1998, p. 41) incisively point out, 'the major defect of such market-based models of exchange is simply that they do not convey the richness and messiness of the exchange experience' in the advanced economies. Drawing upon the earlier work of Polanyi (1944), the formalist anthropology approach that assumed price-fixing and profit-motivated markets to be the universal economic mechanism in western economies has started to be challenged from a 'substantivist' anthropological position that argues how economic relations are always socially embedded (see Crang, 1996; Crewe and Gregson, 1998; Davies, 1992; Lee, 2000a; Zelizer, 1994). As Bourdieu (2001, pp. 280–1) states,

> It is in fact impossible to account for the structure and functioning of the social world unless one reintroduces capital in all its forms and not solely in the one form recognized by economic theory. Economic theory has allowed to be foisted upon it a definition of the economy of practices which is the historical invention of capitalism; and by reducing the universe of exchanges to mercantile exchange, which is objectively and subjectively oriented toward the maximization of profit, … , it has implicitly defined the other forms of exchange as noneconomic, and therefore disinterested. In particular, it defines as disinterested those forms of exchange which ensure the transubstantiation whereby the most material types of capital – those which are economic in the restricted sense – can present themselves in the immaterial form of cultural capital or social capital and vice versa.

The result of such a cultural rereading of monetary exchange is the emergence of a stream of writing that has sought to unpack the messy and complex nature of monetary exchange in late capitalist societies by showing the alternative work relations, motives and pricing mechanisms that prevail (e.g. Bourdieu, 2001; Community Economies Collective, 2001; Cornelieau, 2002; Crang, 1996; Crewe and Gregson, 1998; Lee, 1996, 1997, 2000a,b; Davis, 1992; Slater and Tonkiss, 2001).

The outcome has been a raft of studies that have investigated 'alternative economic spaces' (Leyshon *et al.*, 2003). To display the complex characters and logics of monetary exchange and/or to illuminate alternative futures for monetary transactions, studies have begun to investigate sites such as the garage sale (Soiffer and Herrmann, 1987), the car boot sale (Crewe and Gregson, 1998) and local currency schemes (Boyle, 1999; Lee, 1996; North, 1999; Offe and Heinze, 1992; Williams *et al.*, 2001a,b,c). These uncover different work relations, motivations and pricing mechanisms of exchange that are not always and necessarily market-like and imbued with the profit-motive.

For example, Crewe and Gregson (1998), in their study of the car boot sale, highlight how these 'marginal and/or resistant spaces' have been neglected resulting in partial theorisations of exchange. They explore how conventions of the market-place are suspended here and replaced by forms of sourcing, commodity circulation, transaction codes, pricing mechanisms and value quite different from those that typify more conventional exchange, thus showing how exchange is socially, culturally and geographically embedded. Similarly, a burgeoning literature on local currencies has revealed how it is wholly feasible for monetary exchanges to take place under alternative economic relations beyond market-like exchange and for motives other than profit (e.g. Cahn, 2000; Lee, 1996; North, 1999; Offe and Heinze, 1992; Williams *et al.*, 2001a).

The problem with the studies so far conducted of particular alternative economic spaces of course, is that they investigate only small spaces that are viewed by most people as existing on the 'margins' of the mainstream economy. As such, these studies that unpack how monetised exchange does not have to be profit-motivated fail to provide any significant challenge to the hegemonic ideology that imbues monetised exchange with the profit motive. Such sites where the profit motive is absent can be simply explained away as minor or marginal practices existing on the outer edges of the mainstream commodity economy, and labelled 'peripheral' or even 'superfluous' spaces.

If the view that there is an inextricable relationship between monetary transactions and the profit motive is to be more forcefully challenged therefore, it is necessary to analyse larger spaces of monetised exchange than has hitherto been the case. The study of cash-in-hand work represents one such realm. This is a sphere of economic activity that not only constitutes somewhere between 7 and 16 per cent of GDP in the advanced economies (European Commission, 1998) but is also a sphere that is seen to epitomise profit-motivated market-like exchange. Unpacking the heterogeneous relations and motives involved in this sphere thus enables not only a fuller understanding of cash-in-hand work to be achieved but also enables significant progress to be made in decentring market-based readings of monetised exchange.

Market-centred readings of the nature of cash-in-hand work

In conventional discourse, to repeat, cash-in-hand work has been viewed as conducted under economic relations akin to formal employment for the purpose of profit. The intention here, however, and drawing inspiration from the above cultural analyses of monetised exchange, is to subject this view to critical scrutiny. At first glance, it would not appear that the study of cash-in-hand work would offer much of a contribution to this process of deconstructing the view of monetary transactions as always profit motivated. After all, this sphere has been near enough universally viewed as a form of monetised exchange conducted under market-like relations for profit-motivated purposes by both suppliers and customers.

This reading of cash-in-hand work prevails whatever part of the world is studied (e.g. Castells and Portes, 1989; De Soto, 1989; Lagos, 1995; Lemieux *et al.*, 1994; Matthews, 1983). So too does it pertain equally whether such work is viewed in a positive or negative light. For neoliberals focusing upon the more autonomous microscale activities of petty entrepreneurs in both advanced and under-developed economies, such exchange is seen as a form of self-employment that informal labourers pursue as rational economic actors confronted by rules and regulations that are inherently unfair (De Soto, 1989; Matthews, 1983; Sauvy, 1984). For those of a political economy persuasion focusing upon its organised forms, meanwhile, it is perceived as a form of exploitative employment that a weak and unprotected workforce is obliged to undertake for unscrupulous employers (Amin, 1996; Castells and Portes, 1989; Frank, 1996; Portes, 1994; Ybarra, 1989). Such a market-based reading even predominates when multiple types of cash-in-hand work have been recognized ranging from its 'organised' to 'autonomous' forms (e.g. Fortin *et al.*, 1996; Jensen *et al.*, 1995; Jordan, 1998; Jordan and Redley, 1994; MacDonald, 1994; Leonard, 1994; 1998b; MacDonald, 1984; Pahl, 1984; Renooy, 1990; Williams and Windebank, 1998).

This market-centred reading even applies, by and large, whatever groups are considered as partaking in such work. Whether one accepts that such work is conducted by marginalised populations (e.g. Blair and Endres, 1994; Button, 1984; Castells and Portes, 1989; Elkin and McLaren, 1991; Gutmann, 1978; Kesteloot and Meert, 1999; Matthews, 1983; Portes, 1994; Rosanvallon, 1980) or recognises that it can also be undertaken and even concentrated amongst more affluent populations (e.g. Fortin *et al.*, 1996; Jensen *et al.*, 1995; Mingione, 1991; Pahl, 1984,

Renooy, 1990; Williams and Windebank, 1998, 2001a), such exchange is primarily viewed as embedded in profit-motivated market-orientated relations.

Yet once one starts to unpack the nature of cash-in-hand work in those few studies that have sought to understand the relations within which such work is conducted and the motives of the participants, a very different reading starts to come to light.

Rereading the nature of cash-in-hand work

Until now, a market-centred reading of the economic relations and motives underpinning cash-in-hand work has been simply accepted without investigation. As Travers (2002, p. 2) asserts, 'most research on informal economic activity gives short shrift to the motivations of people to do this work. It is usually said that people do the work to earn extra money and left at that.' Take, for example, the finding that much of this work is low paid. When identified, it is simply interpreted that this means that such work must be exploitative (e.g. International Labour Office, 2002; Sassen, 1997). The economic relations within which low-paid cash-in-hand work is embedded and/or the motives of the suppliers and/or customers are seldom, if ever, investigated. In the few instances where such relations and motives have been explored, however, some remarkable findings have been identified that call into question the conventional market-centred reading of cash-in-hand work.

In a study of incomers to new towns in France for example, Cornuel and Duriez (1985) find that some respondents were engaging in cash-in-hand work for their neighbours not for the purpose of making money but so as to develop their social networks in order to forge greater trust and the opportunity for reciprocity. Similarly, a study in rural Pennsylvania by Jensen *et al.* (1995) discovers that many who were participating in cash-in-hand work voiced reasons for engaging in such work that had little or nothing to do with profit. By far the most extensive research that has been conducted on this issue, however, is that in lower- and higher-income urban and rural neighbourhoods in England, or what throughout this book is referred to as the English Localities Survey (Williams and Windebank, 2001a, 2002b, 2003a).

As part of their study of 'household work practices' in urban and rural England, Williams and Windebank (2003a) examined the social relations and motives involved in work conducted on a cash-in-hand basis. Respondents were questioned about both the cash-in-hand work that they received as customers and the work that household members

Table 2.1   Character of suppliers of cash-in-hand work in
English localities

% of cash-in-hand work conducted by	All areas
Firm/unknown person	30
Friend/neighbour	33
Kin	30
Household member	7
Total	100

Source: English Localities Survey.

undertook on a cash-in-hand basis (see Chapter 3). Although later chapters will analyse the findings with regard to the socio-economic, spatial
and gender variations identified, the intention here is to analyse for the
first time the overall findings across the 861 households interviewed. To
do this, first, the relations within which cash-in-hand is embedded are
analysed and second, the motives of the suppliers and customers.

Starting with the economic relations within which cash-in-hand work
is embedded, the finding of this study was that just 30 per cent of the
cash-in-hand work received by these 861 households was conducted by
formal firms and/or self-employed people (see Table 2.1). The type of
work conducted using this labour ranged from home maintenance and
improvement tasks such as installing a bathroom, plumbing and electrical work, through routine housework (e.g. cleaning and ironing) to the
receipt of gardening and car repair services.

Friends, neighbours and kin thus supplied some 70 per cent of all
cash-in-hand tasks. When these closer social relations were involved,
economic gain hardly figured in the primary rationales of customers.
Instead, this labour was employed on a cash-in-hand basis to carry out
the tasks for primarily non-economic reasons, such as sociality or redistribution. As will now be revealed, the result is that cash-in-hand work
can no longer be depicted simply as a form of employment that is
motivated by profit-seeking behaviour (e.g. Castells and Portes, 1989;
Portes, 1994). To show this, first, consumers' motivations for using cash-
in-hand work are analysed followed by an analysis of suppliers' motives.

Motives of purchasers

Table 2.2 reports the motives of purchasers when seeking to get work
completed on a cash-in-hand basis. This reveals that in those 30 per cent
of instances where cash-in-hand tasks are conducted by either firms
and/or self-employed people previously unknown to the customer, in

Table 2.2 Motives of purchasers of cash-in-hand work in English
localities

% of cash-in-hand work supplied primarily to	All areas
Save money	31
Financially help the supplier	22
Build community networks	47
Total	100

Source: English Localities Survey.

nearly every case, saving money or economic gain is the rationale. There
is thus a strong correlation between the desire to get jobs done cheaper
than would be the case if somebody were formally employed and the use
of unknown firms and people to do the work. For example, the motive
whenever building firms, plumbers or electricians previously unknown
to the purchaser were paid on a cash-in-hand basis was always to save
money compared with paying formal labour to do the job. This was similarly the case whenever domestic cleaners, gardeners and private tuition
were paid for on a cash-in-hand basis. When there is social distance
between the purchaser and supplier, therefore, the profit motive prevails
in purchasers' rationales.

Examining purchasers' primary reasons for paying on a cash-in-hand
basis when closer social relations are involved, however, some very different motivations emerge. When consumers used the cash-in-hand
labour of friends, neighbours, kin and other household members, their
primary motivation revolved around either 'community-building' or
'redistribution'.

'Community-building' rationales predominate where consumers pay
friends or neighbours (rather than kin) so as to maintain or create a
social relationship with them. This is perhaps unsurprising. After all,
exchange is a principal nexus through which social relations are forged
and maintained in contemporary society (Burns and Taylor, 1998;
Morris, 1995). Why, however, is monetary payment involved? Payment
was often preferred due to both wariness about engaging in unpaid
exchange and the embeddedness of payment in norms of reciprocity.
First, people did not want to feel that they owed others a favour. As an
unemployed single parent put it, 'I usually like to pay people who do
work for me, so if I need to, I can feel free ... but a friend laid my carpet
and wouldn't take money. I owe him now and I really hate that hanging
over me.' Second, there was a feeling that you could no longer rely on

people to return favours, indicating the demise of trust in at least some of these neighbourhoods. As a middle-aged unemployed man asserted, 'most people don't return favours these days so I don't do anything for anyone else unless I'm paid for it'. Therefore, cash was seen as a necessary medium when maintaining or building community networks, especially when neighbours or friends were involved. Rather than allow such relations to turn sour if and when they reneged on their commitments, the exchange of cash prevented such a situation arising. If social capital is to be more fully understood, by which is here meant the 'networks, norms and social trust that facilitate co-ordination and co-operation for mutual benefit' (Putnam, 1993, p. 67), then it appears to be necessary to investigate not only unpaid but also cash-in-hand exchanges. Norms of reciprocity, it seems, often involve cash that acts as a substitute for trust in the formation and maintenance of networks of reciprocity, at least in some populations (see Part II).

'Redistributive' rationales, meanwhile, usually apply when kin conduct the work. Here, paying is often viewed as a means of giving them the much needed spending money, such as when they are unemployed. Indeed, asking kin to do a task in order to give them some needed money was the principal rationale behind 22 per cent of all cash-in-hand work. As a man in a dual-earner household stated, 'my brother was skint and we needed it [decorating] doing so it was natural to ask him'. Or as a single employed woman put it, 'it was a little job to give him [her uncle] some pocket money'. Cash-in-hand work was thus a way of giving money to kin that avoided all connotations of charity, even if this was their intention. As Kempson (1996) has previously revealed, people avoid accepting charity at all costs. This was well understood by the populations in the English localities surveyed. As a result, anybody wishing to give aid paid them for doing a task to 'help them out'.

In sum, although consumers of cash-in-hand work provided by firms and/or self-employed people previously unknown to them used it as a cheaper alternative to formal employment, this was not the case when closer social relations are involved. Such work was conducted primarily in order to either cement or consolidate social bonds or for redistributive reasons.

Motives of suppliers

Until now, the few studies that have explored the motives and attitudes of cash-in-hand workers have drawn attention to the fact that they adopt a different attitude to their own cash-in-hand work compared with such work more generally. In Quebec, for example, Fortin *et al*.

(1996) find that just 9.4 per cent of cash-in-hand workers saw their activity as immoral. In Dean and Melrose's (1996) study of welfare fiddlers in London and Luton, moreover, respondents distinguished between their own cash-in-hand work that they felt to be harmless and more serious or organised forms of fraud that they did not. This was also the finding of MacDonald (1994) in Cleveland in the North-East of England. The 214 unemployed respondents interviewed in 1990 and 1992 saw their own cash-in-hand work as morally justifiable and contrasted it with more serious cases of fraud that they did not. Indeed, according to Rowlingson *et al.* (1997), most claimants who break the rules do not think that they were committing a crime. This finding is echoed in the work of Jordan and Redley (1994) in the south-west of England. Henry (1978), who reports that the ability of people who fiddled to justify their activities was an important determinant of continued fiddling, also made such a differentiation.

Until now, it has been argued that such a distinction is made because people differentiate between 'serious' and 'trivial' fraud (e.g. MacDonald, 1994). Here, however, I wish to argue that another reason for such a distinction is perhaps because for the most part, respondents are considering their own participation in a 'hidden economy of favours' for friends, kin and neighbours, which constitutes the majority of cash-in-hand work, and comparing this with participation in the more organised underground sector that dominates the popular imagination of what is meant by cash-in-hand work, but represents only a small proportion of all cash-in-hand work. For these cash-in-hand workers, their 'trivial' cash-in-hand work is seen to be of a totally different order of magnitude to the organised cash-in-hand that they perceive as constituting the majority of such work due to the received image of this activity in the popular imagination.

To understand this, the rationales of suppliers of cash-in-hand work need to be analysed. (See Table 2.3). In only half of all cases (50 per cent) did they assert that cash-in-hand work was undertaken principally to make money. Indeed, even when monetary gain was given as the principal reason for undertaking cash-in-hand work, it was frequently qualified with other statements when this work was conducted for friends, kin, neighbours or other household members. Representative of the vast majority of such statements were the following quotes: 'I did it for the money but it was only pocket money really and it was a chance to help them out at the same time' (employed woman); 'I did it for the money I suppose but it was also a chance to get out of the house' (unemployed man) and 'It was to make some money but I was also doing it

Table 2.3   Motives of suppliers of cash-in-hand work in English localities

% of cash-in-hand work supplied primarily to	Whole sample
Make money	50
Help out the customer	22
Build community networks	28
Total	100

Source: English Localities Survey.

[mending a leaking tap] for them because they were desperate to get it repaired' (employed man).

Although profit was the principal motive when working for firms 'on the side' (5 per cent of all cash-in-hand work) and engaging in self-employed activity for people they do not know well (25 per cent of all such work), it was not so when doing work for closer social relations, which covers 70 per cent of cash-in-hand work. Contrary to the conventional view that cash-in-hand work involves low-paid work conducted for and by formal or informal businesses, therefore, it was found that just 5 per cent of cash-in-hand work was of this type. This 'organised' underground economic activity included such jobs as cleaning a truck for £10 which took 3 hours, doing bar work for 2 weeks for £50, working in a restaurant for £2.00 per hour, working early mornings in a small bakery for £20 per month, working for three weeks in a canteen on a building site for £50, staffing an ice-cream stall for £2.80 per hour and refurbishing a pub for one week for £100.

The 25 per cent of work conducted on a self-employed basis for people previously unknown to the supplier, meanwhile, again covers a diverse array of activities. It includes activities ranging from the provision of various professional advisory services in spheres such as architecture, landscaping and financial planning through gardening services to household cleaning for people previously unknown to the self-employed person. This, moreover, was sometimes very well paid work and in 90 per cent of cases was undertaken purely to make money although there were again caveats often.

In very few instances where such labour was supplied to neighbours, friends, kin or other household members however, was it asserted to be primarily for the purpose of making money. Instead, non-economic rationales dominated. First, there are again community-building rationales. Many offered to do a job for a friend, neighbour or kin as a means of either maintaining or forging their social networks with them. Doing a job for a small payment was a way of mixing with and helping people they knew and at the same time, making a little money on the side. Second, suppliers also had 'redistributive' motives when undertaking cash-in-hand work for closer social relations. Many asserted that they already knew the customer and had conducted the work because the person would not otherwise have been able to do it. In these instances, which constituted 22 per cent of all cash-in-hand work supplied, those involved were either mainly people with professional craft skills (e.g. plumbers, electricians) and often employed who supplied these skills to close social relations for a fee well under the market price, or else they were unemployed or early retired people who saw themselves as helping out those who had less free time than themselves by supplying their time.

On the one hand, those with professional craft skills (e.g. plumbers, electricians) and often employed (and men) supplied these skills to close social relations. As these suppliers asserted, 'I helped out because they couldn't afford to do the job any other way' (male employed electrician), 'without my help, they would have been stuck' (male employed plumber) and 'they have not got any money so the least I could do was help them out' (male self-employed decorator). In no case, however, was this work offered for free because the supplier was conscious that this would be unacceptable to the family receiving the work. Instead, a fee was charged which, although well above constituting a token gesture, was well below the normal market price. Indeed, the general tendency was that the price charged fell below the market norm to a greater extent the closer the social relationship between the customer and supplier.

The second type of redistributive supplier is normally unemployed or an early retired person (and often women) who helped out those who had less free time than them by supplying their time. As such, whilst these suppliers saw themselves as helping out by giving their time, the rationale of the customer was one of redistributing cash to these people. Consequently, this 'trade' between 'time rich–money poor' and 'money rich–time poor' people, far from being seen as exploitative in the eyes of participants, was more perceived as involving mutual reciprocity. Each partner was giving the resource that they possessed in relatively greater amounts to the other.

Therefore, even if there has been the penetration of monetary relations into ever more spheres of social life (cf. Harvey, 1989; Sayer, 1997), these exchanges are by no means everywhere characterised by market-like relations. At least in the realm of cash-in-hand work, monetary exchange is not always profit-motivated. Instead, this form of work, often seen as the exemplar of the worst excesses of profit-motivated market exchange, displays how it is wholly feasible to have monetary transactions that are embedded in alternative work relations and motives. As Zelizer (1994, p. 215) puts it, 'Money has not become the free, neutral and dangerous destroyer of social relations', at least in some cases.

Given that a lot of this monetised exchange does not atomise people simply into the commodity labour or buyer, it is perhaps little surprise that the pricing mechanism used to determine value is not wholly grounded in market norms. Instead, there is a fluidity of prices and pricing arrangements depending on the socio-economic context and social relationship between the seller and purchaser. These norms concerning price arrangements are complex and often implicit, as Zelizer (1994) has previously found when discussing how money is earmarked for different purposes.

One key determinant of the price, for instance, is the closeness of the social relations, such as whether the seller and/or buyer are close kin or a more distant friend and/or neighbour. Prices diverge from market norms to a much greater degree when close social relations such as kin are involved than when more distant social relations are the transacting partners, such as a friend-of-a-friend. As social relations between the supplier and customer become more distant in a social sense, the more convergence there is to market norms, as Leonard (1994) has previously shown on a West Belfast council estate. Another key determinant of price is the socio-economic context, especially the socio-economic status of the recipient and/or seller of the cash-in-hand work relative to the seller and/or recipient respectively. This socio-economic context, moreover, combines with the social relationship aspect to produce complex pricing structures. For instance, if the recipient is unemployed and the seller an employed craft person, as well as kin, then the price tends to diverge markedly from the market norm.

In sum, the conventional market price is the point of reference, or measuring rod, for quantifying what will be charged. It is the fixed point used to provide the basis for the more fluid and transient modes of determining value. In contrast to Offer's (1997, p. 453) reading of reciprocity, therefore, this study does not find any evidence that in 'the long term … the exchange value will approximate not to the use value (expressed by the demand curve) but to the market value'. Rather, different pricing mechanisms are identified embedded in socio-economic norms, relations and contexts that continuously override any convergence towards market norms.

As such, despite the popular view that cash-in-hand work is conducted for unadulterated economic reasons, studies of the motives of suppliers and customers reveal that such a market-orientated reading of cash-in-hand work is necessary but insufficient for fully understanding the cash-in-hand sphere. It appears that monetary relations are being penetrated by alternative logics that lie outside the profit motive and are humanising the money system by harnessing it to pursue redistribution and sociality at the micro-level. As such, this study from England highlights the demonstrable construction and practice of relations of production and consumption based on monetary exchange beyond the profit motive. This raises the fascinating notion that participants in this hidden economy of favours are largely stepping aside from the norms of market relations when engaging in monetary exchanges in a distinctive and possibly suggestive world of production and consumption. They are constructing monetary exchanges where profit-driven market relations are largely absent and in so doing, displaying that the relationship between monetary exchange and the profit motive is not hermetically sealed. The outcome is that new possibilities for transforming exchange relations are being opened up within this paid social economy of favours. One of the key tasks throughout this book, in consequence, is to begin to map out not only the nature of this so far unrecognised hidden economy of favours that challenges the hegemony of capitalist relations in the realm of monetised exchange, but also to identify where this social economy of favours is to be found, who engages in it and why they do so. Before concluding this chapter, however, it is necessary to briefly introduce some of the implications of this re-theorisation of cash-in-hand work for a body of work that superficially, appears to have little to do with the study of cash-in-hand work, namely the social capital literature.

Implications for the study of social capital

Ever since the studies by Stack (1974) and Young and Wilmott (1975), social networks have been recognised as resources that people can draw upon. Indeed, the study of social capital has a long history in social scientific thought (Coleman, 1988; Portes, 1998). During the past few years, however, the seminal work of Robert Putnam (2000) on social capital has placed the resources stored in personal relationships firmly on the policy agenda (e.g. Home Office, 1999; Social Exclusion Unit, 2000). Defining social capital as 'connections among individuals – social networks and the norms of reciprocity and trustworthiness that arise from them' (Putnam, 2000, p. 19), there has been a growing concern that kinship and non-kinship bonds are dwindling (e.g. Cattell and

Evans, 1999; Forrest and Kearns, 1999; Silburn *et al.*, 1999; Williams and Windebank, 2000a,c,d, 2001d; Wood and Vamplew, 1999). The reasons why this is seen to be happening, however, are multifarious. First, there are a range of economic processes such as longer working hours leading to time famine and an inability to participate in activities outside employment, the increased mobility of labour leading to the inability to put down roots and the demise of small locally owned businesses. Second, there are a host of socio-cultural processes such as the increasingly rapid pace of family formation and disintegration, the demise of the extended family, the increased use of private cars and the shift from active leisure in the public sphere to passive leisure in the home. Third and finally, there are environmental reasons ranging from poor housing estate design and the loss of public spaces, through the shift towards out-of-town shopping facilities and the decline of local services, to inappropriate policies on social housing allocation. Although different emphases are given to individual sets of factors, the common perception is that there has been a decline in the resources stored in personal relationships that people can draw upon.

Earlier work on this issue focused upon the benefits of maintaining and developing close ties between people who already know each other (e.g. Stack, 1974; Young and Wilmott, 1975). The new wave of thinking associated with social capital, however, emphasises the beneficial effects of ties between people who do not know each other very well, or what Granovetter (1973) calls the 'strength of weak ties'. In other words, there has been a shift from emphasising 'bonding' to 'bridging' social capital (Gittell and Vidal, 1998; Putnam, 1995a,b, 2000). The assumption is that the more people connect with each other, the more they will trust each other and the better off they will become both individually and collectively.

How, therefore, do current policy approaches seek to develop social capital? The increasing emphasis in policy and grant-giving circles is on enhancing those formal community-based groups that already exist, or what is here called 'third sector' community engagement. In part, this is purely because funding such groups is simpler than attempting either to expand more informal forms of co-operative endeavour and/or to create new associations and thus to risk the consequences of challenging the current voluntary sector lobby (see MacGillivray *et al.*, 2001). In other part, it is because community or voluntary participation is conceptualised in terms of a 'ladder' of activities. At the top are seen to be 'formal' voluntary organisations while under them are progressively more informal forms of community action with one-to-one exchange between family and neighbours at the 'bottom' (Home Office, 1999; Social Exclusion Unit, 2000). Based on a 'stages of growth' model, formal voluntary organisations are seen as a 'mature' form of co-operative endeavour that other activities will evolve into as they develop. The notion that this may be a spectrum of activity rather than a ladder is not seriously entertained. As a result, few pay attention to harnessing one-to-one reciprocity. Often, this is also quite simply because policy-makers do not know how to do so. Giving money to formal community or voluntary organisations and evaluating them, in contrast, is something that they know how to do. Viewing them as a mature form of co-operative endeavour is thus a useful post-hoc rationalisation to justify policies to concentrate resources on their development rather than resource 'lower order' activities.

The English Localities Survey, however, suggests that this 'third sector' route of developing existing community-based groups might not be the most effective way to bolster social capital and that a 'fourth sector' route of developing one-to-one aid needs to be more seriously considered. If the intention of bolstering social capital is to facilitate forms of reciprocity that provide a source of material aid, then the study of the rural areas in the English Localities Survey suggests that one-to-one aid rather than third sector groups needs to become the focus of initiatives to develop social capital. In 99 per cent of circumstances where material aid was provided via acts of reciprocity, this occurred on a one-to-one basis. Third sector groups were primarily used as a source of sociality (Williams, 2002b,d, 2003c; Williams and Windebank, 1999c,d, 2001g, 2002a,b). This study, therefore, strongly supports the finding of McGlone *et al.* (1998) that community-based groups as sources of material aid hardly figure in people's coping practices.

To explain this, the attitudes towards giving and receiving material help in rural populations were examined. First, it was found that there was a widespread perception that 'charity' should be avoided (cf. Berking, 1999; Kempson, 1996). People shunned both receiving and giving one-way help. Not only did people not want to be seen as a 'charity case' but also the population widely understood the negative implications of giving charity to others. As such, the potential of voluntarism, at least in the realm of material support, was found to be severely limited whether this was in the form of community-based groups wishing to deliver material aid or it was in the form of one-way giving and receiving.

Attitudes towards two-way one-to-one giving and receiving (i.e. reciprocity), meanwhile, depended upon the social relations involved. Although there was widespread acceptance of providing unpaid help on a one-to-one basis to and for kin, unlike earlier studies (e.g. Young and Wilmott, 1975), a general wariness was identified in relation to the provision of unpaid help to friends, neighbours and others in the community. Instead, payment was involved in 54 per cent of all cases. Indeed, unpaid aid was provided only when it was considered unacceptable, inappropriate or impossible to pay somebody (Burns *et al.*, 2004). To ignore this paid mutual aid, or what has been called above a 'hidden economy of favours', is thus to ignore a large amount of the reciprocal exchange that takes place in contemporary advanced economies. Indeed, studying solely unpaid mutual aid may well cause the resulting maps of inequality with regard to social capital to be skewed if the contours of paid mutual aid are such that they work in opposition to the prevalence of mutual aid. As such, if social capital is to be more fully understood as well as its uneven contours, then the study of this hidden economy of favours, as will be shown throughout this book, will need to be integrated into the study of social capital. Until now, such activity has been off the radar screen of social capital analysts.

Conclusions

This chapter has reviewed previous conceptualisations of cash-in-hand work so as to situate the theoretical framework developed in this book. Analysing the past literature on cash-in-hand work, the general tendency has been to focus upon the magnitude of the underground sector and how this varies socially and geographically. Using the marginality thesis as the referent, that asserts how cash-in-hand work is concentrated amongst marginalised groups and areas, a Popperian-like approach has ensued whereby most studies have done little more than affirm or falsify this thesis, with the majority showing that such work is not concentrated amongst marginalised groups and/or areas but is instead a means of accumulating advantage for more affluent groups and areas.

To escape this narrow approach to knowledge advancement, this chapter has started to investigate the nature of cash-in-hand work. Recently, the cultural turn/s across the social sciences have resulted in a rethinking of whether monetised exchange is always embedded in profit-motivated behaviour. Until now, however, such studies have been shown usually to confine themselves to rather marginal small-scale spaces. Here, therefore, cash-in-hand work has been analysed that is sometimes seen to be an exemplar of unbridled profit-motivated capitalism and nearly always viewed as a form of employment heavily imbued with profit motivations on the part of both the consumer and supplier. This has revealed that such abstract universal hues oversimplify and obscure the heterogeneous nature of cash-in-hand work. If cash-in-hand work in contemporary advanced economies is to be more fully understood, then the totalising economic discourse that portrays monetary exchange in general, and cash-in-hand work in particular, as universally market-like and profit-motivated will need to be replaced with a more socially, culturally and geographically embedded appreciation of monetised exchange. Here, it has been uncovered that although some cash-in-hand work is of this variety, such work is also often undertaken under social relations more akin to mutual aid for friends, neighbours and kin for non-profit reasons. As such, cash-in-hand work is here theorised to be composed of not only an 'underground economy' of market-like, profit-motivated, cash-in-hand work but also a 'hidden' or 'social' economy of favours where such work is conducted under social relations and for purposes more akin to unpaid mutual aid.

This finding that mutual aid is composed not only of unpaid giving and receiving but also monetised exchanges conducted for non-economic reasons has important implications for understanding the nature of social capital that have not so far been considered in the literature. Here, in consequence, it has been argued that if social capital is to be more fully understood, then this body of knowledge needs to further expand its scope to incorporate the 'hidden economy of favours'. The issue of the variable nature of cash-in-hand work will be returned to in Part II where this subject will be analysed in some depth. Chapter 3 considers the various methodologies that have been used to examine cash-in-hand work so as to evaluate their appropriateness for understanding the character of such work.

3
Methodologies for Measuring Cash-in-hand Work

Introduction

As outlined in Chapter 2, this book seeks to move the study of cash-in-hand work beyond the conventional focus upon assessing the variable magnitude of cash-in-hand work and towards the largely uncharted terrain of the economic relations within which such work is embedded and the motives of suppliers and purchasers. Here, in consequence, the range of methods that has been used in the past to study cash-in-hand work are evaluated critically in terms of their ability not only to measure the volume of cash-in-hand work but also the economic relations and motives underpinning such work.

These methodologies for measuring cash-in-hand work lie on a spectrum ranging from indirect to direct techniques. Those assuming that research participants will not be forthcoming about whether or not they engage in cash-in-hand work have tended to seek evidence indirectly in macroeconomic data collected and/or constructed for other purposes. The belief is that even if cash-in-hand workers wish to hide their incomes, their work will be nonetheless revealed at the macroeconomic level and it is these statistical traces of their cash-in-hand work that are examined by indirect approaches. At the other end of the spectrum are those who assume that despite the illicit nature of cash-in-hand work, reliable data can be directly collected from research participants. These analysts thus conduct mostly intensive investigations on small samples, such as through locality studies, of the nature and extent of cash-in-hand work using direct survey methods. Evaluating critically the range of methods that lie on this continuum, this chapter will reveal that, as a general rule of thumb, indirect techniques are not only inaccurate as a measure of the volume of cash-in-hand work in society but also wholly inappropriate for understanding the economic relations and motives involved in such work. Resulting from this finding, the chapter then outlines the direct survey methods available and the approach developed and used by the author to generate the results that are reported in this book.

Before evaluating critically the contrasting methodologies that can be used to examine cash-in-hand work, however, it is important to make the rather obvious point that care should be taken to consider the methodology used whenever reporting results. This is because different methods produce remarkably different results. Take, for example, the magnitude of cash-in-hand work. For the same nation in the same year, estimates have ranged from 1.5–27 per cent of GDP in the United States, 2–22 per cent in the United Kingdom and 2–35 per cent in France (Barthelemy, 1991; Thomas, 1988). Estimates of cash-in-hand work in the United States in 1976, for example, ranged from 3.5 per cent of GNP (Tanzi, 1982) to 22 per cent (Feige, 1979). Similarly, estimates for the United Kingdom in 1979 range from 2 per cent (O'Higgins, 1981) to 14 per cent (Bhattacharrya, 1990) of GNP, whilst for Sweden in 1978 they range from 3 per cent (Hansson, 1982) to 15 per cent (Frey and Pommerehne, 1984) and in Germany in the same year, they range from 3 per cent (Kirchgassner, 1981) through to 16 per cent (Petersen, 1982). Unless the measurement technique being used in each case is understood, the reasons underlying these variations will not be appreciated. Nor will one realize how many of the assertions about the nature of cash-in-hand work are assumptions, rather than findings, of the specific technique being used.

Indeed, unless detailed attention is paid to the methods employed before reading-off trends from results, all attempts to review the size and character of cash-in-hand work will end in confusion over how to interpret apparently contradictory findings. It is only by unpacking the methods utilised in each study and interpreting the results in terms of these techniques that a clear understanding of the size and nature of cash-in-hand work can be achieved. To provide an overview and critical evaluation of these contrasting methods of researching cash-in-hand work, therefore, First, the relatively indirect methods of the macro-economic approaches are analysed and second, the more direct survey methods.

Indirect methods

The relatively indirect methods used to evaluate cash-in-hand work are of three kinds. First, there are those that seek statistical traces of such work in non-monetary indicators such as the discrepancies in labour supply figures or the number of very small firms. Second, there are those that track down evidence of cash-in-hand work in monetary indicators collected for other purposes, and third and finally, there are those that investigate discrepancies between income and expenditure levels either at the aggregate or household level. Each is here considered in turn. The problem with all of these approaches, as will be shown, is that these so-called 'traces' of cash-in-hand work not only provide an unreliable and inaccurate proxy of the volume of this work but also provide very little information on the nature of such work. Instead, in most cases, they are driven by some very crude assumptions concerning its character that are far from proven.

Indirect non-monetary methods

Two of the most common indirect approaches that use non-monetary surrogate indicators to estimate the extent of cash-in-hand work in advanced economies are first, those that seek out traces of informal employees in formal labour force statistics and second, those that use very small enterprises as a proxy for the existence of cash-in-hand work.

Labour force estimates

Methods that seek to measure cash-in-hand work from formal labour force statistics are of two types. First, there are those that identify various types of employment (e.g. self-employment, second-job holding) as proxy indicators of the existence of cash-in-hand work and then look for unaccountable increases in the official labour force statistical data on the numbers employed in these categories (e.g. Alden, 1982; Crnkovic-Pozaic, 1999; Del Boca and Forte, 1982; Hellberger and Schwarze, 1986). The problem, however, is that the idea that cash-in-hand work prevails in these categories of employment is an assumption, rather than finding, of the technique, and there is no way of discerning the extent to which it is cash-in-hand work, rather than other factors, that has led to an increase in these categories of employment. The growth of self-employment, for instance, is not simply a result of the rise in cash-in-hand work. It has also been due to such trends as the rise of an enterprise culture, increased subcontracting in the production process and the advent of other forms of flexible production arrangement since the early 1980s, when most studies using this method were undertaken. Second-job holding, furthermore, is by no means directly a result of cash-in-hand work except if such job holding is illegal *per se*. It is also in part the combined result of broader economic and cultural restructuring processes such as the demise of the 'breadwinner wage' and the proliferation of part-time work. To identify the proportion of growth in either self-employment or multiple-job holding attributable to such processes and the share attributable to cash-in-hand work at a particular moment is thus a difficult if not impossible task.

Second, therefore, those who analyse official employment data for evidence of cash-in-hand work have sought discrepancies in the results of different surveys used to compile official employment statistics. In the United States, for example, the Census Bureau's Current Population Survey (CPS) has been compared with the Bureau of Labor Statistics (BLS) survey of firms. The CPS includes a monthly sampling of about 60 000 households that asks questions about the work status of their occupants and everyone is classified as employed, unemployed or not in the labour force, whilst the BLS survey examines establishments to determine the number on the payroll. The comparison of the two data sets has been premised on the assumption that those working on a cash-in-hand basis would declare themselves, or be declared as job holders, in the household survey but would not show up on the books of business enterprises. The discrepancy in the numbers between the two surveys has been thus taken as the number employed on a cash-in-hand basis, with changes in the difference between the two sets of figures seen as a measure of its growth or decline (e.g. Denison, 1982; Mattera, 1985; US Congress Joint Economic Committee, 1983). Similar methods have also been adopted in Portugal by the Instituto de Pesquisa Social Daniao de Gois which examined the number of cash-in-hand workers by exploring the difference between the total number of people registered as salaried workers and the total number of workers registered in the Ministry of Work statistics (see Lobo, 1990b).

However, many problems exist with this approach. In terms of its relevance for measuring the volume of cash-in-hand work, the first problem as both Bajada (2002) and Williams and Windebank (1998) highlight, is that it erroneously assumes that each individual is either a formal or cash-in-hand worker and in so doing, misses a vast amount of cash-in-hand work conducted by those who have a formal job. Second, by analysing only those employed in businesses, it assumes that all cash-in-hand work is conducted on an 'organised' basis and misses both more autonomous forms of underground sector activity as well as cash-in-hand work conducted for households. Third, there is no reason to assume that a cash-in-hand worker will describe him/herself as employed in a household survey whilst the employer will not in a business survey. And fourth and finally, the fact that such analyses have resulted in contradictory results, with some studies showing no change in the size of cash-in-hand work in the post-war years (e.g. Denison, 1982) and others showing growth (US Congress Joint Economic Committee, 1983) intimates the need for great caution. Identifying the magnitude of cash-in-hand work through formal labour force statistics, in sum, is beset by problems that cannot be easily transcended and this method has waned in popularity since its heyday in the early 1980s.

When seeking to understand the nature (rather than volume) of cash-in-hand work, moreover, this approach suffers from the problems created by its own assumptions. Its premise that all cash-in-hand work is a form of employment leads to a failure to get to grips with the many one-off tasks undertaken on a cash-in-hand basis, whether in the underground sector or the hidden economy of favours. In consequence, such an approach provides little, if any, information on the character of cash-in-hand work since it is from the outset stifled by a priori assumptions about its characteristics.

Very small enterprise (VSE) approach

Indirect non-monetary methods are not just composed of techniques that seek evidence of cash-in-hand work in formal labour force statistics. Various other non-monetary proxy indicators are also used. For many commentators, very small enterprises (VSEs) represent a useful alternative non-monetary proxy (e.g. Fernandez-Kelly and Garcia, 1989; International Labour Office, 2002; Portes and Sassen-Koob, 1987; Sassen and Smith, 1992; US General Accounting Office, 1989). The assumption is that in advanced economies, most cash-in-hand work takes place in smaller enterprises because of their reduced visibility, greater flexibility and better opportunities to escape state controls. Larger firms, meanwhile, are viewed as subject to more state regulation and risk-averse to the potential penalties so will be less likely to directly employ cash-in-hand workers, although they are purported to subcontract to smaller firms who use such labour.

As an indicator of cash-in-hand work, however, the VSE approach is subject to two contradictory assumptions. On the one hand, not all VSEs engage in cash-in-hand practices, which could lead to an overestimate. On the other hand, fully informal VSEs will escape government record keeping that could lead to an underestimate (Portes, 1994). Moreover, it seems likely that the extent to which VSEs participate either wholly or partly in cash-in-hand practices will vary according to the geographical context in which they are operating (Williams and Windebank,

1998). As such, estimates of both the size and growth/decline of cash-in-hand work using this proxy indicator can only be very approximate. More importantly, such a proxy totally ignores more individualised forms of cash-in-hand work conducted by people on a one-to-one basis to meet final demand. As Portes (1994, p. 440–1) thus concludes,

> By themselves, ... such series represent a very imperfect measure of the extent of informal activity. It is impossible to tell from them which firms actually engage in irregular practices and the character of these practices. All that can be said is that small firms, assumed to be the principal locus of informality, are not declining fast and actually appear to increase significantly during periods of economic recession.

Yet despite the inappropriateness of this indicator, it is still widely used. The International Labour Office, for example, collects data from 54 countries on 'informal sector enterprise' (International Labour Office, 2002). Despite the existence of an internationally agreed definition adopted by the Fifteenth International Conference of Labour Statisticians (ICLS), most of these 54 countries still adhere to their own national definitions, 21 of which use the criterion of non-registration of the enterprise, either alone or in combination with other criteria such as small size or type of workplace location, while 33 countries use small size as a criterion, either alone or in combination with non-registration or workplace location. In consequence, variants of the VSE approach are still in common usage and it should not be thought that this indirect non-monetary approach is in abeyance. If anything, and as shown by the International Labour Office, quite the opposite is the case, despite its inappropriateness to understanding the full range of cash-in-hand work in contemporary societies.

Although the labour force and VSE measures are the most popular non-monetary indicators used to measure cash-in-hand work, they are not the only one's employed. Recent years have seen various other non-monetary indicators adopted to measure cash-in-hand work, such as electricity demand (e.g. Friedman *et al.*, 2000; Lacko, 1999). Ultimately, however, and whichever indicator is employed, indirect non-monetary proxy measures all suffer from the same problems. They provide little more than a crude indicator of the extent of cash-in-hand work and little, if any, information about the nature of cash-in-hand work. As such, other analysts have turned to monetary indicators in the belief that this will enable a much closer estimate of cash-in-hand work.

Indirect monetary methods

Methods seeking evidence of cash-in-hand work in indirect monetary indicators have concentrated largely on three proxies, namely large denomination notes, the cash-deposit ratio and money transactions.

Large denomination notes approach

In this approach, the circulation of high denomination bank notes is seen as a key indicator of the prevalence of cash-in-hand work (Carter, 1984; Freud, 1979; Henry, 1976; Matthews, 1982). This methodology, used principally during the 1970s and early 1980s, but now falling out of favour, is embedded in a portrayal that views cash-in-hand workers carrying around a fat roll of bank notes. It assumes not only that they use cash exclusively in their transactions but also that they handle large quantities of cash and exchange high denomination bank notes. For example, Henry (1976) asserts that the rise in demand for $50 and $100 notes in the US between 1960 and 1970, a period which saw a rapid increase in non-cash methods of payment such as personal cheque accounts and credit cards, could only be explained in terms of an expansion in profit-oriented crime and tax evasion. His view is that these activities require extra cash so as to avoid leaving traceable records. Taking into account factors such as price levels, personal consumption expenditures and federal income tax revenues, he estimates that the extra demand for large denomination notes (US$50 and over) resulting from tax evasion to be as high as US$30 billion in 1973.

However, this method is problematic for at least three reasons. First, it cannot separate the use of large denomination notes for crime from their use in cash-in-hand work, meaning that one has no way of knowing the proportion used for crime and the share for cash-in-hand work. Second, there is little evidence that those engaged in cash-in-hand work use large denomination notes. Indeed, many cash-in-hand transactions are for relatively small amounts of money (e.g. Cornuel and Duriez, 1985; Evason and Woods, 1995; Tanzi, 1982) and do not necessarily even involve the use of cash in transactions (see below). Using high denomination bank notes, therefore, seems to be not only a poor proxy indicator of the level of cash-in-hand work but also grounded in a conceptualisation of its nature that is, at the very best, a description of only a very small segment of all cash-in-hand work.

Third and finally, there are a multitude of other factors that may account for the increased use of large denomination bank notes in contemporary society. On the one hand, inflation needs to be taken into account. Porter and Bayer (1989) in the United States present strong econometric evidence for a relationship between per capita holdings of $100 bills and the price level. In the United Kingdom, meanwhile, the increase in large denomination notes has been less than the rate of inflation. Between 1972 and 1982, the retail price index rose by 290 per cent whilst the average value of the denomination of bank notes only rose by 120 per cent, meaning that the average value of the denomination has declined by 40 per cent over this period when inflation is taken into account (Trundle, 1982). In Canada, moreover, Mirus and Smith (1989) note little change in real terms.

On the other hand, since this approach was propagated, profound transformations have taken place in both attitudes and behaviour towards cash payments. First, major alterations in modes of payment (e.g. credit and debit cards, store cards) have occurred resulting in a decline in cash usage. Second, a restructuring of formal financial services in the advanced economies, reflected in the 'flight of financial institutions' from poorer populations (Collard *et al.*, 2001; Kempson and Whyley, 1999; Leyshon and Thrift, 1994), has necessitated increased cash usage amongst the financially excluded. These counter-tendencies thus make it difficult to discern whether alterations in cash usage are due to the restructuring of formal financial services, shifts in attitudes and behaviour, or the growth/decline of cash-in-hand work.

The large denomination notes method, in sum, represents a very unreliable indicator of the extent and changing magnitude of cash-in-hand work and makes some heroic and erroneous assumptions about the overall character of this work. It is, in conclusion, of little use so far as understanding the nature of cash-in-hand work in contemporary society is concerned, especially if one wants to get to grips with the economic relations and motives underpinning such exchange.

The cash–deposit ratio approach

Rather than analyse the volume of large denomination bank notes in circulation, another indirect monetary method used to measure cash-in-hand work has involved examining the ratio of currency in circulation to demand deposits. Again grounded in the assumption that in order to conceal income, illegitimate transactions will occur in cash, this approach seeks an estimate of the currency in circulation required by legal activities and subtracts this figure from the actual money in circulation. The difference, multiplied by the velocity of money, is an estimate of the magnitude of cash-in-hand work. The ratio of this figure to the observed GNP then provides a measure of the proportion of the national economy represented by cash-in-hand work.

Indeed, it was this approach that Gutmann (1977, 1978) used in the United States in his seminal papers to bring cash-in-hand work to the attention of the North American public. He estimated that this work was worth some US$176 billion in 1976. Making the courageous assumption that there was no cash-in-hand work in the United States prior to the Second World War since levels of taxation were so low as to make tax evasion strategies unnecessary, he takes the ratio for this period as the baseline norm and then finds that the ratio rose substantially by the mid-1970s so that US$29 billion was in circulation beyond the figure required for legitimate transactions, assuming that the illegitimate cash circulated at the same velocity as the legitimate transactions. Cash-in-hand work was argued to represent more than 10 per cent of the officially calculated national income and the amount of currency in circulation was asserted to be equivalent to US$1522.72 for a family of four. Such findings proved very influential with politicians and the media, and this approach was subsequently widely adopted (Atkins, 1999; Caridi and Passerini, 2001; Cocco and Santos, 1984; Matthews, 1983; Matthews and Rastogi, 1985; Meadows and Pihera, 1981; Santos, 1983; Tanzi, 1980).

However, it is a method that suffers from serious problems. First, cash is not always the medium for undeclared monetised exchange. There is plenty of evidence that undeclared work utilises cheques and credit cards as well (see below). Indeed, in some countries such as Italy, laws have precluded the disclosure of information concerning bank accounts, so it is unnecessary to use only cash in cash-in-hand work (Contini, 1982). Moreover, and as Smith (1985) identifies in the United States, whether an undeclared payment is made in cash or by cheque depends on the same factors as determine the mode of payment in formal employment (i.e. the size of the transaction and the seller's confidence in the purchaser's cheque). Second, this approach again has no way of distinguishing what share of the illegitimate cash circulation is due to cash-in-hand work and what proportion is due to crime, nor how it is changing over time. Third, the choice of the cash–deposit ratio as a measure of cash-in-hand work is an arbitrary one that is not derived from economic theory (e.g. Trundle, 1982) and it is not clear why this was chosen rather than others.

Fourth, and again similar to the high denomination notes approach, the cash–deposit ratio is influenced not only by the level of cash-in-hand work but a myriad of other tendencies, often working in opposite directions to one another. As already stated, whilst methods of payment have changed, with credit cards and new interest-bearing assets reducing cash usage (e.g. Bajada, 2002), increasing financial exclusion (e.g. refusal of credit cards and cheque accounts to the poor) resulting from the banks 'flight' to affluent markets, has increased the use of cash amongst some populations. Mattera (1985) echoes these criticisms arguing that Gutmann fails to take account of factors other than those to do with cash-in-hand work, which might have contributed to the decline of the currency ratio. To take into account these factors, some commentators have refined this method. Matthews (1983), Matthews and Rastogi (1985) and Tanzi (1980), rather than attributing the entire increase in cash usage to greater levels of cash-in-hand work, instead focus upon only the proportion of the increase that can be shown to result from cash-in-hand work. These approaches, although more sophisticated, are not without their critics. Smith (1986) for instance, questions the appropriateness and value of the statistical variables employed by Matthews (1983), such as the identification of a positive causal relationship between rises in unemployment levels and the growth of cash-in-hand work. Even using Matthews' own figures, cash-in-hand work expanded most rapidly at a time when unemployment increased comparatively little (Smith, 1986). Thomas (1988), moreover, details some stark differences between the results obtained in Matthews (1983) and Matthews and Rastogi (1985), which neither study attempted to explain.

Fifth, the choice of a base period when cash-in-hand work supposedly did not exist is problematic, especially given the sensitivity of the results to which base year is chosen. O'Higgins (1981) shows in the United Kingdom that if 1974 is taken as the base year, 16.5 per cent of the currency in circulation was fuelling cash-in-hand work in 1978. However, if 1963 is taken as the base year, cash-in-hand work became negative in 1978. Thomas (1988) highlights the problems associated with the need to locate a year when cash-in-hand work did not exist. For him, the choice seems to be determined more by the availability of data than by any other factor and is somewhat *ad hoc*.

Indeed, there is little evidence that some period exists in history where cash-in-hand work was zero. Such work has been in existence as long as there have been rules and regulations with regard to employment. Henry (1978), for example, cites examples of fiddling and tax evasion from the time of Aristotle, whilst Houghton (1979, p. 91) shows that in 1905, when tax was at a uniform rate of less than one shilling (5 pence) in the pound in the United Kingdom, a departmental committee reported that 'In the sphere in which self-assessment is still requisite, there is a substantial amount of fraud and evasion.' Smithies (1984), moreover, in a detailed case study of cash-in-hand work in five towns (Barnsley, Birkenhead, Brighton and Hove, Walsall and part of North London) between 1914 to 1970, clearly demonstrates a continuity in the prevalence of such activity. Any method which measures the size of cash-in-hand work based on the assumption that there was a time when it did not exist is thus founded on suspect grounds (see Henry, 1978). Sixth, to convert the estimates of undeclared cash into undeclared income, it is necessary to know the velocity of cash circulation in the cash-in-hand sphere. Given the lack of data, the standard approach assumes the same velocity as in the formal sphere. However, there is no evidence that the two velocities are the same (Frey and Weck, 1983). Seventh, it is impossible to determine how much of the currency of a country is held domestically and how much abroad. Some of the cash which the cash–deposit ratio assumes is held domestically will be doubtless located abroad causing an exaggeration in the estimate of cash-in-hand work. Finally, and perhaps most importantly so far as the purposes of this book are concerned, this approach does not allow one to consider the nature of cash-in-hand work in terms of either the economic relations within which the work is conducted or the motives of the participants. In a bid to overcome one of problems with this approach (i.e. that informal transactions are assumed to occur in cash), the next approach relaxes this assumption.

The money transactions approach

Recognising that cheques as well as cash are used in 'cash-in-hand' transactions, Feige (1979) measures its magnitude by estimating the extent to which the total quantity of monetary transactions exceeds what would be predicted in the absence of cash-in-hand work. As evidence that cheques as well as cash are used in undeclared transactions in the United States, Feige (1990) quotes a study by the Internal Revenue Service (IRS) showing that between a quarter and third of unreported income was paid by cheque rather than currency. Many other studies identify similar tendencies. In Norway, for instance, Isachsen *et al.* (1982) find that in 1980, about 20 per cent of informal services were paid for by cheque, whilst in Detroit, Smith (1985) provides a higher estimate in the realm of informal home repair, displaying that bills were settled roughly equally in cheques and cash.

By relaxing this cash-only assumption, the unsurprising result is that monetary-transaction approaches generally produce much higher estimates of the size of cash-in-hand work than other approaches. For instance, Feige (1990) reports that the US underground economy as a proportion of total reported adjusted gross income (AGI) rose from 0 in

1940 (the base year) to 20 per cent in 1945, declined subsequently to about 6 per cent in 1960, increased rapidly to reach 24 per cent in 1983 and then declined again to about 18 per cent in 1986.

Before accepting such findings, however, it must be recognised that this approach suffers exactly the same problems as the cash–deposit approach. The only problem it overcomes is the acceptance that cheques can be used in undeclared transactions. Here, in consequence, the criticisms are not repeated. Instead, and to conclude this review of the indirect monetary methods, two key points are made. First, there are inherent problems with all of these indirect methods for evaluating the volume of cash-in-hand work that raise grave doubts about the validity of their findings (see Tanzi, 1999; Thomas, 1999; Williams and Windebank, 1998). Yet despite this, such approaches continue to be used to measure its magnitude (e.g. Bhattacharya, 1999; Dixon, 1999; Gadea and Serrano-Sanz, 2002; Giles, 1999, 2001, 2002; Hill, 2002; OECD, 1997, 2000, 2002). Second, and most importantly for the purposes of this book, none of these approaches appear capable of providing information on the nature of cash-in-hand work, at least so far as the economic relations and motives underpinning such work are concerned. Given that 'the methodology underlying the monetary approaches ... rests upon questionable and generally untestable assumptions and ... the estimates they have generated are of dubious validity' (Thomas, 1988, p. 180), the only conclusion that can be reached is that 'Estimates of the size of the black economy based on cash indicators are best ignored' (Smith, 1986, p. 106). Here, therefore, another method of assessing cash-in-hand work that again uses monetary methods but in a more direct manner is evaluated.

Income/expenditure discrepancies

Another way of measuring the volume and nature of cash-in-hand work is to analyse differences in expenditure and income either at the aggregate national level or through detailed microeconomic studies of different types of individuals or households. This approach is premised on the assumption that even if cash-in-hand workers can conceal their incomes, they cannot hide their expenditures. An assessment of income/expenditure discrepancies is thus considered to reveal the extent of cash-in-hand work and where it is to be found.

First, there are aggregate level studies that analyse the discrepancy between national expenditure and national income so as to estimate the size of cash-in-hand work. Such studies have been conducted in Germany (e.g. Langfelt, 1989), Sweden (e.g. Hansson, 1982; Park, 1979), the United Kingdom (O'Higgins, 1981) and the United States (e.g. Macafee, 1980; Paglin, 1994). In the United States, for example, Paglin (1994) examines the discrepancy between household expenditure and income surveys published annually in the Bureau of Labor Statistics Consumer Expenditure Survey (CES). He finds that between 1984 and 1992, cash-in-hand work declined from 12.4 per cent of personal income in 1984 to 9.6 per cent in 1992, or from 10.2 per cent to 8.1 per cent of GDP over this period. This, he asserts, is principally due to the growth of formal employment during the 1980s in the United States. Nevertheless, he finds that in 1992, 10.2 per cent of households were income-poor but consumption-rich and views this to be a product of the existence of cash-in-hand work. Paglin (1994) finds that the poorest 20 per cent of households had an average after-tax income of US$5648 in 1991 but an average expenditure level of US$13 464. He then takes a major logical leap to conclude that a sizeable number of the income-poor households are engaged in cash-in-hand work, failing to consider whether this could be due to other factors (e.g. retirement household spending, households between jobs, major one-off expenditures on costly items).

Second, others study income/expenditure discrepancies at the household level. In the UK, the Family Expenditure Survey (FES) has been analysed (see Dilnot and Morris, 1981; Macafee, 1980; O'Higgins, 1981). Comparing households' income and expenditure in 1000 out of the 7200 households surveyed for the 1977 FES so as to examine whether some households appear to live beyond their means, Dilnot and Morris (1981) employ a variety of 'traps' to exclude discrepancies that might be explained by factors other than cash-in-hand work (e.g. high expenditure due to an unusual major purchase or to the running down of accumulated wealth). After all adjustments, Dilnot and Morris (1981), assuming that tax evasion existed in any household whose expenditure exceeded its reported income by more than 15 per cent, derived upper and lower estimates of its extent. They reveal that 9.6–14.8 per cent of households evaded taxes and that tax evasion was equivalent to 2.3–3.0 per cent of the GNP in 1977. Such evasion, moreover, was found to be more prevalent amongst the self-employed (who understate their income by between 10 and 15 per cent) and part-time employees than those in full-time employment. Smith (1986) further reinforces this in a study of the 1982 FES, concluding that the self-employed understate their income by between 10 and 20 per cent.

O'Higgins (1981), however, casts doubt over the accuracy of this method. He suggests that it could be an underestimate because 30 per cent of households refuse to participate in the FES, and it is possible and plausible both that a greater proportion of non-respondents participate in cash-in-hand work than the 9.6 per cent of respondents suggested by the lower-bound estimate of Dilnot and Morris (1981) and probably to a greater extent than the identified average weekly figure of £31. As O'Higgins (1981) argues, even if as few as 25 per cent of non-respondents engage in cash-in-hand work to the extent of £31 weekly, the lower-bound estimate would be raised by almost half, yielding an adjusted lower estimate of 3.5 per cent of GNP.

Although this method has advantages over other indirect monetary methods, not least its reliance on relatively direct and statistically representative survey data, its problems remain manifold (see Thomas, 1988, 1992; Smith, 1986). For the discrepancy to represent a reasonable measure of the level of cash-in-hand work, one has to make a number of assumptions about the accuracy of the income and expenditure data. Take, for example, the expenditure side of the equation. Estimates such as those made by Dilnot and Morris (1981) depend upon the accurate declaration of expenditure to government interviewers by respondents. Mattera (1985) suggests that it is somewhat naive to assume that this is the case. Equally convincing is the criticism that, for most people, spending is either over- or under-estimated during a survey because records are kept by few members of the population compared with income, which for employees comes in regular recorded uniform instalments. Moreover, at an aggregate level at least, such expenditure will omit informal purchases by both declared and undeclared incomes (Dallago, 1991). Household-level expenditure studies also suffer from the fatal flaw of only examining final demand (i.e. consumer expenditure), not intermediate demand (i.e. business expenditure) for cash-in-hand goods and services. As such, it ignores cash-in-hand produced intermediate demand, such as cash-in-hand subcontracting as well as off-the-books employment by formal enterprises (Portes, 1994).

On the income side, meanwhile, these studies cannot decipher whether the income derives from criminal or cash-in-hand activities, or even whether it derives from wealth accumulated earlier such as money savings. In addition, and so far as studies such as the FES are concerned, there are problems of non-response as well as under-reporting (Thomas, 1992).

Consequently, it is difficult to accumulate accurate data on the extent of cash-in-hand work using this method. Weck-Hannemann and Frey (1985) in Switzerland bring such problems to the fore when they report that the national income tends to be larger than expenditure. According to this method, Swiss cash-in-hand work is negative. This is nonsensical and reveals that the discrepancy does not display the level of cash-in-hand work but is due to other factors. As Frey and Weck (1983, p. 24) conclude about these monetary methods 'One of the main shortcomings of all these approaches is that they do not concentrate on the causes and circumstances in which a shadow economy arises and exists.' Nor, moreover, do they explore the character of cash-in-hand work beyond crude estimates of its sectoral or occupational concentrations. To answer such issues, it is the more direct approaches to investigating cash-in-hand work that thus need to be examined.

Direct survey methods

Direct survey methods have been employed to evaluate the magnitude and/or character of cash-in-hand work in many nations, including Belgium (Pestieau, 1983; Kesteloot and Meert, 1999), Canada (Fortin *et al.*, 1996), Germany (Frey *et al.*, 1982), Italy (Censis, 1976), Norway (Isachsen and Strom, 1985), the Netherlands (e.g. Renooy, 1990; Van Eck and Kazemier, 1985), the United Kingdom (e.g. Leonard, 1994; Pahl, 1984; Williams and Windebank, 2003a) and the United States (Ross, 1978; Jensen *et al.*, 1995; Nelson and Smith, 1999; Tickamyer and Wood, 1998). To survey directly the magnitude and character of cash-in-hand work, one can in theory ask suppliers and/or purchasers of cash-in-hand work about the volume or the value of their exchanges, what they did/received, for/from whom and why.

Starting with the *volume* of cash-in-hand work, studies can directly or indirectly ask either households or businesses whether they have used cash-in-hand work to acquire specific goods and/or services. Alternatively, one can ask people about their supply of cash-in-hand work in specific activities. In practice, much of the research to assess the volume of cash-in-hand work has been conducted on a household level and has requested information from respondents both as suppliers and purchasers of cash-in-hand work (e.g. Leonard, 1994; Pahl, 1984; Warde, 1990). To explore the *value* of undeclared purchases and/or sales, meanwhile, the amount of money earned by sellers, or spent by consumers, with regard to cash-in-hand work can be examined. Again, most studies have tended to investigate respondents as both purchasers and sellers (e.g. Fortin *et al.*, 1996; Isachsen *et al.*, 1982; Lemieux *et al.*, 1994), although some examine respondents only as purchasers (e.g. McCrohan *et al.*, 1991; Smith, 1985).

This data can be collected, moreover, through either mail-shot questionnaires (e.g. Fortin *et al.*, 1996) or through face-to-face interviews that range from the relatively unstructured (e.g. Howe, 1988) to the relatively structured variety (e.g. Williams and Windebank, 2001a) using either open- and/or closed-ended questions. On the whole, and perhaps reflecting the lack of data available on this subject, most studies have used relatively quantitative approaches composed largely of closed-ended questions and then frequently employed a variety of more open-ended questions and/or qualitative methods for in-depth exploration of the findings (e.g. Leonard, 1994; Pahl, 1984). Indeed, even studies relying primarily on ethnography, such as that by Howe (1988), conduct some interviews as a quantitative precursor for their ethnographic material. Pahl (1984), meanwhile, used follow-up in-depth interviews with a limited number of households to explore specific issues.

Although direct studies could be carried out on either national, regional or local population samples, in most instances they have tended to be applied to particular localities (e.g. Barthe, 1985; Fortin *et al.*, 1996; Leonard, 1994; Pahl, 1984; Renooy, 1990; Warde, 1990; Williams and Windebank, 2003a), socio-economic groups such as home-workers (e.g. Phizacklea and Wolkowitz, 1995) or industrial sectors such as garment manufacturing (e.g. Lin, 1995). Indeed, unless governments decide to invest in conducting such direct studies, it seems unlikely that direct studies will move beyond the case study approach in the near future.

Examining criticisms of these direct survey methods, it is telling that these derive almost exclusively from those commentators using indirect approaches. Their major criticism is that researchers naively assume that people will reveal to them, or even know, the character and magnitude of cash-in-hand work in their lives. It is intimated on the one hand, that purchasers may not even know if such work is being offered informally or formally and on the other hand, that sellers will be reticent about disclosing the nature and extent of their cash-in-hand work since it is illegal activity.

The former point might be correct. For example, if a purchaser has his/her external windows cleaned or purchases some goods from a market stall, s/he might assume that this money is not declared when this is not necessarily the case, or *vice versa*. In other words, although consumers may often assume that goods and services bought in certain contexts are purchased on a cash-in-hand basis whilst in other contexts they are not, their assumptions might not be correct. Goods acquired in formal retail outlets, for example, may not only have been produced on a cash-in-hand basis but may even be sold in such a manner (e.g. in illegally inhabited shop premises) without the knowledge of the consumer. Not all those dealing in cash meanwhile, may necessarily be working on a cash-in-hand basis (e.g. they may not have confidence in the purchaser's cheque), just as some accepting cheques may be tax evaders. On the whole, therefore, although people who purchase goods and services may be more willing to reveal whether they think it has been bought on a cash-in-hand basis, they cannot necessarily be sure whether this is indeed the case unless the supplier informs them that this is so.

Despite the assertions of those critical of direct surveys, however, it is not necessarily the case that those supplying cash-in-hand work will be untruthful in their dealings with researchers. Indeed, such a criticism has been refuted many times although it continues to be raised. Pahl (1984), in his study of the Isle of Sheppey, questioned people both as suppliers and purchasers. He found that when the results from individuals as suppliers and purchasers were compared, the same level of cash-in-hand work was discovered. The implication, therefore, is that individuals are not so secretive as sometimes assumed about their cash-in-hand work. Just because it is activity hidden from or unregistered by the state for tax, social security and/or labour law purposes, it does not mean that people will hide it from each other or even from academic researchers. It also intimates that customers are not as wrong as might be considered about whether or not a supplier is working on a cash-in-hand basis.

Similar conclusions have been drawn concerning the openness of research participants in Canada (Fortin *et al.*, 1996) and the United Kingdom (Evason and Woods, 1995; Leonard, 1994; MacDonald, 1994). As MacDonald (1994) reveals in his study of cash-in-hand work amongst the unemployed, 'fiddling work' was not a provocative subject from their perspective. They happily talked about it in the same breath as discussing, for instance, their experiences of starting up in self-employment or of voluntary work. This willingness of people to talk about their cash-in-hand work was also identified by Leonard (1994) in Belfast.

Perhaps a more salient criticism is that the direct approaches have so far largely investigated only cash-in-hand work used in relation to final demand (spending by consumers on goods and services), not intermediate demand (spending by businesses). Final demand, however, accounts for only some two-thirds of total spending in most advanced economies. Such direct methods are thus missing the cash-in-hand work that takes place in the other third of the economy. This is a valid criticism of those studies that focus upon only households as customers of cash-in-hand work. Where respondents as suppliers of cash-in-hand work are considered, however, it is to be expected that this would gather data on work that not only met final but also intermediate demand.

To conclude, therefore, the particular strength of direct survey methods, compared with their indirect counterparts, is that they are specifically designed to generate data on cash-in-hand work rather than make sense of data collected for other purposes (Harding and Jenkins, 1989). The result is that they can be tailored to meet the needs of the particular research problem being investigated. This is particularly the case when it comes to exploring the character of cash-in-hand work, such as its distribution by gender, employment status, income and ethnicity, and the motivations underpinning engagement in cash-in-hand work. In consequence, and given the focus of this book, it is the data collected using these direct methods that are largely the focus herein. To enable the reader to understand some of the data in the forthcoming chapters, the next section thus focuses upon how this direct survey method has been put into operation in the English Localities Survey of cash-in-hand work.

Implementing direct methods: the English Localities Survey

Throughout this book, reference will be continuously made to the findings of the English Localities Survey of cash-in-hand work. Here, therefore, the methodology used to collect data is highlighted. Between 1998 and 2001, this survey collected primary data on cash-in-hand work using a 'household work practices' approach (see Nelson and Smith, 1999; Pahl, 1984; Sik, 1993; Smith, 2002; Wallace, 2002). This takes the household as the unit of analysis and then examines both the economic practices that households employ in order to undertake domestic service tasks and the work supplied on a paid and unpaid basis to others.

To do this, and despite the apparent success of mail-shot questionnaires in some other nations such as Canada (Fortin *et al.*, 1996), the English Localities Survey used face-to-face interviews. A pilot study based on a relatively unstructured interview schedule, however, revealed that interviewees found it both difficult to recall instances of cash-in-hand work and that comparative data was not being collected. In consequence, a relatively structured interview schedule was designed. This was centred on a list of 44 common services (see Table 3.1). The starting point in generating this list were the tasks used by Pahl (1984) in his seminal study of household work practices on the Isle of Sheppey. Unlike this earlier study, however, the motivations of suppliers and consumers were also investigated.

Table 3.1   List of tasks investigated in the English Localities Survey

House maintenance
–outdoor painting
–indoor painting
–wallpapering
–plastering
–mending a broken widow
–maintenance of appliances

Housework
–routine housework
–cleaning windows outdoors
–spring cleaning
–cleaning windows indoors
–doing the shopping
–washing clothes and sheets
–ironing
–cooking meals
–washing dishes
–hairdressing
–household administration

Car maintenance
–washing car
–repairing car
–car maintenance

Caring activities
–daytime baby-sitting
–night-time baby sitting
–educational activities
–pet care

Home improvement
–putting in double glazing
–plumbing
–electrical work
–house insulation
–putting in a bathroom suite
–building a garage
–building an extension
–putting in central heating
–carpentry

Making and repairing goods
–making clothes
–repairing clothes
–knitting
–making or repairing furniture
–making or repairing garden
    equipment
–making curtains

Gardening
–care of indoor plants
–outdoor borders
–outdoor vegetables
–lawn mowing

To identify cash-in-hand work conducted for households, the first issue analysed was the sources of labour used by the household to get these 44 tasks completed. The interviewee was asked whether each task had been undertaken in the household during the previous five years/year/month/week (depending on the activity). If not, they were asked why not. If it had been undertaken, however, they were asked: Who had conducted the task (e.g. a household member, kin living outside the household, a friend, neighbour, firm, landlord, etc); whether the person had been unpaid or paid; and if paid, whether it was 'cash-in-hand' or not, as well as how much they had been given. For each task completed, moreover, the respondent was asked in an open-ended manner why they had decided to get the work done using that source of labour so as to enable their motives to be understood and how they would have got the task done if they had not employed this labour.

Following this, the supply of both cash-in-hand work and unpaid community exchange by household members was examined. The interviewee was asked whether a household member had conducted each of the 44 tasks for another household and if so, who had done it, for whom, whether they had received money, how much they had received and why they had decided to do the task. To collect data on other types of cash-in-hand work conducted and received, meanwhile, a series of open-ended questions were used to elicit information with probes. Similar to previous studies (e.g. Leonard, 1994; Pahl, 1984), the finding was that the interviewees had little reticence in openly talking about this work. Just because it is hidden from government authorities does not mean that people hide it from each other or even academic researchers.

This perception of a lack of reticence by interviewees, moreover, is confirmed by the results. The total amount customers reported spending on cash-in-hand work in deprived urban neighbourhoods for example was £23 354 and this was near enough exactly the same amount that suppliers of cash-in-hand work asserted that they had received (£22 986). So too was the mean price customers paid (£90.24) broadly equitable with the mean price suppliers asserted that they received (£84.48). It was similarly the case when affluent suburbs and rural areas were analysed. From this, one might conclude that there is little evidence either of suppliers greatly under-reporting such work and their income from this activity, or of customers falsely allocating economic activity to cash-in-hand work when this was not the case. Given that the order of magnitude of customer and supplier responses are approximately the same, there are few grounds for believing that these results under-report either the level of this work or the income from such activity.

Throughout Part II, the results of this English Localities Survey will be reported to investigate specific issues such as the geographical variations in the extent and nature of cash-in-hand work. Here, therefore, it is useful to provide a brief overview of the areas studied. As can be seen in Table 3.2, a broad regional spread of deprived and affluent neighbourhoods in both urban and rural English localities were surveyed. The rationale for using the urban/rural and level of affluence variables to select localities to be studied was quite simply that previous research has indicated both of these to have important influences on cash-in-hand work (e.g. Jensen *et al.*, 1995; Kesteloot and Meert, 1999; Pahl, 1984; Renooy, 1990).

To select areas for study, a maximum variation sampling technique was employed. First, two cities were chosen that starkly varied in terms

Table 3.2 Overview of areas studied in the English Localities Survey

Area-Type	Locality	Description of area	Number of Interviews
Affluent rural	Fulbourn, Cambridgeshire	'Picture postcard' rural village in high-tech sub-region	70
Affluent rural	Chalford, Gloucestershire	Rural village in Cotswolds.	70
Deprived rural	Grimethorpe, South Yorkshire	Ex-pit village with very high unemployment.	70
Deprived rural	Wigston, Cumbria	Village with one factory dominating the local labour market.	70
Deprived rural	St Blazey, Cornwall	Village in a tourist region	70
Affluent suburb	Fulwood, Sheffield	Suburb in south-west Sheffield	50
Affluent suburb	Basset/Chilworth, Southampton	Sole affluent suburb within the city of Southampton	61
Deprived urban	Manor, Sheffield	Social housing estate with high unemployment	100
Deprived urban	Pitsmoor, Sheffield	Inner city area in deindustrialising city with high levels of private sector rented accommodation and high unemployment	100
Deprived urban	St Mary's, Southampton	Inner city locality in affluent southern city with high levels of private sector rented accommodation and high unemployment	100
Deprived urban	Hightown, Southampton	Social housing estate with high unemployment	100

of their level of affluence. Southampton is a successful service-oriented economy with low unemployment rates in the affluent south east of England whilst Sheffield is a poorer northern English city, once famous for steel making but now suffering relatively high rates of unemployment. Continuing this desire for maximum variation sampling, three neighbourhood-types in each city were then chosen using the Index of Multiple Deprivation of the Department of Local Government, Transport and the Regions (DLTR) that ranks all wards in England and Wales according to the level of their deprivation (DLTR, 2000). In each city, two of the most deprived wards and the most affluent ward were selected. Following this, and to provide a stark contrast with the urban areas, a range of rural localities was chosen with a broad regional spread. Again, some very affluent and deprived rural localities were chosen for investigation, continuing the theme of maximum variation sampling.

To select households for interview in each area, meanwhile, a spatially stratified sampling procedure was used (Kitchin and Tate, 2001). The researcher called at every nth dwelling in each street, depending on the size of the neighbourhood and the number of interviews sought. In consequence, if there were 1000 households in the ward and 100 interviews were sought, then every tenth household was visited. If there was no response, then the researcher called back once. If there was still no response and/or they were refused an interview, then the eleventh house was surveyed (again with one call back), then the ninth dwelling, twelfth and so on. This provided a representative sample of the neighbourhood in terms of tenure and type of housing and prevented any skewness in the sample towards certain tenures, types of dwelling and different parts of the neighbourhood being interviewed rather than a spatially representative sample of the whole neighbourhood.

All target households had a covering letter put through their door a day or so prior to the researcher calling in order to provide information about the nature of the interview and to hopefully increase the response rate (30 per cent overall for the first choice household). This letter described the researcher as being interested in finding out how households manage to get everyday tasks completed and what prevents them being able to do more for themselves and others. Interviews took place not only during daytime hours on weekdays but also in the early evening and at weekends in order to capture working households. Although these interviews resulted in a wide array of data on unpaid work as well as overall household coping capabilities and work practices (see Williams and Windebank, 2003a), this book focuses upon solely its findings with regard to cash-in-hand work, particularly how the economic relations and motives underpinning cash-in-hand work vary across different geographical areas and social groups.

Conclusions

In order to lay the foundations for understanding cash-in-hand work in the advanced economies, this chapter has evaluated the contrasting methods used to measure the magnitude and character of such activity. This has revealed that for the purposes of this book where the focus is upon understanding the relations within which cash-in-hand work is conducted and the motives of suppliers and customers, the indirect techniques are of little use. These methods are more the product of various untested assumptions about the nature of cash-in-hand work rather than a means of acquiring understanding about the character of such work. If knowledge is to be acquired on the nature of cash-in-hand work, such as the work relations involved and the motives of participants, then it is to the direct methods that those with a desire to understand these issues have to turn.

Part II

Socio-spatial Variations in the Nature of Cash-in-hand Work

4
Employment Status and Cash-in-hand Work

Introduction

In Chapter 2, it was argued that if cash-in-hand work is to be more fully understood, it is necessary to distinguish between the 'underground economy' (market-like cash-in-hand work conducted for profit-motivated purposes) and the 'hidden economy of favours' (cash-in-hand work conducted under work relations akin to mutual aid for non-profit reasons) and to unpack the variable nature of cash-in-hand work in different contexts. To do this, Part II of this book investigates how the preponderance of these forms of cash-in-hand work varies according to the employment status, gender and location of the participants.

To commence this unravelling of the variable nature of cash-in-hand work, this chapter explores the relationship between employment status and cash-in-hand work. This will reveal that people in formal employment not only conduct more cash-in-hand work than the unemployed but also that their cash-in-hand work is more frequently market-like and profit-motivated than amongst the unemployed where such work is more often embedded in work relations and motives akin to mutual aid.

In order to show this, this chapter first reviews findings on the extent of cash-in-hand work in the advanced economies according to the employment status of participants. Revealing how the long-held view that cash-in-hand work is concentrated amongst the unemployed has been widely refuted in recent years (e.g. Ahn and Rica, 1997; Marcelli et al., 1999; Pahl, 1984; Renooy, 1990; Williams, 2001b; Williams and Windebank, 1998, 1999b, 2001e,g, 2002b, 2003a), it will be shown that questions have started to be asked concerning the character of such work. Given that it is the formally employed rather than the unemployed who disproportionately participate in and gain from cash-in-hand work, the traditional view of cash-in-hand work as low-paid and conducted under 'organised' exploitative conditions has started to be put under the spotlight. The result, it will be shown, is the recognition that cash-in-hand work is not always low paid and can be conducted under 'autonomous' as well as 'organised' economic relations. Remaining unchallenged so far, however, are the beliefs that cash-in-hand work is always conducted under relations akin to formal employment and that it is universally undertaken for profit-motivated purposes. To begin to contest these tenets that remain at the core of the vast majority of literature on cash-in-hand work, this chapter draws upon evidence to reveal that although the unemployed conduct only a small proportion of all cash-in-hand work, when they do engage in such work, it is not found to be always low-paid employment conducted for unadulterated economic reasons. Even though some of their cash-in-hand work is of this variety and they are the principal participants in exploitative forms of low-paid informal employment, the majority of their cash-in-hand work is found to be carried out for friends, kin and neighbours in order to either help them out and/or to cement or forge social networks. For the employed, meanwhile, the vast bulk of their cash-in-hand work is found to be market-like and conducted for profit-motivated purposes.

To conclude, therefore, the implications of this finding for understanding social capital are analysed. This will argue that although cash-in-hand work plays a relatively minor role in understanding social capital amongst the employed, this is not the case amongst the unemployed. For this latter group, the hidden economy of favours will be shown to represent one of the principal vehicles through which bridging and bonding social capital is built and as such, to ignore it is to misunderstand the uneven contours of social capital in contemporary society as well as what needs to be done to bolster it.

Level of participation in cash-in-hand work: by employment status

A long-standing view is that the unemployed participate in and gain from cash-in-hand work disproportionately relative to the employed. This view gained currency during the 1970s and 1980s (e.g. Gutmann, 1978; Henry, 1982; Isachsen and Strom, 1985; Matthews, 1983; Parker, 1982; Petersen, 1982; Rosanvallon, 1980) and has remained popular throughout the 1990s (e.g. Blair and Endres, 1994; Lagos, 1995; Maldonado, 1995) until the present day (e.g. Office of the Deputy Prime Minister, 2003).

In France, for example, Rosanvallon (1980) asserted that high unemployment at the end of the 1970s did not result in the traditional French reaction of rioting in the streets because the unemployed, many of whom were not entitled to any benefits at all at the time, must be working on a cash-in-hand basis. In the recession of the early 1980s in the United Kingdom, meanwhile, Parker (1982, p. 33) claimed that 'with high unemployment more and more people are getting caught up in the web of the underground economy', whilst in the heyday of *laissez-faire* free marketeers, Robson (1988, p. 55) asserted that 'the informal economy is more feasible as an alternative prop to those who are out of work ...'. In the United States, similarly, Stauffer (1995, p. 1) argued that 'the informal sector can act as an important buffer against unemployment', whilst Blair and Endres (1994, p. 288) asserted that 'The role of the informal sector in providing a source of support for unemployed workers or individuals receiving public assistance is an important function of the unobserved sector.' The assumption underlying many analyses, therefore, has been that 'a significant percentage of the officially unemployed are in reality working "off the books", being paid in cash without intercession of a tax collector' (Gutmann, 1978, p. 26).

This discourse persists today. To see its continuing prevalence, consider how the call in 2003 by Ministers in the UK government for greater understanding of the 'informal economy' have been taken on board by the civil service. The responsibility for co-ordinating a systematic review of this subject was allocated to civil servants in a project team whose overarching brief is to look at what can be done to reduce joblessness in deprived neighbourhoods, based on the view that cash-in-hand work and joblessness are inextricably inter-related (Office of the Deputy Prime Minister, 2003).

Yet the validity of this long-held view that the unemployed disproportionately participate in, and benefit from, cash-in-hand work has been widely refuted in recent years throughout the advanced economies. Take, for example, studies conducted in northern European Union (EU) nations using direct surveys. In the Netherlands, for example, Van Geuns *et al.* (1987) find in all the six localities studied that the unemployed generally do not participate in cash-in-hand work to the same extent as the employed. This is additionally found to be the case in the Netherlands by Van Eck and Kazemeir (1985) and Koopmans (1989). It is also repeated in studies carried out in France (Barthe, 1988; Cornuel and Duriez, 1985; Foudi *et al.*, 1982; Tievant, 1982), Germany (Glatzer and Berger, 1988; Hellberger and Schwarze, 1987) and in Britain (Economist Intelligence Unit, 1982; Howe, 1990; Morris, 1994; Pahl, 1984;

Warde, 1990). In these northern EU nations, therefore, the overwhelming conclusion of direct surveys is that cash-in-hand work is primarily a means of accumulating advantage for those in formal employment and that only a very small proportion of cash-in-hand workers are regular 'working claimants'.

In southern EU nations, a similar conclusion has been reached. The unemployed claiming benefit have been found to be only a small proportion of all cash-in-hand workers. In Spain, the Ministry of the Economy estimates that 29 per cent of those in formal employment also work on a cash-in-hand basis (in Hadjimichalis and Vaiou, 1989), whilst Lobo (1990a) finds that just 12 per cent of those claiming benefit engage in cash-in-hand work. Benton (1990) thus surmises that 65.7 per cent of all cash-in-hand workers in Spain have a formal job, just 5.2 per cent are receiving social security benefit and 29 per cent are those unemployed and not entitled to benefit. As Lobo (1990a) concludes, most cash-in-hand work is conducted by the employed or those unemployed and not claiming benefit rather than by the unemployed receiving benefit. In Greece, similarly, the Ministry of Planning recognises that it is the formally employed rather than the unemployed who engage in cash-in-hand work when it states that 40 per cent of those employed in the private sector also have non-declared jobs as do 20 per cent of those in public sector jobs (in Hadjimichalis and Vaiou, 1989). In Italy, meanwhile, the majority of studies again reinforce both the finding that the formally employed rather than the unemployed are the vast bulk of the cash-in-hand workforce and that those in formal employment are more likely to engage in cash-in-hand work than the unemployed (Cappechi, 1989; Mingione, 1991, 1994; Mingione and Morlicchio, 1993; Warren, 1994). There is even evidence that the participation rates of the employed and unemployed in cash-in-hand work are widening over time (Mingione and Magatti, 1995).

This finding does not only prevail across Europe but also North America (Fortin *et al.*, 1996; Jensen *et al.*, 1995; Lemieux *et al.*, 1994; Lozano, 1989; Marcelli *et al.*, 1999; Nelson and Smith, 1999). In a study of cash-in-hand work in the San Francisco Bay area, Lozano (1989) finds that it is not the unemployed who engage in cash-in-hand work but, rather, people who are driven by tensions on the shop and office floor, where frustration with managerial authority and bureaucratic control lead them to seek an escape through cash-in-hand work. Therefore, in this relatively wealthy region, engagement in such work is shown to be a choice on the part of participants, the majority of which are in higher-income households. Jensen *et al.* (1995) in the very different context of rural Pennsylvania come to similar conclusions when they find that it is more likely to be those in employment than the unemployed who engage in cash-in-hand work whilst the extensive survey conducted by Fortin *et al.* (1996) in Quebec provides confirmation that the formally employed constitute a much larger proportion of the cash-in-hand workforce than the unemployed.

Throughout all of these studies, nevertheless, a distinction is often drawn between different categories of the unemployed. This varies according to the nations under discussion. In southern EU nations, for example, a distinction is drawn between the unemployed who are claiming benefits and those who are not when discussing cash-in-hand work. The reason for this, as Reissert (1994) reveals, is that a much lower percentage of the total unemployed in southern EU states have traditionally received unemployment compensation benefits compared to northern EU nations. Examining the European Labour Force Survey, he finds that in 1990 the benefit recipient quotas (i.e. the number of benefit recipients as a proportion of the total unemployed) ranged from less than 20 per cent in southern EU nations such as Greece, Portugal and Italy to more than 80 per cent in Denmark and Belgium. Those not receiving social assistance are found to engage in cash-in-hand work to a greater extent than those who receive it (e.g. Lobo, 1990a,b). In the United States, a similar differentiation is again drawn resulting in the same finding (Blair and Endres, 1994).

In northern EU nations, meanwhile, a distinction is drawn between the long- and short-term unemployed. In Germany, for example, Hellberger and Schwarze (1987) find that whilst 16.7 per cent of the temporarily unemployed engage in cash-in-hand work, this is the case for only 5.8 per cent of the permanently unemployed. Engberson *et al.* (1993) comes to a similar conclusion in the Netherlands, as does Morris (1995) in Britain, stating that this is perhaps because the short-term or temporarily unemployed retain many of the contacts, resources and skills that they gained from their employment.

These findings concerning whether it is the employed or unemployed who engage in cash-in-hand work as well as the need for a distinction to be drawn between the short- and long-term unemployed have been reinforced by the results of the English Localities Survey. As Table 4.1 reveals, the formally employed (36 per cent of the sampled population) supplied 70 per cent of the work provided on a cash-in-hand basis. The non-employed (64 per cent of the sample), which includes homemakers and the retired as well as the registered unemployed, thus undertook just 30 per cent of all such work. Breaking the non-employed down into

Table 4.1 Proportion of cash-in-hand work conducted by the employed and non-employed in England

	% of sampled population	% of all cash-in-hand work
Employed	36	70
All non-employed	64	30
Registered unemployed	16	4
Long-term registered unemployed	5	< 1

Source: English Localities Survey.

their subgroups, moreover, the registered unemployed (16 per cent of the sampled population) conducted just 4 per cent of all cash-in-hand work and those who were long-term registered unemployed (4 per cent of the sample) undertook less than 1 per cent of all cash-in-hand work. 'Working whilst claiming,' therefore, especially amongst the long-term registered unemployed, constitutes only a very minor proportion of all cash-in-hand work in England.

Explaining the lack of participation of the unemployed

To explain this lack of participation of the unemployed in cash-in-hand work compared with those in formal employment, five conditions have been commonly cited. Taken together, these constitute a cocktail of factors that combine to produce a barrier to entry to cash-in-hand work for the unemployed. First, there is the economic factor that the unemployed lack the money to acquire the goods and resources necessary to engage in cash-in-hand work (Miles, 1983; Pahl, 1984; Smith, 1986; Thomas, 1992). For example, without access to a car, they cannot always travel to where the work is available, whilst without the tools necessary to undertake the work (e.g. ladders, workbenches, power tools, workrooms), they cannot conduct a wide range of cash-in-hand activities. The result is that the unemployed have fewer opportunities than the formally employed to engage in autonomous cash-in-hand work or even gain access to organised work due to their lack of economic capital.

A second barrier is their lack of social network capital. The reduction in the size of social networks following redundancy means that the unemployed have fewer opportunities for undertaking work or for receiving help (Engbersen *et al.*, 1993; Howe, 1990; Miles, 1983; Mingione, 1991; Morris, 1993, 1995; Renooy, 1990; Thomas, 1992). Given that the long-term unemployed, moreover, mix mostly with other long-term unemployed, have relatively few friends or acquaintances who are employed (Morris, 1995), and that the majority of cash-in-hand work is found through acquaintances and employment (Van Eck and Kazemeier, 1985), the result is that the unemployed again have fewer opportunities for getting to know about cash-in-hand work than those in employment, especially opportunities for autonomous cash-in-hand work. As Komter (1996) finds in the Netherlands, and contrary to popular belief, not only are the social networks of the employed often more numerous and extensive than those of the unemployed, but cash-in-hand work is used as a way of maintaining them. Similar findings have been identified on new estates in France where cash exchanges occur as much for social as for economic reasons (Cornuel and Duriez, 1985).

A third barrier to entry to cash-in-hand work for the unemployed compared with the employed is their lack of human capital (Fortin *et al.*, 1996; Howe, 1990; Lysestol, 1995; Mingione, 1991; Renooy, 1990; Smith, 1986). If their skills and competencies are inappropriate for finding formal employment, there is no reason to believe that they can sell them on a cash-in-hand basis. So, besides lacking economic and social network capital, it can be argued that many of the unemployed also lack the human capital necessary to engage in cash-in-hand work. The consequence is that they are relegated to engaging only in unskilled or semi-skilled cash-in-hand work. Having a formal job means that the outside world recognises a person as having a skill to offer and is a legitimisation of these skills in the eyes of potential customers. This applies as much to conducting cash-in-hand work for friends, neighbours and kin as it does to selling one's labour to businesses and people previously unknown to the supplier. After all, one is more likely to wish to employ somebody known to you if one knows that they are capable of doing a job and being employed in a trade is a mark that they possess these capabilities.

A fourth barrier to participation in cash-in-hand work, particularly of benefit claimants, is that they feel more inhibited about engaging in such work for fear of being reported to the authorities and having their benefit curtailed. Given that working on a cash-in-hand basis whilst claiming social security is considered in many advanced economies to be a more serious offence than engaging in tax evasion (Aitken and Bonneville, 1980; Cook, 1997; Deane and Melrose, 1996; Jordan *et al.*, 1992; Keenan and Dean, 1980; Weatherley, 1993), the result is that the claimant unemployed are less likely to engage in cash-in-hand work than the employed. This 'institutional' factor is particularly relevant in welfare regimes which have both universal and comprehensive social security benefits as well as strict enforcement of social security regulations and punitive measures for those caught, such as Germany, Norway, Denmark and the United Kingdom (Grabiner, 2000; Hellberger and Schwarze, 1987; Lysestol, 1995; Mogensen, 1990; Wenig, 1990).

Finally, there is what might be called an environmental or geographical barrier to participation. A greater proportion of the unemployed live in deprived areas (Morris, 1994; Pahl, 1984; Smith, 1986) where less disposable income exists to pay for cash-in-hand work. There is little point, for example, being a window-cleaner working on a cash-in-hand basis in such areas if nobody can afford to have their windows cleaned (Coffield *et al.*, 1983). As such, and given the spatial concentration of the unemployed (e.g. Dorling and Woodward, 1996; Green and Owen, 1998), there is simply less demand for cash-in-hand work in these areas than in others.

Therefore, the unemployed possess the free time but lack the additional resources and opportunities necessary to conduct cash-in-hand work. Conversely, those in formal employment have fewer fears about the authorities, more money to acquire the necessary tools and materials, wider social networks, more chance of hearing about cash-in-hand work and greater scope for undertaking such work in the areas in which they live. Pahl (1988, p. 255) refers to this as 'the Matthew effect': to them that hath, more is given, whereas to them that have little, even that which they have is taken away.

However, not all of these factors always apply in every situation and this perhaps explains why a number of studies identify either similar levels of cash-in-hand work amongst the employed and unemployed (Ferman *et al.*, 1978; Hellberger and Schwarze, 1987; Mogensen, 1990; Wenig, 1990) or even higher participation rates amongst the unemployed than the employed (e.g. Howe, 1988; Kesteloot and Meert, 1994, 1999; Leonard, 1994; Pestieau, 1985). In Germany, for example, where similar participation rates in cash-in-hand work have been identified amongst the employed and unemployed, the World Values Survey identifies that tax fraud is seen as less justifiable than benefit fraud, reflecting differences in benefit system structures, culture, beliefs and politics (Weatherley, 1993). This will impact on the participation rates of the unemployed and employed in such work compared with nations where benefit fraud is seen as less justifiable than tax fraud. Similarly, on the West Belfast estate studied by Leonard (1994), the socio-political rejection of the validity of the state as well as the presence of a 'shadow state', meant that the institutional barrier described above is of minimal importance.

It is important to realise, nevertheless, that these are exceptions. As such, although there is a need to avoid over-simplistic generalisations and explanations concerning the barriers towards participation of the unemployed in cash-in-hand work and to move towards context-bound understandings, in the vast majority of localities in the advanced economies, most of the above barriers apply and this is why it is so common to find that the unemployed conduct less cash-in-hand work than the employed in advanced economies.

Until now, the focus has been upon the extent of participation of the employed and unemployed. In major part, this reflects the broader literature. A key issue that needs to be considered, however, is whether there is a difference in the nature of the cash-in-hand work executed by those in formal employment compared with that done by the unemployed.

Nature of cash-in-hand work: by employment status

The recognition that participation in cash-in-hand work is not confined to the unemployed has led many commentators to reconsider whether the conventional view of such work as a low-paid organised form of employment is a valid description of its character. The outcome is that some analysts have begun to unpack the heterogeneous character of cash-in-hand work (e.g. Fortin *et al.*, 1996; Jensen *et al.*, 1995; Laguerre, 1994; Leonard, 1994; 1998a,b; Pahl, 1984, Renooy, 1990; Waldinger and Lapp, 1993; Williams and Windebank, 1998). On the whole, and as shown in Chapter 2, this has been achieved by referring to a continuum of types of cash-in-hand work. At one end are more 'organised' forms of cash-in-hand work, often low-paid and undertaken by cash-in-hand employees for a business that conducts some or all of its activity on a cash-in-hand basis. At the other end are more 'individual' or 'autonomous' forms of better-paid cash-in-hand work (Jordan, 1998; Leonard, 1994,1998a,b; MacDonald, 1994; Williams and Windebank, 1998). A view has thus come to the fore that cash-in-hand work can no longer be seen as existing at the bottom of a hierarchy of types of employment. Instead, it is seen to have a hierarchy of its own, as displayed in the idea of a 'segmented informal labour market' (Williams and Windebank, 1998).

Examining the place of the formally employed and unemployed in this segmented informal labour market, the widespread view has been that the formally employed engage in relatively well-paid cash-in-hand work, often of the autonomous variety, whilst the unemployed are viewed generally to engage in relatively low-paid organised cash-in-hand work (e.g. Fortin *et al.*, 1996; Howe, 1990; Lemieux *et al.*, 1994; Lobo, 1990a,b; Pahl, 1984; Renooy, 1990; MacDonald, 1994; Williams and Windebank, 1998; Windebank and Williams, 1997).

Take, for example, the analysis by Lobo (1990b) of cash-in-hand work in the service sector in Portugal. He distinguishes between two types of cash-in-hand worker. On the one hand, there are well-qualified self-employed cash-in-hand workers, engaged in activities such as domestic repairs (e.g. washing machines, televisions and radios), who have the opportunity to undertake this kind of work because they also have a formal job, usually full-time. On the other hand, there are cash-in-hand workers (e.g. in catering, retailing) who usually do not have a formal job and are female, young and poorly qualified. Many of these tend to work in very precarious jobs (Izquierdo *et al.*, 1987) with low earnings (Rusega and de Blas, 1985) or for very long hours when their income is compared with the employed (Lopez, 1986). For Lobo (1990a), therefore, there is a close relationship between employment status and one's position in this segmented informal labour market and it is one in which the employed conduct autonomous work and the unemployed the more organised forms of cash-in-hand activity.

Until now, however, this allocation of the employed and unemployed to the autonomous and organised sectors of the cash-in-hand sphere respectively has been seldom based on detailed empirical study of the types of work conducted by these groups. Instead, such a view has been simply extrapolated from the finding that the unemployed receive lower wage rates than the employed for their cash-in-hand work (Fortin *et al.*, 1996; Hellberger and Schwarze, 1986; Mattera, 1980; Renooy, 1990; Van Eck and Kazemeier, 1985).

Take, for example, the work of Fortin *et al.* (1996) in Quebec. As Table 4.2 reveals, the employed in 1993 earned an average of C$10.66 per hour from cash-in-hand work whilst the unemployed earned C$7.94, that is, just 74 per cent of the level of the employed. Between 1985 and 1993, moreover, whilst the hourly informal wage rate of the unemployed increased by 13.3 per cent, it rose by 15.8 per cent for the employed, displaying the increasing polarisation of hourly wage rates between the employed and unemployed. At the same time, the percentage of all unemployed working informally decreased drastically from 24.5 per cent to 8.5 per cent (mostly due to the stricter enforcement of rules concerning working whilst claiming). The result is that the proportion of all cash-in-hand earnings going to the employed rose from 41.4 per cent to 43.1 per cent between 1985 and 1993. Cash-in-hand work, therefore, increasingly became a vehicle for ameliorating the earnings of the employed in this region.

Table 4.2 Wage rates for cash-in-hand work in Quebec region: by employment status, 1993 and 1985

1993 (1985 in parentheses)	% doing cash-in-hand work	% of all cash-in-hand workers	Average wage/hr (C$)	% of cash-in-hand work by	
				Hours	Value C$
All	4.8 (6.0)	100.0 (100.0)	7.66 (7.28)	100.0	100.0
Student	13.5 (19.4)	42.7 (31.2)	8.00 (6.65)	33.7 (31.5)	32.1 (27.4)
Retired	1.0 (1.0)	2.1 (0.9)	9.01 (N/A)	2.3(—)	2.2 (0.2)
housekeeper	4.5 (5.0)	9.4 (14.3)	5.06 (5.62)	13.4 (23.9)	9.4 (19.7)
Unemployed	8.5 (24.5)	11.5 (11.6)	7.94 (7.01)	13.2 (12.2)	13.2 (11.8)
Employed	2.9 (3.9)	34.4 (41.9)	10.66 (9.20)	36.5 (32.3)	43.1 (41.4)

Source: Derived from Fortin *et al.* (1996, tables 3.1 and 4.2).

Table 4.3 Mean wage rate for cash-in-hand work in England: by employment status of individuals and households

Household type	Mean cash-in-hand wage rate per hour (£)
By number of earners in household	
No-earner households	2.60
Single-earner households	3.94
Multiple-earner households	5.75
By employment status	
Registered unemployed	2.40
All non-employed	3.20
Employed	5.15

Source: English Localities Survey.

Similar findings that the unemployed are relatively poorly paid compared with the employed are identified in the English Localities Survey (see Table 4.3). Jobless households, for example, earn an average of £2.60 per hour for their cash-in-hand work compared with £5.75 in multiple-earner households. Similarly, the average hourly wage rate of the registered unemployed (£2.40) is lower than that of the employed (£5.15). Given that the minimum hourly wage rate for formal employment was £3.60 at the time, this clearly displays that whilst the unemployed were earning on average below the formal minimum wage rate, this was not the case for the formally employed.

However, just because the unemployed are lower-paid does not mean that they are necessarily engaged in exploitative low-paid 'organised' kinds of cash-in-hand work. And just because the employed are well paid does not mean that they are largely engaged in autonomous varieties of such work. To assert this is to make a logical leap that has no justification. Indeed, a first clue that it is invalid to link the low pay amongst the unemployed with their participation in organised forms of cash-in-hand work is the finding by Van Eck and Kazemeier (1985) that the unemployed usually engage in work for closer social relations which tends to be lower paid than that undertaken for businesses. The average wage for cash-in-hand work conducted for one's family is Dfl 10, for acquaintances it is Dfl 14, for colleagues Dfl 20 and for employers Dfl 33.

Just because the unemployed are poorly reimbursed, therefore, does not mean that they are necessarily and inevitably engaged largely in exploitative 'sweatshop' work for formal or informal businesses whilst the employed are engaged in more autonomous cash-in-hand work, as previously assumed by the segmented informal labour market thesis. To use the low pay of the unemployed as a proxy indicator for their participation in organized, exploitative work relations in this cash-in-hand sphere is, as will be now shown, an erroneous conclusion.

In England, as Table 4.4 reveals, it is simply not the case that the formally employed engage in autonomous varieties of cash-in-hand work and the unemployed in organised forms of such work. Just 5 per cent of the cash-in-hand work conducted by the registered unemployed was on an organised basis for formal or informal businesses (compared with 20 per cent for those in formal employment). To portray the cash-in-hand work of the unemployed as conducted for businesses is thus a gross misnomer. Some 95 per cent of the cash-in-hand work of the unemployed is conducted on a self-employed basis.

Table 4.4 Types of cash-in-hand work of the registered unemployed and employed in English areas: by nature of customer

% of cash-in-hand work supplied to	Registered unemployed	Employed	All
Informal or formal businesses	5	20	18
Unknown people on self-employed basis	15	32	28
Friends, neighbours, kin	80	48	54
Total	100	100	100

Source: English Localities Survey.

Yet the finding that the unemployed are low-paid relative to their employed counterparts still stands. How, therefore, can this be explained? Is it really the case that callous profit-motivation has entered into even these social relations between kin, friends and neighbours? Or are different motives prevalent when such work is conducted meaning that the low wage rate cannot be taken as indicator of exploitative work relations? Until now, and based on the assumption that all cash-in-hand work is conducted under work relations akin to those found in employment, the notion has been that low pay represents a proxy indicator of exploitative work conditions. Here, however, by relaxing this assumption, a new understanding is achieved.

Before exploring this, however, it is important to be clear that this section is not arguing that the unemployed never engage in exploitative organised forms of cash-in-hand work for unscrupulous employers. As shown, some 5 per cent of all cash-in-hand work conducted by the unemployed in the English Localities Survey was for informal and formal businesses and the average hourly wage is just £2.30 compared with the national minimum wage of £3.60. There is little doubt, therefore, that the unemployed do conduct some highly exploitative low-paid cash-in-hand work for informal and formal businesses. Moreover, there is no doubt that if only this type of cash-in-hand work is considered, then it is near enough solely the unemployed who conduct such work. The point being made here, however, is that this is not the only type of cash-in-hand work that the unemployed conduct and overall, such work represents but a small segment of the whole cash-in-hand sphere.

If the cash-in-hand work of the employed and unemployed is to be more fully understood, therefore, one has to consider the contrasting work relations involved and the varying reasons why the employed and unemployed engage in such work. It can no longer simply be assumed for example, that all of the cash-in-hand work of the unemployed is for informal and formal businesses and conducted in order to earn some badly needed cash and that it is unscrupulous employers seeking to make money who employ them.

Motives for participating in cash-in-hand work: by employment status

It has already been shown that the way in which the nature of cash-in-hand work differs between the employed and unemployed is often based on little more than supposition derived from data on the wage rates involved. It is similarly the case when it comes to motives. The

view originating in the marginality thesis that cash-in-hand work is conducted for unadulterated economic purposes by both the employed and
unemployed (Hessing *et al.*, 1993) has been seldom tested.

In the past, although a few studies raised queries about whether this
was always the case, the authors never really attempted to mount any
serious challenge to this received canon of wisdom. Cornuel and Duriez
(1985), for example, found in their study of relatively affluent incomers
in a French small town that such affluent groups sometimes engaged in
cash-in-hand exchanges in order to forge new relationships and develop
reciprocity and trust. Komter (1996) finds much the same in the
Netherlands. So far, however, such findings have been largely treated as
a mildly interesting exception that pinpoints how the affluent sometimes engage in cash-in-hand work for reasons other than profit.

Here, however, the data from the English Localities Survey is drawn
upon to show that this finding is not only more widely applicable than
has so far been assumed but also how non-profit motives are more
prevalent when unemployed people engage in cash-in-hand work than
when the formally employed do so. In this survey, for each task conducted on a cash-in-hand basis, the supplier was asked why they had
engaged in this work. The finding was that just 19 per cent of the cash-
in-hand tasks undertaken by the unemployed and 57 per cent of the
tasks conducted by the employed are undertaken primarily in order to
make money (see Table 4.5). Examining the work relations involved
when this is the primary motive, moreover, it was found to prevail near
enough entirely when the registered unemployed and employed either
conduct work for formal or informal businesses or on an autonomous
basis for people unknown to them.

Table 4.5   Reasons for engaging in cash-in-hand work in English
localities: by employment status

% of cash-in-hand work work supplied primarily to	Unemployed	Employed	All
Make money	19	57	50
Help out others	40	20	22
Build community networks	41	23	28
Total	100	100	100

Source: English Localities Survey.

The remaining 81 per cent and 43 per cent of cash-in-hand activities conducted by the unemployed and employed respectively are thus primarily motivated by rationales other than profit. First, there are community-building rationales, particularly when an unemployed or employed person conducts work for a friend or neighbour. Here, cash-in-hand work is supplied in order to pursue longer-term motives associated with developing social capital. Viewing social networks as a resource to draw upon (c.f., Blau, 1994; Coleman, 1988; Gittell and Vidal, 1998; Portes, 1998), the unemployed and employed use cash-in-hand work as a means of either developing closer ties with those they already know (i.e. to develop 'bonding' social capital) or instigating associations with people who they do not know very well (i.e. to build 'bridging' social capital).

As an unemployed woman explained her cash-in-hand work for a neighbour, 'I helped her out, so she'll help me later when I need a hand'. Developing closer ties is therefore economically orientated behaviour but it is embedded in longer-term mutual co-operation, not short-term profit-motivated behaviour. The outcome, and this is important for understanding the finding that the unemployed receive lower 'wages' for cash-in-hand work, is that constructions of value often widely diverge from the market price. Prices in these situations are often well below the market price but well above what would constitute a token gesture. Indeed, where exchanges are explained in terms of forging closer ties with people that they already know (i.e. developing 'bonding' social capital), the average price paid is the lowest of all forms of cash-in-hand work. This is not the case, however, when the rationale is to forge associations with people that an unemployed person does not know very well (i.e. building bridging social capital). Here, much greater care has to be taken that the price approximates to market norms so that the person with whom one is trying to develop greater reciprocity and trust is not insulted. If it is too high, one will be seen as 'ripping them off' and if it is too low, it will be seen as 'charity'. Given that a greater proportion of the cash-in-hand work of the unemployed is conducted for such community-building objectives, especially for closer social relations, it is thus perhaps little surprise that their cash-in-hand wage rates are lower than amongst the employed whose cash-in-hand work is conducted mainly for unknown customers and for businesses in order to make money. To use low wage rates as a proxy indicator of exploitative work relations is thus to miss the point that much cash-in-hand work is conducted for close social relations and that such work often involves only token payments by the customer.

Besides community-building rationales, the registered unemployed and employed provide cash-in-hand work in order to help others out. This rationale mostly prevails where the registered unemployed conduct work for employed kin. The perception of the registered unemployed is that they are helping out those who have less free time by supplying their time, a resource that they have in relative abundance. For them, a 'trade' is taking place between somebody who is relatively 'time rich-money poor' and 'money rich-time poor' people and each party is giving the resource that they possess in relatively greater amounts to the other.

Motives for employing the unemployed and employed on a cash-in-hand basis

In previous research, the perception has been that employers pay both the registered unemployed and employed on a cash-in-hand basis in order to save money. Although this is doubtless the chief rationale for owners of informal and formal businesses, it is not the usual primary motivation when individual consumers employ people on a cash-in-hand basis (see Table 4.6). In these circumstances (which cover 95 per cent and 82 per cent of the cash-in-hand work of the registered unemployed and employed respectively), the rationale was to save money in just 10 per cent and 33 per cent of cases respectively. Instead, not-for-profit rationales on the part of the 'employer' prevailed in 90 per cent of the cases where the registered unemployed were paid on a cash-in-hand basis and 67 per cent of the instances where the formally employed were paid cash-in-hand.

In 35 per cent of cases where the unemployed worked on a cash-in-hand basis and 49 per cent of cases where the employed worked on such a basis, the 'employer' asked them to do the work for primarily community-building reasons. In these circumstances, the employer was usually a

Table 4.6 Motives of employers when using unemployed and employed cash-in-hand workers

% of cash-in-hand used primarily to	Unemployed	Employed	All
Save/make money	10	33	31
Help out the person	55	18	22
Build community networks	35	49	47
Total	100	100	100

Source: English Localities Survey.

friend or neighbour and they were either instigating paid exchanges or returning a previous favour. In nearly every case, however, this involved monetary payment due to wariness about partaking in unpaid exchange and the embeddedness of payment in norms of reciprocity, reflecting the penetration of monetary exchange into spheres of life previously founded upon non-monetised exchange. Indeed, 53 per cent of all community exchanges involved payments and when the registered unemployed were involved, this figure was even higher at 65 per cent.

In 55 per cent of the cases where the registered unemployed were used to do cash-in-hand work and 18 per cent of cases where the employed were used, however, the motive of the employer, who was normally kin, was to help them out. For example, one employed man in a dual-earner household who needed his home decorating thought it 'natural' to employ his unemployed brother and pay him for the work 'to help him out' while an employed woman in a single-person household stated that asking her uncle to tidy her garden was a deliberate ploy 'to give him some pocket money'. For most employers, in consequence, paying kin to do a job was a way giving them money while avoiding any explicit notion of charity, even though this was the intention.

Little of this work, moreover, was deleterious to the creation of formal jobs. Indeed, of all cash-in-hand work conducted by the registered unemployed, 70 per cent would either have been undertaken by the consumer themselves or not done at all if the registered unemployed person had not been paid to do the work. Similarly, some 45 per cent of the cash-in-hand work conducted by the employed would not have been conducted on a formal basis if the person had not conducted the work. This is because both the 'employers' and the 'workers' are engaging in cash-in-hand work in order to help out others and/or to cement or forge social networks, and this is particularly the case where the unemployed are involved. This has major implications for understanding social capital.

Implications for understanding social capital

Until now, and as stated in Chapter 2, cash-in-hand work has not been considered as having anything to do with the issue of developing reciprocal exchange, trust and social networks. Here, however, it has been revealed that this is a mistake, particularly with regard to the unemployed. If the way in which social capital operates in contemporary society is to be more fully understood, then cash-in-hand work can no longer be ignored.

When studying community involvement, the tendency until now has been to study only participation in community-based groups (what I call 'third sector' community involvement) and participation in one-to-one unpaid aid (what is here referred to as 'fourth sector' community involvement). The principal finding has been that the unemployed engage in both third and fourth sector forms of community involvement to a lesser extent than the employed (e.g., Coulthard *et al.*, 2002; Davis Smith, 1998; Krishnamurthy *et al.*, 2001; Prime *et al.*, 2002).

Here, however, it has been shown that adding-in paid mutual aid reduces the disparities between the employed and unemployed so far as social capital is concerned. Given that the unemployed engage in paid mutual aid to a far greater extent than the employed, and that cash is given for favours in some two-thirds (65 per cent) of all instances where unemployed people engage in exchange for family, friends and neighbours (compared with 41 per cent of cases for an employed person), the integration of paid mutual aid into the study of social capital somewhat reduces the differences between the employed and unemployed in terms of the extent to which they are involved in community exchange.

However, this should not lead one to the conclusion that the unemployed are therefore getting-by to a greater extent than has been previously considered the case. Even when paid mutual aid is taken into account, the unemployed are still giving and receiving mutual aid to a lesser extent than the employed. The unemployed in these English localities are still receiving 35 per cent fewer tasks on a mutual-aid basis than the employed (even when paid mutual aid is included) and they are engaging in 32 per cent fewer tasks for others. It still remains the case, therefore, that ways need to be found to develop the social capital of the unemployed. This is particularly the case when it is recognised that some 25 per cent of all of the unemployed were found to not receive even one act of mutual aid on either a paid or unpaid basis in this survey.

What changes, however, due to the above findings, is how social capital might be developed. Once it is recognised that a large proportion of the mutual aid given and received involves cash payments due to the lack of trust that the favour will be repaid and their feeling that they will be unable to return any favours received, then this 'culture of payment' needs to be taken into account when forging policy to harness community exchange, especially amongst the unemployed. If one attempts to immerse the unemployed into either community-based groups as a means of developing social capital, or to develop one-to-one unpaid aid, then initiatives are likely to be unsuccessful. Instead, policy initiatives are required that can substitute for cash-in-hand work by providing alternative mechanisms whereby people can maintain a tally system of favours owed and received.

How this might be achieved will be returned to later in the book. For the moment, it is necessary only to recognise that there exists a hidden economy of paid favours, especially amongst the unemployed, and that this needs to be taken into account when both seeking to understand social capital and forging policy to develop their social capital.

Conclusions

Investigating the relationship between employment status and cash-in-hand work, this chapter has revealed that the formally employed conduct more cash-in-hand work than the unemployed and that their work is also more frequently market-like and profit-motivated than amongst the unemployed where such work is more often embedded in work relations and motives akin to mutual aid. Put another way, the cash-in-hand work of the employed is skewed towards the underground sector and that of the unemployed towards the hidden economy of favours. Exploring the implications of this finding for comprehending social capital, it has been argued that although cash-in-hand work plays a relatively minor role in understanding social capital amongst employed populations, this is not the case amongst the unemployed. For this latter group, the hidden economy of favours represents a principal vehicle through which social capital is maintained and developed and as such, to ignore it is to misunderstand the uneven contours of social capital in contemporary society as well as what needs to be done to bolster social capital amongst the unemployed.

5
Gender Variations in Cash-in-hand Work

Introduction

There is now a voluminous literature on numerous aspects of the gender divisions in employment as well as unpaid work (e.g. Gardiner, 1997; Gershuny *et al.*, 1994; Gregory and Windebank, 2000; Hakim, 1995; Himmelweit, 2000; Vogler, 1994; Walby, 1997; Warde and Hetherington, 1993). In stark contrast, very little work exists on gender disparities in cash-in-hand work. To examine this missing work in the study of gender divisions of labour, therefore, the aim of this chapter is to analyse the extent and character of the participation of men and women in cash-in-hand work.

Until now, the vast majority of research on the disparities in cash-in-hand work has focused upon how it varies across space and socio-economic groups (e.g. Feige, 1990; Fortin *et al.*, 1996; Leonard, 1998; Pahl, 1984; Renooy, 1990; Thomas, 1999; Williams and Windebank, 1998). Although the study of cash-in-hand work has not been entirely 'gender-blind', it is fair to say that the gender dimension has not been given the same prominence as socio-economic and spatial disparities in the literature. Here, in consequence, an attempt is made to review what has so far been written and then to make some significant advances in terms of how the gender divisions of cash-in-hand work are conceptualised.

Where the gender dimension of cash-in-hand work has been considered (e.g. Fortin *et al.*, 1996; Lemieux *et al.*, 1994; MacDonald, 1994; McInnis-Dittrich, 1995; Mingione, 1991; Mogensen, 1985; Pahl, 1984; Renooy, 1990; Van Eck and Kazemeier, 1985; Vinay, 1987), a view that has pervaded the literature is that women cash-in-hand workers engage in low-paid forms of exploitative market-orientated work for the purpose of making additional money 'on the side' so as to help the household get by (e.g. Howe, 1990; Jordan *et al.*, 1992; Leonard, 1994; MacDonald, 1994; Morris, 1987, 1995; Rowlingson *et al.*, 1997). This is seen to be particularly the case when women work as domestic servants, which has become a principal focus of such enquiry (e.g. Anderson, 2001a,b; Boris and Prugl, 1996; Dagg, 1996; Salmi, 1996). Surprisingly, however, and despite such strong intimations being made about the nature of women's cash-in-hand work, there has been little attempt to investigate in any depth the work relations and motives within which women's cash-in-hand work is embedded. Instead, most studies go little further than identifying the amount of cash-in-hand work women conduct, whether they are engaging in such work to a greater extent than men and how much they are paid (e.g. Fortin *et al.*, 1996; Hellberger and Schwarz, 1986; Lemieux *et al.*, 1984; Leonard, 1994; McInnis-Dittrich, 1995).

The work relations and motives underlying women's cash-in-hand work, meanwhile, are simply read-off from the finding that they are low paid (see Fortin *et al.*, 1996). The assumption is that because women are poorly paid, this must be exploitative work (e.g. Castells and Portes, 1989; Sassen, 1989) that these women enter into in order to make ends meet (e.g. Howe, 1990; Jordan *et al.*, 1992; Leonard, 1994; MacDonald, 1994; Morris, 1987, 1995; Rowlingson *et al.*, 1997). Whether this is actually the case has not been investigated in any detail. Here, therefore, research that does not simply accept such views *prima facie* but, rather, attempts to uncover the work relations and motives of women (and men) cash-in-hand workers and their employers, is reported.

This will reveal that although men are usually slightly more likely than women to engage in cash-in-hand work, there are some significant differences in the nature of the cash-in-hand work that they conduct. When men engage in cash-in-hand work, it is much more likely to be of the market-orientated variety in the 'underground sector'. Women's cash-in-hand work, in contrast, is significantly more likely to be conducted for friends, neighbours and kin for rationales other than profit or, put another way, embedded in the hidden or moral economy of favours. The implication, therefore, is that just because the cash-in-hand work of women is low paid does not mean that they are necessarily always engaged in exploitative organised forms of informal employment in the underground sector. Instead, their low pay is also a reflection of the fact that they are the major participants in the hidden economy of favours whose 'wage' rates tend to diverge significantly from market rates.

The outcome will be a call for a less totalising and more gender-differentiated view of cash-in-hand work. Although some cash-in-hand work conducted by women is indeed low-paid market-orientated work conducted for unadulterated economic reasons, the vast majority is conducted for friends, kin and neighbours for the purposes of redistribution and sociality. Men, on the other hand, tend to engage in cash-in-hand work that is market-like and conducted for the purpose of economic gain. This has important implications for understanding social capital. Until now, the view has been that cash-in-hand work needs to be deterred through punitive measures. Here, however, it is argued that although the low-paid forms of informal employment require such a punitive approach, a different policy response is needed towards the cash-in-hand work carried out under work relations and for motives akin to mutual aid, and mostly conducted by women. Indeed, to seek to suppress this moral economy of favours in which women are heavily engaged would be to seek to deter engagement in a significant proportion of the mutual aid that currently takes place.

Level of participation in cash-in-hand work: gender variations

Are women more likely to participate in cash-in-hand work than men? For some adherents to the 'marginality thesis', this is assumed to be the case (e.g. Priest, 1994). However, and similar to the discovery in the last chapter concerning the unemployed, the overarching finding of the vast majority of studies conducted on cash-in-hand work is that the extent of women's participation is less than that of men and that men constitute the majority of the cash-in-hand labour force. This is identified to be the case in the Netherlands (Renooy, 1990; Van Eck and Kazemeier, 1985), the UK (MacDonald, 1994; Pahl, 1984), Italy (Mingione, 1991; Vinay, 1987), Denmark (Mogensen, 1985), the United States (McInnis-Dittrich, 1995) and Canada (Lemieux *et al.*, 1994; Fortin *et al.*, 1996).

It is important to state, nevertheless, that the relative gap in the participation rates of men and women is not great. For example, in three Canadian regions, Fortin *et al.* (1996) find that men constitute just over half of all cash-in-hand workers (51.3–52.6 per cent) and about 1 per cent more men than women engage in cash-in-hand work (see Table 5.1). Similar sized gaps in participation rates are also identified in Denmark (Mogensen, 1985), the Netherlands (Van Eck and Kazemeier, 1985) and Italy (Mingione, 1991). For those who realise that men more frequently engage in paid employment than women in nearly every context, this difference in men's and women's participation rates in cash-in-hand

Table 5.1 Cash-in-hand wage rates in three regions of Canada: by gender, 1993

	Quebec (1985 in parentheses)	Montreal	Bas-du-Fleuve
% engaging in cash-in-hand work:			
men	5.4 (6.4)	6.6	4.1
women	4.2 (5.6)	5.5	3.2
% of all cash-in-hand workers:			
men	52.6 (51.8)	52.1	51.3
women	47.4 (48.2)	47.9	48.7
Average Hours p.a. (C$):			
men	403 (275)	581	309
women	417 (450)	614	317
Average Salary p.a. (C$):			
men	3 093 (2 744)	5 136	2 850
women	3 994 (2 444)	3 949	1 652
Average wage/hour:			
men	7.67 (9.98)	8.83	9.22
women	9.57 (5.43)	6.43	5.21

Source: Derived from Fortin *et al.* (1996: tables 3.1–3.3).

work might come as no surprise. What is interesting, however, is that if anything, the gap between men and women in their participation rates in cash-in-hand work is narrower than the gender gap in formal employment participation rates, revealing that women do indeed find it easier to work on a cash-in-hand basis relative to men than formally.

Exceptions to this general rule regarding who participates, neverthe-less, do exist. Lobo (1990a,b), for example, argues that women rather than men are more likely to conduct cash-in-hand work in Portugal and Spain. Similarly, the English Localities Survey also finds that women conducted a very slightly higher proportion of tasks on a cash-in-hand basis. Although 52 per cent of the sampled population, women con-ducted 55.5 per cent of all the cash-in-hand work. More particularly, it is women living in lower-income households (i.e., with an income of less than £275 gross per week) and unemployed women who most heavily engage in such work. The problem, however, is that this method com-bines work of very different types (see Table 3.2 earlier). For example, in asserting that women conducted 55.5 per cent of the tasks carried out on a cash-in-hand basis, it treats equally the task of building a garage and the task of doing some shopping. To gain a better picture of the distribution of cash-in-hand work, future research will need to also investigate the number of hours spent engaged in such work rather than solely if cash-in-hand work was last used. This research, nevertheless, and as will be shown below, does provide a valuable insight into both the types of work conducted on a cash-in-hand basis by women and men and their contrasting motives.

Character of cash-in-hand work: gender variations

Here, the so far unchallenged assumption that both men and women always conduct cash-in-hand work under market-like relations for the purpose of economic gain is evaluated critically. To do this, the section explores the character of such work when conducted by men and women. This will reveal that although the cash-in-hand work conducted by men tends to be more market-like in terms of the work relations it is embedded within, this is not the case so far as the majority of cash-in-hand work conducted by women is concerned.

Starting with the types of cash-in-hand work that men and women perform, it is striking that women undertake a very different set of tasks than men. Just as there exists gender segmentation by sector in the formal labour market with women heavily concentrated in service sector jobs (e.g. Townsend, 1997), the same is true of the cash-in-hand sphere. As Hellberger and Schwarze (1986) identify in Germany, whilst 12.3 per cent of cash-in-hand workers are in the primary sector, 35.8 per cent in manufacturing and 51.9 per cent in services, these figures are 6.2 per cent, 11.8 per cent and 82.0 per cent for women (and 15.7 per cent, 49.3 per cent and 35.0 per cent for men). It is similar elsewhere. Women tend to engage in service activities such as commercial cleaning, domestic help, child-care and cooking when they undertake cash-in-hand work. Men, on the other hand, tend to undertake what are conventionally seen as 'masculine tasks' such as building and repair work (Fortin *et al.*, 1996; Jensen *et al.*, 1995; Leonard, 1994; Mingione, 1991; Pahl, 1984).

Rather than view the types of cash-in-hand work that men and women conduct solely in relation to the formal sphere, it is perhaps just as salient to view such work through the lens of the unpaid domestic sphere and the gender allocation of responsibilities in this realm. When this is done, the finding is that gender divisions in the cash-in-hand sphere also mirror the gender divisions of domestic labour. As such, the cash-in-hand sphere reflects and reinforces the gender divisions in activities prevalent in not only the formal labour market but also unpaid work.

To see this, the English Localities Survey can be analysed in terms of the types of cash-in-hand work that men and women conduct. Overall, it finds that just under half (45.2 per cent) of all tasks conducted on a cash-in-hand basis were concentrated in six activities (i.e., window cleaning, hairdressing, car repair, appliance maintenance, plumbing and child-care) and that some tasks are much more likely to draw upon cash-in-hand labour to get the work done than others (see Table 5.2). Notable here are making garden furniture, bird tables, etc. (which in 33 per cent of cases was conducted on a cash-in-hand basis), attic conversions (25.0 per cent conducted on a cash-in-hand basis), putting in a new bathroom suite (23.8 per cent), car repair (19.4 per cent), plumbing (12.5 per cent), electrical work and plastering (both 11.8 per cent) and night-time and daytime baby-sitting (11.7 and 11.5 per cent respectively). Indeed, the prominence of baby-sitting here is important since there is now a lot of evidence that Britain relies on a low cash-in-hand system of child-care whereby grandmothers, mothers, sisters, aunts and other women are looking after employed women's children (for a review, see Windebank, 1999). This study displays that at least some of this child-care is reimbursed on a cash-in-hand basis.

More interesting, especially in terms of the gender divisions of cash-in-hand work, is that women undertake tasks on a cash-in-hand basis for which they are largely responsible so far as the gender division of domestic work is concerned. This has been intimated before elsewhere (e.g. Fortin *et al.*, 1996; Hellberger and Schwarze, 1986; Jensen *et al.*, 1995; Leonard, 1994; Mingione, 1991; Pahl, 1984). What is so interesting about these results, however, is that they display how the gender segregation of tasks in the realm of cash-in-hand work is stronger than the gender segregation of unpaid domestic work. For example, women alone conduct 63 per cent of all routine housework tasks when unpaid domestic work is used but 84 per cent when carried out as cash-in-hand work. In contrast, women conduct 37 per cent of house maintenance tasks when domestic work is used but only 19 per cent when carried out as cash-in-hand work. The inequalities prevalent in the gender divisions of domestic work, therefore, are extenuated in the cash-in-hand sphere.

Take, for example, the task of doing the housework. The last time that this was conducted on an unpaid basis, it was a woman alone in 65 per cent of instances. When conducted on a cash-in-hand basis, however, in 93 per cent of instances, it was a woman who had undertaken this work. Payment for such work appears to reinforce the gender segmentation of tasks, not reduce it. This applies to nearly every task surveyed in Table 5.2. It seems, therefore, that women are employed on a cash-in-hand basis to

Table 5.2 Relationship between gender divisions of cash-in-hand work and unpaid domestic work in England: by task

	% of work conducted using cash-in-hand exchange	% of all cash-in-hand exchange	% of cash-in-hand exchange conducted by women	Unpaid domestic work % conducted by		
				Man alone	Woman alone	Shared
House maintenance						
All house maintenance (last 5 yrs)	8	24	19	49	37	14
Outdoor painting	10	4	23	65	22	13
Indoor painting	7	4	19	36	43	21
Wallpapering	6	4	18	39	45	16
Plastering	12	4	11	74	20	6
Mending broken window	7	2	17	93	7	0
Maintenance of appliances	11	6	33	75	23	2
Home improvement						
All home improvement (last 5 yrs)	10	19	3	74	25	1
Double glazing	7	2	0	67	33	0
Plumbing	13	6	0	76	24	0
Electrical work	12	4	0	68	29	3
House insulation	1	0	0	100	0	0
Put in bathroom	24	2	0	100	0	0
Build a garage	0	0	50	100	0	0
Build an extension	0	0	0	100	0	0
Convert attic	25	0	0	100	0	0
Put in central heating	9	1	0	100	0	0
Carpentry	9	4	0	72	27	1
Routine housework						
All routine housework (last week)	3	28	84	17	63	21
Do housework	2	2	93	13	65	22

Table 5.2   Continued

	% of work conducted using cash-in-hand exchange	% of all cash-in-hand exchange	% of cash-in-hand exchange conducted by women	Unpaid domestic work % conducted by		
				Man alone	Woman alone	Shared
Clean the house	2	2	86	25	65	11
Clean Windows	10	9	83	29	64	7
Spring cleaning	2	2	89	13	72	15
Do the shopping	1	1	80	14	50	36
Wash clothes/sheets	1	1	88	11	73	17
Ironing	1	1	80	11	71	18
Cook the meals	1	1	87	12	54	34
Wash dishes	1	1	83	17	53	30
Hairdressing	8	8	80	22	75	3
Administration	1	1	50	28	59	13
Making and repairing goods						
All making and repairing goods	2	3	94	10	89	1
Make clothes	0	0	100	9	91	0
Knitting	0	0	100	2	98	0
Repair clothes	0	0	100	7	91	2
Make furniture	6	1	50	61	39	0
Make garden equipment	33	0	0	50	50	0
Make curtains	8	2	100	3	97	0
Car maintenance						
All car maintenance (last year)	9	12	11	78	15	8
Wash car	6	3	50	68	20	13
Repair the car	19	8	13	100	0	0
Car maintenance	4	2	0	84	12	4
Gardening						
All gardening (last year)	2	3	58	32	59	9
Indoor plants	0	0	86	18	76	6
Outdoor borders	3	2	40	34	53	12

Table 5.2   Continued

	% of work conducted using cash-in-hand exchange	% of all cash-in- hand exchange	% of cash-in-hand exchange conducted by women	Unpaid domestic work % conducted by		
				Man alone	Woman alone	Shared
Outdoor vegetables	0	0	100	41	47	13
Lawn mowing	4	2	50	52	38	10
Caring						
All caring (last month)	8	11	92	11	63	26
Baby sitting (day)	11	5	100	5	74	21
Baby sitting (night)	12	5	92	11	68	21
Courses (e.g. Piano lessons)	0	0	100	22	67	11
Pet care	2	1	50	15	50	35

Source: English Localities Survey.

do tasks 'traditionally' associated with women's work and men to do tasks conventionally associated with men's work. Monetisation, in consequence, does not seem to reduce, but consolidate, gender divisions of labour at least so far as paying on a cash-in-hand basis is concerned.

It is not only the types of cash-in-hand work conducted that differentiate men from women. There is also tentative evidence that in some particular contexts men's participation is more infrequent but full-time than that of women which although continuous tends to be part-time (Leonard, 1994; McInnis-Dittrich, 1995). As Leonard (1994, p. 162) finds in Belfast, 'While the women were usually in constant informal employment compared to the men, whose employment was more casual, nonetheless ... the women tended to work part-time while the men tended to work full time.' In Appalachia, meanwhile, McInnis-Dittrich (1995) arrives at the same conclusion. Women engage in regular small part-time cash-in-hand jobs such as housework, consignment quilting, gardening, child- or elder-care, yard sales, aluminium recycling or work in the tobacco fields, whilst men tended to engage in more irregular full-time jobs, such as in the local sawmill, the sanitary landfill or on the farm. So, not only is cash-in-hand work characterised by the same sector divisions as formal employment, but also the part-time/full-time dichotomy that is often prevalent in formal employment appears to be replicated in the cash-in-hand sphere.

There are also major differences in the formal employment status of men and women who conduct such work. So far as men are concerned, most evidence suggests that cash-in-hand workers tend to be formally employed rather than unemployed. For women, however, it is the non-employed who do much of this work. Take, for example, the study by Pahl (1984) on the Isle of Sheppey. When the 27 informal workers identified in the study were analysed, some salient gender contrasts emerged. Of the 11 men, 10 were in full-time employment. Only one was unemployed. By contrast, of the 16 women, eight were full-time housewives. This difference is largely related to the type of work undertaken. Men, in general, are more likely to do home improvements, which if unemployed is conspicuous to observers, whilst women overwhelmingly provide routine domestic services, which are not so noticeable and are often perceived rightly or wrongly as unpaid activities. In addition, 'full-time housewives' are one step removed from the authorities in the sense that they do not claim benefit themselves, sign on, get called for interviews or even register as unemployed. This unequal evaluation of various tasks is to the advantage of men when they are in formal employment but is held against them if unemployed and work informally (Pahl, 1984). Furthermore, most cash-in-hand work involving men requires skills which unemployed men are viewed as unlikely to possess, whilst most cash-in-hand work for women uses skills which most women are perceived to possess (Renooy, 1990), since these emanate from the family and household, not the employment-place. Indeed, these women are often acting as substitute 'housewives' for other women with more lucrative employment.

Pay rates

The overwhelming finding of the vast majority of studies of cash-in-hand work is that women generally earn lower wages than men (Fortin *et al.*, 1996; Hellberger and Schwarze, 1986; International Labour Office, 2002; Lemieux *et al.*, 1985; McInnis-Dittrich, 1995). Take, for example, the studies by Fortin *et al.* (1996). As Table 5.1 earlier displays, men who engage in cash-in-hand work do fewer hours than women and have higher average total incomes from such work in both Montreal and Bas-du-Fleuve. The result is that the average hourly wage of women informal workers is lower than men's. Although this was also the case in Quebec in 1985, it was not the situation by 1993. Despite men continuing to be over-represented in the informal labour force in 1993, the average number of hours worked by male informal labourers considerably increased between 1985 and 1993 compared with a decline in the average hours of women, yet the average hourly male informal wage drastically reduced whilst for women it underwent a considerable increase. Indeed, by 1993, the average hourly wage of women was higher than that of men.

Although Fortin *et al.* (1996) neither identify nor explain this shift in their original analysis, personal correspondence with the author reveals that they consider this to be due to the recession in Quebec in the early 1990s, which hit men's activities particularly such as in construction and repair, whilst the on-going feminisation of the formal labour force is likely to have led to a shortage of informal labour in what are traditionally perceived as feminine tasks, such as child-care and domestic cleaning, leading to a rise in informal wage rates for conventional women's work. This important exception, nevertheless, despite displaying that there are particular economic and social circumstances in which women can and do receive higher informal wage rates than men, should not distract attention from the fact that women generally earn less than men in cash-in-hand work.

Moreover, and as Table 5.3 reveals in Germany, although women dominate the lower-paid echelons and men the higher-paid spheres of cash-in-hand work, there are men in particular places and circumstances who tend to earn a very poor wage from their cash-in-hand work and women who earn a relatively high hourly wage. For example, in areas where child-care is scarce, one would expect relatively high cash-in-hand incomes from it. Indeed, rates of pay for childminding vary enormously from one suburb to another, let alone one city to another. Indeed, this caution in allocating poorly and well-paid cash-in-hand employment exclusively to women and men respectively is reinforced by findings in Italy. Here, research indicates that some women do fare relatively well from their cash-in-hand work, especially in the Red regions (Cappechi, 1989; Vinay, 1987), such as those women in Umbria who fabricate minimotors for teleprinters in their basements (Mattera, 1985). Consequently, it would be erroneous to characterise the segmented nature of cash-in-hand work in too rigidly gendered terms. Nevertheless, and similar to the formal labour market, the existence of women in executive positions does not undermine the general trend of women being ghettoised at the lower end of the segmented informal labour market. As the International Labour Office (2002, p. 31) state in relation to cash-in-hand work, 'women are concentrated in the lower-income segments'.

Table 5.3 Average hourly wage rates in second-jobs, Germany

DM per hour	% of second-jobs in this income bracket	% of men in second-jobs	% of women in second-jobs
< 5	7.4	7.1	7.9
5–8	11.7	3.9	28.5
8–10	10.2	9.2	11.9
10–12	21.0	24.9	14.1
12–15	10.7	12.9	6.6
> 15	38.1	42.0	31.0

Source: Hellberger and Schwarze (1986, table 2).

Can one thus conclude that this is low-paid market-like work? Although most of the literature takes low wage rates as indicative that this must be the case, a deeper investigation of the work relations and motives underlying this work reveals that the reality is richer and more complex than has been assumed.

Work relations within which cash-in-hand work is embedded

Who do women work for on a cash-in-hand basis? For example, do they work for organised businesses? Examining the evidence from the survey of English localities, the finding is that just 5 per cent of women's cash-in-hand work was undertaken for formal and informal businesses (12 per cent of men's cash-in-hand work) and only 10 per cent (37 per cent amongst men) on a self-employed basis for people previously unknown to them. The vast majority (85 per cent) of women's cash-in-hand work (compared with 51 per cent of men's) is conducted either for kin, friends or neighbours. When women conducted work on a cash-in-hand basis for kin, friends and neighbours, moreover, it was in 95 per cent of cases other women who had employed them. Breaking down this cash-in-hand work conducted for close social relations, 45 per cent of all cash-in-hand work is undertaken for kin (mostly sisters, aunts, grandmothers, cousins) and 40 per cent for friends and neighbours (nearly always other women).

Consequently, although women, especially unemployed women, disproportionately engage in cash-in-hand work and it is low paid, this data on the work relations involved suggests that one needs to pause before extrapolating from this that they are engaged in market-like profit-motivated work. Previous studies are entirely correct that a lot of cash-in-hand work conducted by women is carried out on a short-term part-time basis, is low paid and revolves around tasks associated with women's domestic responsibilities. However, to view this in employment-related terms is a perhaps a misnomer. Given that much of this cash-in-hand work is identified in the context of the English Localities Survey to be undertaken for kin, friends and neighbours, one has to consider whether classifying such work as akin to a form of employment and perceiving it in terms of the hierarchy of forms of employment is an appropriate interpretation of the work relations involved.

Motives of suppliers of cash-in-hand work: gender differences

Examining traditional discourses on how the motives of men and women differ when conducting cash-in-hand work, the overwhelming view is that women conduct cash-in-hand work mainly when the household needs to generate extra cash and when it is the only work available which fits in with their domestic caring responsibilities, such as for children or elderly relatives (Howe, 1990; Jordan *et al.*, 1992; Leonard, 1994; MacDonald, 1994; Morris, 1987, 1995; Rowlingson *et al.*, 1997). Men, on the other hand, undertake cash-in-hand work for very different reasons. For them, it is much more about generating spare cash or pocket money to finance social activities and to differentiate themselves from the domestic realm and women (Leonard, 1994; MacDonald, 1994; Morris, 1987, 1995).

Take, for example, the studies by Morris (1987, 1995) in South Wales and Hartlepool. For men, cash-in-hand work was found to fulfil two social functions: it provides a means of disassociation and differentiation from the domestic sphere and women; and acts as a source of additional earnings that finance a degree of social activity, notably drinking. Cash-in-hand work for women, meanwhile, relates to the conventional gender division of labour and to established norms about gender roles and identities. 'Thus female spending patterns are bound with their association with the domestic sphere, and to be contrasted with men's perceived need for a "public" identity achieved through social spending' (Morris, 1987, p. 100–1). Leonard (1994) finds similar differences in the uses to which men and women put cash-in-hand earnings in Belfast. Women were found to regard their income as the family's wage and use their earnings to provide for the everyday needs of the family. Men, on the other hand, use either part or all of the income derived from working on a cash-in-hand basis to satisfy their personal needs. Some men felt that to give the whole cash-in-hand income to satisfy family needs

Table 5.4 Motives of suppliers of cash-in-hand work in English localities: by gender

% of cash-in-hand work supplied primarily to	Men	Women	Whole sample
Make money	82	20	50
Help out the customer	8	36	22
Build community networks	10	44	28
Total	100	100	100

Source: English Localities Survey.

would mean that they were working for nothing. In this sense, women use such income for primarily economic reasons whilst men use it more for social reasons.

However, such a gendered division of the motivations for conducting cash-in-hand is not so exclusive as suggested above. As Leonard (1994) highlights, women also use such work as a tool to reconstitute continually their social networks. For example, catalogue buying and selling gave women an opportunity to forge networks and cement personal and social ties. Transactions were highly socialised, giving women the opportunity to network with other housewives on the estate. However, and as Leonard (1994) asserts, these personal social relationships between women on the estate were often also manipulated for entrepreneurial advantage. Building up friendships and relationships with others on the estate was frequently a cultural device, strategically used to make money. Similarly, for men, although such work might be undertaken to fund socialising, this can also be seen as a mixture of economic and social reasons since social interaction is seen by many of these men as a basic need and a source of further work.

In the English Localities Survey however, a rather different understanding of the primary motives underpinning such work has started to emerge. Its finding is that only 20 per cent of the cash-in-hand tasks women conduct are undertaken for primarily economic rationales compared with 82 per cent of the cash-in-hand tasks conducted by men (see Table 5.4). These rationales predominate when women (and men) work for firms or engage in self-employed activity for people they do not know well. They do not prevail, however, when they work for friends, relatives and neighbours which constitutes 85 per cent of all cash-in-hand work conducted by women and 47 per cent of all such work conducted by men.

First, and given that many women mostly knew the people for whom they worked, 36 per cent of the tasks conducted on a cash-in-hand basis were undertaken chiefly for 'redistributive' reasons (compared with just 8 per cent of the tasks undertaken a cash-in-hand basis by men). The supplier knew the recipient needed to carry out the task and that they would be unable to get the work completed unless they were helped. This was either because they could not afford to get it done or because they were unable to do it due to age, illness and so forth. These primarily 'redistributive' rationales are to the fore amongst unemployed or early-retired women. The price charged was often well under the market price. Indeed, the closer the social relations, the more likely was the price to diverge from market norms. Given that these rationales prevailed for some 50 per cent of all women's cash-in-hand work, it is not difficult to see one of the principal reasons why women are poorly paid for their cash-in-hand work and it has little to do with the presence of unscrupulous employers seeking to exploit them.

Besides redistributive rationales, another reason women engage in cash-in-hand work revolves around community building. Some 44 per cent of the cash-in-hand work conducted by women (compared with 10 per cent of the cash-in-hand work undertaken by men) is carried out primarily for this reason. Conducting a job informally for a small payment was a way of mixing with and helping people one knew and at the same time, making a little money on the side. As one respondent explained her act of helping out her neighbour with child care,

> I did it because it was a good chance for 'Josh' [her son] to get to know her kids so it was a bit selfish I suppose. But I suppose the main reason was to sort of help her out so she would return the favour one day when I needed one. I didn't really know her that well so it sort of got us started off. I think she paid and paid me near enough proper rates to show that she wasn't trying to play on my good nature.

When the work was conducted for somebody fairly well known to them in order to develop 'bonding' social capital, payment diverged from market norms to a greater extent than for all other forms of cash-in-hand work. However, when women conduct a job for somebody less well known to them in order to develop 'bridging' social capital, as in the example above, the price is often set at just below the market price. This is because, as stated in the last chapter, there is a keen sense of not wanting to insult the person either by charging too much or too little.

Table 5.5 Motives of purchasers of cash-in-hand work in English localities: by gender

% of cash-in-hand work purchased primarily to	Men	Women	All Areas
Save money	45	15	31
Financially help the supplier	13	30	22
Build community networks	42	55	47
Total	100	100	100

Source: English Localities Survey.

Instead, the aim is to charge an amount that leaves the way open to reciprocity but does not oblige it.

Understanding these motives thus enables the gendered nature of cash-in-hand work to be more fully comprehended. When it is asserted, for example, that women are more likely to engage in temporary and part-time cash-in-hand work, and that it is more likely to be low paid, this is not simply because women are engaged in precarious types of exploitative employment. Although they do indeed engage in such cash-in-hand work, it is only a minor segment of all of the cash-in-hand work that they undertake. Rather, the reason that it is part-time, continuous and low-paid is because it is paid mutual aid, or what has been termed a hidden economy of favours.

Motives of employers

Do these 'employers' (i.e., not only formal firms but also other individuals who do not know them and friends, kin and neighbours) simply see women cash-in-hand workers as cheap labour? Or are their rationales more heterogeneous? Economic rationales, such as the desire to save money, were cited as the primary reasons in only 15 per cent of the cases where women had been employed to conduct a task on a cash-in-hand basis, and this was near enough always when women who were working for firms or were strangers, were used (see Table 5.5). When friends, neighbours or kin employed them, however, they asserted explicitly that the purpose was not, could not and should not be to save money. Indeed, when asked how much they had paid a friend, neighbour or relative, the response was nearly always prefaced by phrases like 'we weren't ripping them off but they would only take ...' or 'it wasn't really about money but we gave them ...'. If not about saving money, then what were the rationales underlying these exchanges?

Examining the diverse motives cited by those employing women cash-in-hand workers, two overarching themes prevail within which most of the detailed motives are embedded. These are the desire to develop social capital and the wish to help others out.

The need to get a task completed was often viewed by these 'employers' as an opportunity to be able to engage in an exchange with relatives, friends or neighbours. For participants in the English Localities Survey, cash-in-hand exchange is used as a medium both to forge closer ties with those whom they already know (i.e. to develop 'bonding' social capital) and to initiate links with people who they do not know very well (i.e. to build 'bridging' social capital). Why, however, was payment involved in their attempts to develop social capital? First, it was used because they did not want to feel that if they asked somebody to do something for them that they would owe them a favour. As one woman put it,

> I pay people when they do a favour for me. That way, I am free. If they won't accept money though, you have to force them. Otherwise, you have an obligation hanging over you. You can't allow that to happen. Giving them money is always best. Otherwise, you never know when they'll 'call in' the favour.

For many struggling to get by, the last thing that they wanted was to owe people favours. Using money to pay for favours avoided such obligations 'hanging over them'.

Second, payment was used to pay for favours because the overwhelming perception was that you could no longer rely on people to return favours, indicating the demise of trust in these neighbourhoods. As one woman asserted,

> You cannot trust people to return a favour these days. I don't want the hassle of waiting and seeing if they return it. Me paying stops any rucks when we fall out. I wouldn't be able to go round to theirs if they owed me. They'd think I was pestering them.

Consequently, the exchange of cash was seen as a necessary medium when maintaining or building community networks, especially when neighbours or friends were involved. Rather than provide any opportunity for such relations to deteriorate if and when they failed to reciprocate, the exchange of cash prevented this situation arising. Indeed, monetary exchange was viewed as oiling the wheels of mutual aid in a situation where trust was lacking. Put another way, cash was acting as a substitute for trust. The result was that it was often the norm to give cash in return for favours, especially in deprived neighbourhoods (see next chapter).

Besides maintaining and building social capital, a second reason for paying was to give them cash in a way that avoided any connotation of charity. This 'redistributive' rationale was particularly prevalent when money was provided to kin, such as a sister, cousin, niece or aunt, especially when they were unemployed. As one put it,

> I would have done the job [decorating] myself, but she [her sister] was on the dole so I asked her to do it instead. After all, she needed the money so it was the natural thing to do.

Hence, employing people on a cash-in-hand basis is not simply about economic gain. Although some used it to save money, this normally involved previously unknown people and accounted for only some 31 per cent of all the cash-in-hand work used. The vast majority of the time, women were being paid on a cash-in-hand basis either to help them out (e.g. by providing some cash while avoiding any notion of charity) or to develop closer ties with them. In asserting this, one does not negate the fact that there are unscrupulous employers who exploit vulnerable women in dire need of extra money. The point here is simply that other rationales also exist when women are employed by kin, friends and neighbours and these have little to do with an employer seeking to save or make money.

Implications for the study of social capital

Until now, discussions of the contribution of women and men to the building of social capital have focused almost entirely upon their unpaid community activity. These studies reveal, somewhat surprisingly for those who have believed that women are the social glue who bind communities together, that the contribution of women to building social capital is not that much greater than the contribution of men (e.g. see Putnam, 2000). For example, in the United Kingdom, according to the 2000 General Household Survey (GHS), women are only slightly more likely to either have been involved in a local organisation with responsibilities over the past three years than men (a 14 per cent participation rate compared with 12 per cent) or to have been involved in a local organisation without responsibilities (8 per cent of women compared with 7 per cent of men). If formal volunteering is found to be only marginally greater amongst women than men, participation in informal volunteering reveals similarly minor gender differences. According to the 2000 GHS (Coulthard *et al.*, 2002), exactly the same proportion of women as men have done a favour for a neighbour in the past six months (74 per cent) while the proportion of women receiving a favour is only slightly higher than for men (73 per cent compared with 71 per cent).

It superficially appears to be the case, therefore, that women are not the force, once considered to be the case so far as community involvement is concerned. Here, however, it is argued that a contributory factor leading to this surprising finding might be that only one aspect of community participation is being investigated, namely unpaid community involvement. As monetised exchange has penetrated deeper into very nook and cranny of everyday life in contemporary advanced economies (e.g. Harvey, 1989; Thrift, 2000), could it be the case that some of this mutual aid has transferred from the unpaid to the paid sphere and is thus being missed by social capital analysts? The findings so far revealed in this book regarding the motives that underpin engagement in cash-in-hand work certainly suggest that this might well be the case. Some 70 per cent of cash-in-hand work identified in the English localities survey is primarily conducted not in order to make or save money but so as to forge new relationships, cement existing ones and help people out.

Breaking down the motives underpinning engagement in cash-in-hand work by the gender of the participant, this chapter has indeed revealed that such community-building and redistributive rationales are much more common when women engage in cash-in-hand work than when men do so. As the English Localities Survey reveals, the vast majority (85 per cent) of women's cash-in-hand work (compared with 51 per cent of men's) is conducted either for kin, friends or neighbours. In consequence, the vast majority of the cash-in-hand work conducted by women can be viewed as engagement in a moral economy of favours, whilst about a half of men's involvement in cash-in-hand work is very much more in keeping with the conventional view of such work as an underground economy that is market-like and conducted for the purpose of economic gain. The result is that examining only unpaid community exchanges as a measure of community participation fails to capture what amounts to a sizeable moral economy of favours that has the same objectives as unpaid aid and is the domain of women. Given that some 5 per cent of tasks in these English localities were conducted on an unpaid basis and 5.5 per cent on a paid informal basis (of which

70 per cent is conducted for rationales akin to unpaid mutual aid), this means that social capital theorists are missing what amounts to 44 per cent of all acts of mutual aid by ignoring paid favours.

Given the gender differences in the propensity to engage in paid mutual aid, moreover, the result is that the contribution of women in the realm of mutual aid is being under-emphasised. Examining both paid and unpaid mutual aid together, the finding is that in these English localities, just less than 60 per cent of all acts of mutual aid are still being provided by women. When this is weaved into the equation, therefore, what is commonly known becomes more obvious; namely that women are the glue that binds communities together.

Even more interesting, however, are the public policy implications of this finding. This identification of a moral economy of paid favours, which is engaged in mostly by women, suggests that if a policy of deterring cash-in-hand work is pursued through more stringent regulations and punitive measures, then public policy in relation to cash-in-hand work is in danger of working against that other major realm of public policy which is trying to develop precisely those types of social capital that cash-in-hand policy is seeking to deter. The message of this chapter, therefore, is that perhaps this cash-in-hand work in the moral economy of favours needs to be considered in another light if 'joined up' thinking by government is to occur.

Conclusions

Until now, the majority of studies of the gender divisions of work have considered only the gender disparities in either formal employment and/or unpaid work. Relatively little thought has been given to the gender disparities in cash-in-hand work, despite this being a sizeable sphere of economic activity. This chapter has started to unpack these gender inequalities. Until now, where this has been considered, it has been read-off from the finding that women cash-in-hand workers are relatively low-paid compared with men, that their work in this realm is of a more exploitative variety and that they occupy the lowest rung of jobs in this sphere. Although it has not been the intention of this chapter to deny that some women do engage in highly exploitative cash-in-hand employment in the underground sector for very low pay and that something needs to be done to curtail this type of work, the overall argument is that much greater care needs to be taken over deciphering the nature of the cash-in-hand work conducted by men and women. Rather than simply read-off the existence of exploitative cash-in-hand work from their low pay, this chapter has sought to explore the work relations and motives involved when men and women engage in cash-in-hand work.

This has revealed that there are some significant differences in the nature of the cash-in-hand work they conduct that do not resonate with what has been argued before. It has been found here that when men engage in cash-in-hand work, it is much more likely to be of the market-orientated variety in the 'underground sector'. Women's cash-in-hand work, in contrast, is significantly more likely to be conducted for friends, neighbours and kin for rationales other than profit or, put another way, embedded in a social economy of favours. The implication, therefore, is that just because women are lower paid it does not mean that they are more likely to be found engaged in exploitative low-paid organised forms of informal employment in the underground sector. Instead, it is much more a reflection of the fact that it is largely women who provide the social glue that holds together community in the form of the provision of mutual aid.

This finding has implications for the study of social capital. Somewhat surprisingly for those who have assumed that it is women who hold together communities through their community participation, the social capital literature has so far failed to reveal that this is the case. Focusing upon involvement in unpaid community-based groups and the propensity of women and men to provide unpaid favours to neighbours, the majority of surveys have found little difference in participation rates between men and women. From this, it might be concluded that the view of women as community-builders is a myth. Here, however, it has been argued that one reason why this might not have been found is because this social capital literature has so far not considered the participation of women in the social economy of paid favours. The argument of this chapter has been that as monetised exchange has penetrated deeper into every aspect of social life, it appears that mutual aid that might have been previously conducted on an unpaid basis may well have been transferred into a paid realm of mutual aid. When such paid mutual aid is weaved into the equation, the assumption that women play a more significant role than men in building social capital has been shown to be more prevalent for it is women who conduct the majority of acts of paid mutual aid.

The implication, therefore, is that this finding needs to be taken into account when considering what is to be done about cash-in-hand work. After all, if a deterrence approach is adopted based on more stringent regulations and punitive measures, then one might well find that governments in seeking to deter cash-in-hand work will be also obliterating the very activity that they are wishing to develop in their policies to facilitate greater community involvement. How joined-up policy can be created in what appear to be two mutually contradictory spheres of policy-making will be returned to in Part III of this book. For the moment, attention needs to turn to the third and final dimension considered here regarding the variable nature of cash-in-hand work, namely how such activity differs according to the location in which it takes place.

6
Geographical Variations in Cash-in-hand Work

Introduction

To investigate the geographical variations in cash-in-hand work, first, this chapter reviews the literature on how the magnitude of cash-in-hand work varies geographically both at the cross-national level as well as regionally and locally. Second, previous readings on the geographical variations in the character of cash-in-hand work will be evaluated critically and third, an attempt will be made to unpack the motives underpinning engagement in cash-in-hand work and how these vary across space. Fourth and finally, the implications of these findings for the study of social capital will be explored.

To view cash-in-hand work as everywhere composed of market-like work relations and motivated by profit, it will be shown, oversimplifies and obscures the spatially variable and heterogeneous meanings of cash-in-hand work. Although cash-in-hand work in affluent locality-types is more likely to be undertaken under work relations akin to formal employment for profit-motivated purposes, in deprived locality-types, such work is much more a form of mutual aid conducted for kin, neighbours and friends and embedded in non-market motives. Indeed, drawing upon case study evidence from English localities, it will reveal that such monetised exchange, especially in deprived localities, is now one of the principal ways in which people help each other out, reflecting how mutual aid has become embedded in monetary transactions even if these monetary exchanges are not imbued with profit-motivated rationales. In consequence, the argument of this chapter is that if public policy seeks to deter cash-in-hand work through more stringent regulations and punitive measures, especially in relation to deprived communities, it will run the risk of destroying precisely the forms of community engagement that it is seeking to develop in its initiatives to rebuild social capital.

Extent of cash-in-hand work: geographical disparities

The issue of the geographical variations in the magnitude of cash-in-hand work is a popular topic in the literature. Indeed, there are a multitude of texts that attempt to investigate the uneven contours of cash-in-hand work both at the cross-national level and at the regional and local level. First, therefore, this section outlines the findings concerning cross-national comparative studies and second, the data on the regional and local disparities.

Cross-national variations in cash-in-hand work

Examining the literature on the geographical variations in cash-in-hand work, it would be fair to say that the majority focus upon variations at the cross-national level rather than the regional or local level (e.g. Dallago, 1991; European Commission, 1998; Feige, 1990; Feige and Ott, 1999; Friedman *et al.*, 2000; International Labour Office, 2002; Pederson, 1998; Schneider, 2001; Schneider and Enste, 2000). The vast bulk of this literature, however, and referring back to the discussion in Chapter 3 on methodology, employs indirect approaches when doing so. They seek evidence of cash-in-hand work in macroeconomic data that have been collected and/or constructed for other purposes. Few cross-national comparative studies have been undertaken at the time of writing that use the same direct survey methods to estimate international variations in cash-in-hand work.

The result is that most of these cross-national comparative analyses must be treated with extreme caution. The methodologies used to generate such comparative cross-national data on cash-in-hand work are severely limited in their accuracy. Without repeating in any detail the criticisms of such methods already raised in Chapter 3, some of the problems involved in these indirect survey approaches are that: they cannot differentiate between cash-in-hand work and all other forms of criminal activity and transactions; they are based on unproven assumptions; and different macroeconomic approaches produce dramatically different results in terms of the percentage of Gross National Product (GNP) that cash-in-hand work supposedly represents even within the same country at the same time. Nonetheless, such indirect macroeconomic estimates are currently the only source of information available on cross-national variations in the propensity to undertake cash-in-hand work.

Indeed, even if their accuracy is in some doubt, it is nonetheless interesting that whatever technique is used, a fairly consistent picture emerges with regard to the uneven cross-national contours of cash-in-hand work. For example, and as Barthelemy (1991) notes, indirect monetary approaches always seem to result in a similar hierarchical order in terms of the cross-national variations in the size of cash-in-hand work, suggesting that significant cross-national differences do exist and that these patterns can be detected even if the volume of this activity cannot be measured precisely using such techniques. Although it might be the case that the similarities arise because various indirect approaches tend to make the same (perhaps erroneous) assumptions about the principal drivers of cash-in-hand work, it is nevertheless of interest to portray their findings about the cross-national contours of cash-in-hand work. Table 6.1 accumulates the evidence together of a wide range of studies of the size of cash-in-hand work in particular nations, and displays that these macroeconomic studies find that cash-in-hand work tends to be higher in poorer countries and/or those with weaker welfare states than

Table 6.1 Estimates of the magnitude of cash-in-hand work obtained through indirect methods, as % of GDP

	Smallest	Highest	Average estimate
Ireland	0.5	7.2	3.9
Austria	2.1	6.2	4.2
Norway	1.3	9.0	5.5
Britain	1.0	34.3	6.8
Australia	3.5	13.4	8.4
Germany	3.4	15.0	8.7
Netherlands	9.6	9.6	9.6
Denmark	6.0	12.4	10.1
Sweden	4.5	14.1	10.1
Canada	1.2	29.4	10.7
Belgium	2.1	20.8	10.9
Spain	1.0	22.9	11.1
USA	5.0	28.0	11.3
France	6.0	23.2	11.4
Portugal	11.2	20.0	15.6
Italy	7.5	30.1	17.4
Greece	28.6	30.2	29.4

Sources: Derived from Dallago (1991, table 2.1), Pestieau (1985) and European Commission (1990).

in more affluent nations and/or countries with more comprehensive welfare systems, always assuming that the proportions of cash-in-hand work and criminal activity remain stable across different countries. Take, for example, the nations that comprise the EU. Summarising the findings of the EC Official Expert final synthesis report, *Underground Economy and Irregular Forms of Employment* (European Commission, 1990), the European Commission (1991, p. 130) concludes that in most northern parts of the EU, cash-in-hand work is some 5 per cent of the level of declared work or less, somewhat more in France and Belgium, and possibly reaching 10–20 per cent in the southern EU countries. Hence, these indirect methods appear to validate the suggestion that less affluent nations and/or nations with weaker welfare states (e.g. Greece, Portugal) engage in greater amounts of cash-in-hand work than richer nations and/or countries with more comprehensive welfare systems (e.g. Germany, Norway). The International Labour Office (2002) reinforces this finding on a more global scale. Providing sketch maps of how the size of cash-in-hand work varies across the globe, the assertion is that such work generally tends to be highest in the poorer nations and regions of the world, albeit with a number of caveats due to the different definitions of cash-in-hand work used in various countries.

Nevertheless, although such indirect estimates offer an approximate guide to the pattern of cross-national differences in cash-in-hand work, especially given the current absence of cross-national direct surveys, this is the limit of their usefulness. These cross-national comparative studies using indirect methods reveal nothing about local or regional variations in cash-in-hand work. Nor do they consider whether and how the nature of cash-in-hand work varies across space. To understand these issues, one needs to turn to other literature.

Regional and local variations in cash-in-hand work

Although there have been a number of studies of the regional and local variations in cash-in-hand work that again employ indirect measurement methods (e.g. Button, 1984), the vast majority of studies at this spatial scale comprise direct surveys. Here, therefore, the multitude of direct empirical studies of cash-in-hand work conducted in specific locations in countries across the advanced economies are synthesised in order to draw conclusions concerning the regional and local variations in the volume of cash-in-hand work.

In the past, a common assumption was that just as poorer nations engage in more cash-in-hand work than affluent nations according to indirect survey methods, the same applies on a local and regional level.

Reflecting the dominance of the marginality thesis (see Chapter 2), the popular prejudice was that such work is more prominent in deprived regions and localities. Elkin and McLaren (1991, p. 217), for example, talk of 'disadvantaged localities where cash-in-hand work is often very important', whilst Haughton *et al.* (1993, p. 33) assert that 'the distribution of informal work ... may well be especially important in areas of high unemployment, in part acting as a palliative, in part merely recycling people between employment and unemployment and possibly reducing official unemployment statistics'. For many commentators, therefore, cash-in-hand work is most likely to be found in those areas where such marginalised populations are concentrated: deprived inner city localities (Blair and Endres, 1994; Elkin and McLaren, 1991; Haughton *et al.*, 1993; Robson, 1988) and poorer peripheral regions (Button, 1984; Hadjimichalis and Vaiou, 1989).

The vast majority of direct empirical studies, however, find the opposite to be the case. In the Netherlands, for example, a study of six localities by Van Geuns *et al.* (1987) demonstrates that the higher the rate of unemployment in an area, the lower is the level of cash-in-hand work. In France, meanwhile, studies in both Orly-Choisy (Barthe, 1985) and Lille (Foudi *et al.*, 1982) identify poverty black spots in which the unemployed cannot escape from their deprivation through cash-in-hand work because not only is less money available to pay for cash-in-hand work than in more affluent areas but no informal factories or businesses have emerged to succeed those formal businesses which have closed. Surveys of relatively affluent new towns and commuter areas in France (Cornuel and Duriez, 1985; Tievant, 1982), in contrast, discover a relatively high amount of cash-in-hand work, maintained principally by the more prosperous and professional residents who undertake individual cash-in-hand work ventures as much for social as for economic purposes. In Italy, similarly, direct studies of cash-in-hand work reveal that it is more extensive in the relatively affluent northern regions than in the more deprived southern regions (Mattera, 1980; Mingione, 1991). As Mingione and Morlicchio (1993, p. 424) declare, 'the opportunities of [*sic*] informal work are more numerous, the greater the level of development of the surrounding social and economic context'. This finding is replicated in Britain. A survey of eight localities by Bunker and Dewberry (1984) discovers that those areas with the highest unemployment rates undertake relatively little cash-in-hand work.

This finding concerning the local and regional variations is further reinforced in the English Localities Survey. As Chapter 3 outlined, this examined eleven affluent and deprived localities in both urban and

Table 6.2 Percentage of everyday tasks undertaken using cash-in-hand work in England: by locality-type

Area	% of the 44 tasks last conducted using cash-in-hand work	No. of households surveyed
All areas	5.5	861
Lower income rural areas	5.6	210
Higher-income rural areas	4.1	140
All rural areas	5.0	350
Lower-income areas – Southampton	4.4	200
Higher-income suburb – Southampton	6.5	50
Lower-income areas – Sheffield	5.4	200
Higher-income suburb – Sheffield	11.2	61
All urban areas	5.8	511

Source: English Localities Survey.

rural areas of England. Starting with the consumption side of the equation, the finding was that cash-in-hand work is more likely to be used by those who live in affluent areas. As Table 6.2 reveals, this is the case in both urban and rural areas and whether one evaluates the share of all work that is conducted using cash-in-hand work or the absolute number of tasks received on a cash-in-hand basis. The sites where cash-in-hand work is consumed, therefore, are concentrated in affluent areas.

Does the labour undertaking this work, however, also live in these areas? As Table 6.3 displays, households in affluent areas conduct a disproportionate share of cash-in-hand work and receive much greater monetary rewards than those living in lower-income areas. This applies in both the urban and rural environment. Comparing lower- and higher-income urban areas, for example, the average amount received for conducting a task on a cash-in-hand basis was £90 compared with £1665 respectively; the average hourly wage rate for cash-in-hand work was £3.40 compared with £7.50; and the mean annual household income from cash-in-hand work was £58 compared with £899. For the 40 per cent of households in lower-income neighbourhoods who supplied cash-in-hand labour, meanwhile, the mean annual household income from such work was £115 compared with £2420 in the 18 per cent of households who supplied such work in affluent suburbs. The

Table 6.3   Participation in cash-in-hand work in England: by area

Area-type	No. of house-holds	% of all house-holds surveyed	% of all cash-in-hand tasks conducted	Average pay/cash-in-hand task (£)	Mean household income p.a. from cash-in-hand work (£)
All	861	100	100		
Urban higher income	111	13	37	90	46
Urban lower income	400	47	22	1 665	435
Rural lower income	210	24	16	25	47
Rural higher income	140	16	25	564	921

Source: English Localities Survey.

monetary rewards from cash-in-hand work, therefore, are heavily skewed towards the affluent suburbs.

However, just because demand and supply are concentrated in affluent localities does not mean that the residents of these areas are exchanging work with each other. Examining the tasks demanded and supplied, there is a mismatch. Although some might be supplied to other local residents (e.g. architectural services, music lessons, home improvement, landscape design services), the vast majority is being conducted for commercial businesses, usually on a consultancy basis for money that is not being declared to the tax authorities. Meanwhile, tasks supplied by households in lower-income areas (especially for people that they did not previously know) broadly match those being consumed in the affluent suburbs (e.g. house cleaning, window cleaning, gardening). Therefore, although this study did not ask consumers where the person doing the work lived or suppliers where they had conducted the work, the task list suggests that residents of affluent areas are supplying others in their neighbourhood as well as commercial enterprises with cash-in-hand labour. Concomitantly, those in lower-income neighbourhoods are supplying activities that those in the affluent areas consume. Whether they are directly supplying these affluent areas, nevertheless, is not known.

Table 6.4 Suppliers of cash-in-hand labour in lower- and higher-income English neighbourhoods: by socio-economic status

	No. of households	% of all households	% of all cash-in-hand tasks conducted
Lower-income areas			
By number of earners in household			
Multiple-earner households	94	23.5	35.3
Single-earner households	92	23.0	34.6
No-earner households	214	53.5	30.1
By household income			
< £250 per week	278	72.2	50.1
> £250 per week	108	27.8	49.9
Higher-income areas			
By number of earners in household			
Multiple-earner households	47	42.3	51.0
Single-earner households	33	29.7	31.8
No-earner households	31	27.9	17.2
By household income			
< £250 per week	24	21.7	9.8
> £250 per week	87	78.3	90.2

Source: English Localities Survey.

What type of household, however, supplies cash-in-hand work? The finding in both the deprived and affluent English neighbourhoods is that it is higher-income households (here defined as earning over £250 gross per week) and those with members in employment who conduct a disproportionate share of this work. As Table 6.4 displays, in lower-income areas, households with a gross income of more than £250 per week (17.8 per cent of the sample) supply the labour for 49.9 per cent of all the work conducted on a cash-in-hand basis. In the affluent areas, similarly, higher-income households conduct a disproportionate share of all cash-in-hand work.

Consequently, this study reinforces in the context of contemporary England previous studies conducted elsewhere that challenge the marginality thesis (e.g. Fortin *et al.*, 1996; Jensen *et al.*, 1995; Marcelli *et al.*, 1999; Pahl, 1984). Higher-income populations not only use and supply such work to a greater extent than lower-income populations but also receive a disproportionate share of the income from such work. Here, however, attention turns to some key issues that have not been so far considered to any extent in the literature on the geographies of cash-in-hand work. How do the work relations and motives within which cash-in-hand work is conducted differ across space?

Character of cash-in-hand work: geographical variations

Until now, the assumption has been that cash-in-hand work is a form of work conducted under market-like relations akin to formal employment for the purpose of profit. As such, when the geographical variations in the nature of cash-in-hand work have been highlighted, the tendency has been to assert that residents in affluent areas engage in higher quality cash-in-hand work and the populations of deprived areas in lower quality work (e.g. Williams and Windebank, 1995a). In this view, deprived areas are viewed as conducting greater proportions of poorly paid exploitative organised cash-in-hand work whilst relatively affluent areas are seen to undertake more well paid autonomous cash-in-hand work. Mingione (1991), for example, distinguishes three Italies: the more affluent and industrialised north-west in which autonomous cash-in-hand work is widespread; the north-east and centre in which although cash-in-hand work has developed in order to cut production costs, there is both organised and individual cash-in-hand work conducted under reasonable conditions as well as low cash-in-hand work; and the south in which cash-in-hand work is more exploitative in character than that found in the centre or north of the country and where some of the most exploitative forms of cash-in-hand work (e.g. industrial home-working, illegal manufacturing of forged fashion items) are concentrated. Similar patterns are asserted to exist in Spain (Benton, 1990) and Greece (Hadjimichalis and Vaiou, 1989; Leontidou, 1993; Mingione, 1990).

As such, there has emerged a very particular view about the spatial heterogeneity of cash-in-hand work (Fortin *et al.*, 1996; Jensen *et al.*, 1995; Laguerre, 1994; Leonard, 1994, 1998; Mingione, 1991; Pahl, 1984; Renooy, 1990; Waldinger and Lapp, 1993; Williams and Windebank, 1998). This distinguishes 'organised' kinds of cash-in-hand work conducted for formal and informal businesses, which tends to be low-paid and exploitative in character and are concentrated in deprived areas (e.g. Fortin *et al.*, 1996; Howe, 1990; Lemieux *et al.*, 1994; MacDonald, 1994; Renooy, 1990; Williams and Windebank, 1998), and 'autonomous' forms of cash-in-hand work conducted on a self-employed basis for better pay and which are concentrated in more afflu-ent areas (Cornuel and Duriez, 1985; Jensen *et al.*, 1995; Komter, 1996; Leonard, 1994). From this perspective, all cash-in-hand work is thus market-like in character as displayed by the fact that this spatial division of cash-in-hand work has been referred to as a spatially 'segmented informal labour market' (Williams and Windebank, 1998).

In the English Localities Survey, however, evidence has been gathered that suggests not only that cash-in-hand work might well be conducted under a wider set of work relations than has so far been considered but also how these might be geographically variable. The first clue that this is the case is the data presented in Table 6.5. In a bid to start to evaluate critically the so far unchallenged assumption that cash-in-hand exchange is market-like work (De Soto, 1989; Castells and Portes, 1989; Matthews, 1983; Sassen, 1991), this unravels the work relations involved in these exchanges in different area-types. Examining the nature of the relationship between the supplier and customer, it reveals that in lower-income neighbourhoods over two-thirds of cash-in-hand tasks are provided by kin, neighbours and friends and even in affluent suburbs, some 16 per cent of cash-in-hand tasks are conducted under these social relations. Is it the case, therefore, that even in these circum-stances, market-like work relations akin to formal employment prevail and the motive of participants is economic gain? Is it still market-orientated exchange based on atomistic, impersonal and dis-embedded relations by suppliers and consumers seeking to achieve maximised money gains? To answer these questions, the motives of both consumers and suppliers of such work need to be investigated.

Before doing this, however, it is necessary to state that the intent in highlighting the existence of a hidden economy of favours is in no way to mask or underplay the exploitative working conditions that exist in the underground economy. In lower-income areas in particular, where such work is conducted for firms, the wage rates tend to be below the national minimum wage. However, this low-paid organised cash-in-hand work accounts for just 5 per cent of all cash-in-hand work in these lower-income populations (cf. Castells and Portes, 1989; Sassen, 1989). If this kind of cash-in-hand exchange is the sole focus of investigation, therefore, the caricature of such work as a low-paid form of peripheral employment conducted for economic gain is correct. However, when

Table 6.5 Character of suppliers of cash-in-hand work in England: by area-type

% of all cash-in-hand work conducted by	Rural areas		Southampton		Sheffield		Both cities		All areas
	Higher income	Lower income	Higher income	Lower income	Higher income	Lower income	Higher income	Lower income	
Firm/unknown person	5	8	92	30	76	33	84	32	30
Friend/neighbour	56	52	1	30	20	29	11	29	33
Relative	38	35	7	29	1	21	4	24	30
Household member	1	5	0	11	3	17	1	15	7
Total	100	100	100	100	100	100	100	100	100
No. of households surveyed	140	210	50	200	61	200	111	400	861

Source: English Localities Survey.

Table 6.6   Motives for employing cash-in-hand workers in England: by type of area

% of cash-in-hand work conducted primarily to	Urban		Rural		All areas
	Lower income	Higher income	Lower income	Higher income	
Save money	18	80	6	20	31
Financially help the supplier	11	6	34	32	22
Build community networks	71	14	60	48	47
Total	100	100	100	100	100
No. of households surveyed	400	111	210	140	861

Source: English Localities Survey.

cash-in-hand exchange conducted on a self-employed basis for people unknown to them is included along with exchange between friends, relatives and neighbours, it becomes apparent that this is a gross over-simplification of the rich and complex characteristics and motives of cash-in-hand exchange in contemporary England.

To explore why people engage in cash-in-hand exchange, first, the rationales underlying consumers' decisions to use such work are analysed and second, the motivations of suppliers. This will display that more variegated and complex exchange relations are prevalent, especially in lower-income neighbourhoods, than has been assumed in much previous discourse.

Motivations of purchasers: geographical variations

Do consumers employ people on a cash-in-hand basis simply in order to save money? Examining the rationales of those who employed cash-in-hand labour in the English Localities Survey, the finding is that the profit motive is not always to the fore. As Table 6.6 reveals, less than a third (31 per cent) of all the tasks paid for on a cash-in-hand basis employed such labour for primarily profit-motivated purposes. However, there are some significant geographical variations in the motives of purchasers. Such a motive is much more prevalent in higher- than lower-income areas as well as urban rather than rural areas. In nearly every case where the principal rationale is to use cash-in-hand work as a cheaper alternative to formal employment, nevertheless, it is firms and/or self-employed people not known by the household who are employed to do this work in all localities.

This significant variation in consumers' motives in higher- and lower-income areas, and rural and urban areas, is for two reasons. First, and as detailed above, affluent and urban areas make far greater use of firms and/or self-employed people not known by the household, thus resulting in the greater prevalence of economic motivations. Second, residents of affluent and urban areas are more likely to turn to formal suppliers where cash-in-hand labour is not used, and so are more likely to cite cheapness as the reason for using such labour. In lower-income and rural areas where the alternative is either self-provisioning or more usually not conducting the task at all, cheapness is less likely to be the chief reason for using cash-in-hand labour.

When saving money is the major rationale, furthermore, consumers significantly differ in affluent and urban areas compared with lower-income and rural areas in terms of how they perceive the work relations between themselves and the cash-in-hand worker. In affluent and urban areas, consumers perceived themselves as having chosen to get the work completed in this manner and saw the supplier, who was perceived to be of 'unequal' status to them (e.g. in socio-economic terms), as grateful for this favour. In lower-income and rural areas, however, consumers saw themselves as having little choice but to complete the work on a cash-in-hand basis and the supplier was seen as doing them a favour. The result was that whilst residents of affluent and urban areas often demanded additional favours from the cash-in-hand worker, as Gregson and Lowe (1994) have shown in the context of nannies, residents of lower-income and rural areas saw little scope for negotiating what would be provided, how and when. Residents of lower- and higher-income areas as well as urban and rural areas thus position themselves differently in relation to the supplier when consuming cash-in-hand work. In major part, this is a product of the alternatives that they perceive as available to them.

Economic rationales, however, are not the only reason for using cash-in-hand work, especially in lower-income and rural areas. Customers had a well-formulated understanding that when friends, neighbours or kin were employed, cash-in-hand work was not, could not and should not be used to save money. Indeed, and as described in earlier chapters, when asked how much they had paid a friend, neighbour or kin, the response was nearly always prefaced by caveats. If not about saving money, then what were the rationales underlying these exchanges?

Examining the diverse motives cited by consumers, two overarching themes prevail within which most of the detailed motives are embedded. These are the desire to develop social capital and the wish to help others out, and the proportion of cash-in-hand work premised upon these two broad motives displays distinct spatial variations, as will now be shown.

This study finds that when a task needs completing, consumers often view this as an opportunity to engage kin, friends or neighbours as suppliers in order to pursue longer-term motives associated with developing bridging and/or bonding social capital. This type of rationale tends to prevail mostly when consumers pay friends or neighbours (rather than kin) and is much more common in lower- than higher-income areas, and urban rather than rural areas.

An employed male on an urban council estate explained his use of a friend to do some work by stating, 'why give the money to someone I don't know. If I give it to my own, then they'll do the same for me.' This forging of closer ties with friends, neighbours and relatives through cash-in-hand exchange is thus economically orientated but is grounded in longer-term mutual co-operation. The outcome is that constructions of value often widely diverge from the market price when 'bonding' social capital is the motivation. Here, the average price paid is the lowest of all forms of cash-in-hand work. For example, one customer paid just £20 for his neighbour to dismantle a garage and take it away, a task that took two days to complete. However, it was not seen as low-paid work since it was conducted neither under market-like conditions nor for profit. In affluent suburbs in contrast, exchanges conducted under the auspices of 'bonding' social capital are often 'paid' at rates far higher than the market rate, usually in the form of gifts rather than money. One customer in an affluent urban area, for example, had given a work colleague who lived nearby a bottle of whisky and some Belgian chocolates merely for delivering their work mail to their home ready for when they returned from their holiday, a task that had taken five minutes.

When the primary motive is to initiate links with people one does not know (i.e. to build bridging social capital), however, such divergence in wage rates from the market norm is not found. In lower-income and rural areas, rates generally tend to conform to the market price so that the cash-in-hand worker, with whom one is trying to develop greater reciprocity and trust, is not insulted. In affluent and urban areas, it is much more so that the person who one sees as less equal in socio-economic terms (e.g. a gardener, decorator, builder) will return in the future.

Investigating why payment is involved, the finding was that in deprived areas, although unpaid exchange occurred between kin, it seldom took place between friends and neighbours. When asked about providing unpaid help to non-kinship relations, for example, the common response, especially in deprived urban communities, was that 'they can f—ing look after themselves'. Indeed, the only reason such unpaid non-kinship exchange occurred was because payment in that particular situation was seen as unacceptable, inappropriate or impossible. This applied either when the task was too small to warrant a payment (e.g. when somebody lends a hammer) or when the social relations mitigate against payment (e.g. when customer may not be able to afford to pay and has no choice but to offer a favour in return). Whenever possible, therefore, people avoided unpaid exchange relations when friends and neighbours were involved and used monetary payment.

Paying avoided any obligation to reciprocate favours but at the same time, it oiled the wheels for the maintenance or creation of closer relations through exchange. In major part, payments were indicative of the demise of trust in these areas. Monetary payment was acting as a substitute for the trust. Consequently, there was a sense that the exchange of cash was a necessary medium when maintaining or building community networks, especially when neighbours or friends were involved. Rather than provide any opportunity for such relations to turn sour if and when they reneged on their commitments, the exchange of cash in lower-income areas and gifts in affluent suburbs prevented such a situation arising.

Where such primary rationales predominate, nevertheless, users did not see this work as substituting for formal employment. On the whole, they would have done the work themselves or not done it at all had they not employed somebody on a cash-in-hand basis. In affluent suburbs, meanwhile, those few instances where bridging social capital was the rationale for using informal labour, the work would have been otherwise conducted by formally employed labour. Where bonding social capital was the rationale in such suburbs, the work would not have been conducted at all or done by the household themselves if they had not used informal labour.

Besides developing social capital, the second theme underlying consumers' rationales for using cash-in-hand work involved redistribution. This usually applied when kin were conducting the work. In these instances, payments did not involve one spouse paying another (and thus the monetisation of the gender division of domestic labour between spouses). Rather, it was either children or a relation such as a brother, sister or parent who was paid, often as a way of giving them spending money. Indeed, using kin to do tasks in order to give them money was much more prevalent as a rationale for cash-in-hand work in deprived than affluent localities.

Again, little of this work was substituting for formal employment. In the vast majority of cases, the users would have done the work themselves if the person had not been paid on a cash-in-hand basis. They were paying solely to give money to kin in order to help them out. In affluent suburbs, this mostly involved paying one's pre-adult children to 'teach them the value of money'. In lower-income areas, however, a wider variety of kin were involved and the intention was much more explicitly to help them out.

In sum, customers were primarily motivated to use cash-in-hand exchange in affluent areas by a desire to save money, with some limited work conducted by friends and neighbours in order to develop closer social bonds for which gifts were given and some undertaken by children in order to redistribute cash and teach them the value of money. In lower-income areas, however, only a minor amount of cash-in-hand work was conducted primarily to save money. Most was undertaken by friends, neighbours and kin either to cement or consolidate social bonds with the supplier or to help them out for redistributive reasons. Therefore, to envisage all customers as 'unscrupulous' employers who oblige a weak and unprotected workforce to undertake precarious cash-in-hand work under exploitative conditions for low wages is far from the reality, especially in lower-income areas (cf. Castells and Portes, 1989; Portes, 1994). Although such motives are evident, especially in affluent suburbs and amongst firms employing organised informal labour living in lower-income areas, they constitute only a small minority of all 'employers' of cash-in-hand workers, especially in lower-income areas.

Motivations of suppliers: geographical variations

Turning to the rationales of those who supply cash-in-hand work, there are again significant variations between those living in higher- and lower-income areas. In both urban and rural areas, nearly twice the proportion of cash-in-hand work is conducted for profit-motivated purposes in higher- compared with lower-income areas. In the urban environment, for example, some 51 per cent is conducted for the purpose of economic gain in lower-income urban neighbourhoods but 90 per cent in the affluent suburbs.

Some caution is required, however, concerning these results. Although respondents who supplied cash-in-hand work were quick to assert that they had conducted this work in order to make money, especially in the interviews in the urban areas, in over half (52 per cent) of all instances where money was given as the chief reason, caveats were again given. In the urban areas, this type of qualification was much more frequently voiced in the deprived urban neighbourhoods. It was seldom heard, however, amongst residents of affluent suburbs who were supplying cash-in-hand work, doubtless because a much larger proportion of such work is conducted either for businesses or on a self-employed basis for people previously unknown to them, in stark contrast to deprived urban neighbourhoods where most of the work is conducted for friends, kin and neighbours. When conducted under these latter social relations, few suppliers cite money as the principal motivating factor. This tends only to apply when conducting work for businesses or for people previously unknown. Indeed, this is perhaps the reason why the profit-motive is much less prevalent in rural areas, where a much smaller proportion of all cash-in-hand work is conducted for business or on a self-employed basis for people previously unknown to the supplier.

Indeed, it appears that in rural areas, respondents were more forthcoming from the outset about their reasons for engaging in such work. Perhaps bolstered by the stereotype that rural areas possess strong social bonds and community spirit, respondents seemed to be more forthright that such work was not conducted for purely profit-motivated reasons and that other rationales were prominent in explaining their cash-in-hand work. In major part, however, this is also perhaps because a much higher proportion of the suppliers claimed to have some prior acquaintance with the customer so for them, such work was on the whole embedded in closer social relations than in urban areas. Whatever the reason for the lesser emphasis on profit in rural areas compared with urban areas, however, the important point is that overall, profit was mentioned as the primary motive in only half of all instances where people worked on a cash-in-hand basis. Indeed, when those who made qualifying statements are extracted, just 25 per cent of all cash-in-hand work was conducted purely for the purpose of economic gain (19 per cent and 79 per cent in deprived and affluent urban areas, and 12 per cent and 29 per cent in affluent and deprived rural areas respectively). Beyond making money, suppliers of cash-in-hand work, similar to customers, conducted such work primarily either in order to help out somebody else or as a means of cementing, building or maintaining

Table 6.7 Motives of suppliers of cash-in-hand work in English localities

% of all cash-in-hand work supplied primarily to	Urban		Rural		All areas
	Lower income	Higher income	Lower income	Higher income	
Make money	51	90	26	48	50
Help the customer	13	5	30	32	22
Build community networks	36	5	44	20	28
Total	100	100	100	100	100
No. of households surveyed	400	111	210	140	861

Source: English Localities Survey.

social networks. Here, the ways in which the preponderance to assert these motives vary spatially are explored.

First, there is the finding that suppliers tended to use community-building rationales. Overall, and as Table 6.7 reveals, such community-building motives were far more prevalent in lower- than higher-income areas and in rural compared with urban areas. It appears to be the case, therefore, that the tendency to engage in cash for favours in order to build social capital, whether of the bonding or bridging variety, is more characteristic of poorer and rural areas. To some extent, this is due to the absence of trust, especially in deprived areas.

Besides community-building rationales, suppliers also display 'redistributive' motivations when conducting cash-in-hand work. Again, this was more commonly cited in both lower-income and rural areas than in affluent and urban areas. In sum, although the vast majority of cash-in-hand work in higher-income areas is primarily conducted to save/make money by both customers and suppliers and is mostly acting as a substitute for formal employment, this is not the case in lower-income areas. Here, cash-in-hand work is more likely to be conducted by friends, neighbours and kin for the purpose of developing social capital and/or redistribution. The fascinating consequence of this finding is that just because cash-in-hand work is poorly paid in lower-income areas, it does not follow that such work is low-paid employment. Given that such exchanges are largely conducted under social relations akin to unpaid mutual aid and involve community-building and redistributive rationales, one cannot overlay market-oriented consequences onto such work.

Implications for the study of social capital

As outlined in previous chapters, it has long been recognised in social scientific enquiry that social networks represent resources that people can draw upon (e.g. Stack, 1974; Young and Wilmott, 1975). What is so important about this geographical research on the variable nature of cash-in-hand work reported here is that it has implications for how one goes about developing social capital.

Throughout the advanced economies, the belief until now has been that community involvement can and should be nurtured through the development of community-based groups (e.g. Dekker and Van Den Broek, 1998; Merrett, 2001; Salamon *et al.*, 1999; Stoll, 2001). Indeed, fostering community involvement and nurturing community-based groups are often seen as synonymous. Little consideration is given to the fact that there may be other forms of community involvement beyond participating in such local organisations. This is particularly the case in Britain. Here, the UK government's policy approach towards nurturing community involvement focuses almost entirely on developing community-based groups. Indeed, this focus is justified in UK government policy documents by referral to a 'ladder of community involvement' in which participation in community-based groups (formal community involvement) is seen as an expression of a more mature participatory culture whilst one-to-one acts of good neighbourliness (informal community involvement) are seen as 'simple' acts characteristic of immature cultures of engagement (Home Office, 1999). As such, the UK government in adopting a 'ladder' metaphor to characterise community involvement has drawn upon a symbolic representation of community development that has a long and contested history since it was first proposed by Arnstein (1969).

To evaluate the implications and legitimacy of both such a hierarchical depiction of the different forms of community involvement and the resulting emphasis on nurturing community-based groups, a recent paper (Williams, 2003a) analyses data from the 2000 General Household Survey (GHS). This reveals the existence of contrasting local and regional cultures of community engagement in the United Kingdom, with regions such as London and the south east as well as affluent wards possessing more formal cultures of community involvement, and northern regions and deprived wards having more informal participatory cultures.

As Table 6.8 clearly indicates, the rate of participation in both formal and informal community involvement is lower in deprived wards. Just

Table 6.8 Spatial variations in the extent of participation in formal and informal community involvement: by Index of Deprivation (grouped by deciles, % of respondents)

| | Most deprived wards | | | | | | | | | Least deprived wards | All | χ^2 |
	1	2	3	4	5	6	7	8	9	10		
Been involved in a local organisation, with responsibilities	7	7	12	12	15	12	15	22	20	18	13	116.82
Been involved in a local organisation without responsibilities	7	5	7	7	8	7	9	8	7	11	8	20.65
Done favour for a neighbour in past 6 months	65	72	73	78	76	74	71	77	77	78	74	15.98
Received favour from a neighbour in past 6 months	64	68	71	77	75	74	71	74	74	76	72	16.06

Source: General Household Survey 2000.

14 per cent of people participated in groups in the last three years in the most deprived wards compared with 29 per cent of the population in the most affluent wards. Similarly, merely 65 per cent did a favour for a neighbour in the past six months in the most deprived wards compared with 78 per cent in the most affluent wards (and this difference between deprived and affluent wards is even smaller when the most deprived decile of wards are extracted). Consequently, while more than twice the proportion of the total population engage in community-based groups in the most affluent compared with the most deprived wards, the proportion of the total population engaging in informal community involvement in the most affluent and deprived wards differs by a much smaller overall amount: 78 per cent compared with 65 per cent (or 78 per cent compared with 72 per cent if the most deprived decile of wards are excluded).

Examining whether ward-level variations in the rate of participation in formal and informal community involvement are statistically significant, a chi-square analysis reveals no significant spatial variation in the participation rate in informal community involvement across these ten types of ward. However, there is a statistically significant variation in the participation rate in local organisations across these affluent and deprived wards. In the most deprived 10 per cent of wards in England and Wales, just 7 per cent of respondents participated in a local organisation with responsibilities over the last three years (compared for example with a peak of 22 per cent in the eighth decile of least deprived wards, tailing off to 20 per cent in the ninth decile and 18 per cent in the most affluent wards) and 7 per cent without responsibilities (11 per cent in the most affluent wards). To seek to develop community involvement by nurturing groups is thus to attempt to cultivate a vehicle in which only a small proportion of the population in the most deprived wards participate. This ladder of involvement approach has as its focus the development of a specific form of participation (and participatory culture) that is relatively unfamiliar to most of the population in deprived wards and at the same time, pays no heed to further bolstering the type of community involvement in which two-thirds (65 per cent) of people in deprived wards are already involved, namely one-to-one aid.

Participating in community-based groups in consequence, is much more a part of the participatory culture of affluent compared with deprived wards and this variation is statistically significant. Deprived wards in contrast have a more informally orientated participatory culture. It is not only a comparison of wards according to their level of multiple deprivation, however, that reveals significant geographical variations in cultures of community involvement.

Table 6.9 Regional variations in the extent of formal and informal community involvement, in the United Kingdom (% of respondents)

Government office region	Involvement in local organisation with responsibilities in last 3 years	Involvement in local organisation without responsibilities in last 3 years	Done favour for neighbour in past 6 months	Received favour from neighbour in past 6 months
North East	7	6	71	72
North West	9	9	77	74
Merseyside	11	7	77	73
Yorkshire & Humberside	13	6	74	74
East Midlands	14	10	74	71
West Midlands	17	5	71	69
Eastern	11	8	73	73
London	15	7	70	65
South East	19	8	73	72
South West	13	8	78	79
Wales	15	9	75	73
Scotland	13	7	77	75
All	13	8	74	72

Sources: General Household Survey, 2000; derived from Coulthard *et al.* (2002, tables 2.14 and 3.14).

Table 6.9 documents the regional variations in the extent and nature of community involvement. Starting with how the level of participation in formal community engagement differs across regions, the 2000 GHS provides one of the first insights into the existence of distinct regional cultures in contemporary Britain so far as the extent of participation in organisations and the size of this civic core are concerned. As this table displays, this is a form of community participation that is far more widespread in some regions than others. In the South East, Eastern and London regions for example, some 19 per cent, 17 per cent and 15 per cent of respondents respectively had been actively involved in at least one organisation during the past three years, but this was the case for just 7 per cent of the population responding in the North East and 9 per cent in the North West. Active involvement in local organisations is thus very much part of the participatory culture of regions such as the South East but is poorly developed in other regions such as the North East and North West. Comparing how informal community involvement varies across regions, meanwhile, the 2000 GHS again provides a useful insight into the regional differences in participatory cultures. Although London, as mentioned, has relatively higher rates of participation in formal forms of community engagement compared with other regions, it has the lowest rate of engagement in informal community involvement. While 72 per cent of respondents nationally had received a favour from a neighbour in the past six months, this was the case for just 65 per cent of Londoners (compared with 79 per cent in the South West). Similarly, while the South East has the highest rates of formal community participation, its rate of informal engagement is below the national average so far as receiving favours from neighbours are concerned.

The North West, in contrast, despite having amongst the lowest rates of formal participation, is amongst those regions displaying the highest rates of engagement in informal forms of giving and receiving. In consequence, the participatory culture of regions such as London and the South East is orientated towards formal forms of community involvement and regions such as the North East and North West towards informal engagement.

The result, it seems, is that such a hierarchical policy approach ends up denigrating as 'simple' the cultures of community involvement in these northern regions and deprived wards, and seeks to parachute into such areas a relatively alien culture of engagement in order to transform them into more 'mature' participatory cultures. For Williams (2002c,e; 2003a,b,e), therefore, there is a need for shift in the focus of public policy so far as fostering community involvement is concerned. Rather than emphasise the development of community-based groups, there is a need to cultivate informal community involvement.

If community involvement is to be nurtured in ways less regionally and locally biased, therefore, Williams (2003a) argues that a conceptual shift is required from viewing forms of community engagement in terms of a hierarchy to recognising these forms as a spectrum and thus the existence of a plurality of participatory cultures. Once this non-hierarchical re-conceptualisation of the contrasting local and regional cultures of community involvement is adopted, it follows that a spatially variegated policy approach is required so as to prevent alien forms of community engagement from being imposed onto the existing participatory cultures of some northern regions and deprived wards.

In order to nurture such informal participatory cultures, however, this chapter has revealed that it is first necessary to get to grips with an essential fact about informal community involvement in deprived neighbourhoods and regions, at least so far as Britain is concerned. Such one-to-one mutual aid is often undertaken on a paid basis due to the absence of trust. Token payments lubricate the wheels and enable exchange to occur in situations where trust is lacking and where such exchange would otherwise not take place. Unless it is recognised that there is a culture of payment in such deprived neighbourhoods when-ever acts of mutual aid take place, then there seems little likelihood that further progress can be made in developing social capital. How this can be taken on board will be returned to in Part III.

Conclusions

Until now, most of the literature on the geographies of cash-in-hand work has concentrated on how its magnitude varies mostly on a cross-national level as also regionally and locally. Here, however, the focus has been upon identifying the geographical variations in the nature of cash-in-hand work. In the few instances where this has been previously considered, the conclusion has been that cash-in-hand work in deprived areas is characterised by low-paid exploitative forms of 'organ-ised' cash-in-hand work conducted for informal or formal businesses, whilst cash-in-hand work in affluent areas tends to be composed of more 'autonomous' better paid forms of cash-in-hand work conducted on a self-employed basis. However, this chapter has argued that such a view of cash-in-hand work as being always embedded in market-like work rela-tions akin to formal employment misrepresents not only the nature of cash-in-hand work but also the spatial heterogeneity of such work.

Reporting evidence from English localities, this chapter has revealed that although cash-in-hand work in affluent areas is more likely to be conducted under social relations akin to employment and motivated by economic gain, in deprived areas the majority is undertaken for and by close social relations for redistributive and social reasons. In conse-quence, there is a need to recognise the different meanings of cash-in-hand work in different geographical contexts. Indeed, these findings have significant implications for policy. Viewing cash-in-hand work as market-like and profit-motivated, the widespread response has been to seek to deter it through the introduction of more stringent regulations and punitive measures (e.g. European Commission, 1998; Grabiner, 2000; Hasseldine and Zhuhong, 1999; International Labour Office, 1996, 2002; OECD, 1994). Recognising that cash-in-hand is also con-ducted for and by friends, neighbours and kin so as to help each other out and develop social networks, however, it is evident that the current deterrence approach may be inappropriate *per se* as a policy response, especially in deprived neighbourhoods.

The key point is that because much cash-in-hand work is akin to unpaid community exchange in terms of its motives, especially in deprived neighbourhoods, a fuller exploration is required of the policy implications of this finding. Indeed, unless this occurs, deprived populations may well find themselves ever more deterred from engaging in community exchange with friends, kin and neighbours by a state intent on not only promoting forms of community engagement 'foreign' to their participatory cultures but also deterring the principal form of community engagement currently used in such areas.

Part III

Evaluating the Implications
of the Policy Options

7
Deterring Cash-in-hand Work

Introduction

This chapter evaluates critically the dominant policy approach towards cash-in-hand work that seeks to deter such activity using stringent regulations and punitive measures so as to achieve full-employment and/or comprehensive formal welfare provision. The argument here, however, is that not only is deterring cash-in-hand work through tougher regulations and punitive measures both ineffective and undesirable, but it is also highly unlikely that full-employment and/or comprehensive formal welfare provision will be there in the near future or even beyond to meet the material needs currently found in the cash-in-hand sphere.

To see this, the chapter commences by reviewing the arguments of the deterrence approach and following this, evaluates critically first, its vision of the future of work, second, its vision of the future of welfare and third and finally, the consequences of pursuing its approach towards eradicating cash-in-hand work. This will reveal that this approach is a direct product of viewing cash-in-hand work as having purely negative consequences and as such, it will be only through a fuller recognition of the positive features of such work, along with the impracticality of the full-employment/comprehensive welfare state scenario, that this approach will start to be transcended.

The deterrence approach towards cash-in-hand work

Like all other approaches towards cash-in-hand work, the objective of this policy option is to eradicate such work. The difference between this dominant approach and others, however, rotates largely around how it seeks to achieve this and what it envisages as being there to meet the material needs currently found in the cash-in-hand sphere. In this approach, grounded in its view that cash-in-hand work has purely negative consequences, the belief is that eradication can be achieved by using tougher regulations and more punitive measures so as to deter people from engaging in cash-in-hand work. First, therefore, it is necessary to outline how it views cash-in-hand work along with what it considers to be the major consequences arising from its existence and following this, the nature of the deterrence approach can be analysed.

On the issue of how cash-in-hand work is conceptualised in this approach, it is largely the case that a market-centred reading is adopted. Such work is seen as a form of employment conducted under market-like relations, often involving low pay and exploitative conditions, with unadulterated economic motives being the driving force of both employers and suppliers. Both cash-in-hand workers and employers are characterised as making a rational economic decision to engage in this work. As such, the way to eradicate this activity is to ensure that the expected cost of being caught and punished is greater than the economic benefit of participating in such activity. This can be achieved through the use of more stringent regulations and punitive measures so as to change the cost-benefit calculation of participants (e.g. Allingham and Sandmo, 1972; Falkinger, 1988; Hasseldine and Zhuhong, 1999; Milliron and Toy, 1988; Sandford, 1999).

This deterrence approach is widely believed to be the appropriate response and is adopted by most national governments (e.g. Hasseldine and Zhuhong, 1999), supra-national agencies (e.g. European Commission, 1998; OECD 1994; International Labour Office, 1996, 2002) and many academic commentators (e.g. Castells and Portes, 1989; Mingione, 1991; Sassen, 1989). For adherents to this approach, the notion that cash-in-hand work is perhaps not always conducted for unadulterated economic reasons is not entertained. Nor is the idea that cash-in-hand work might have positive as well as negative consequences. The inevitable outcome of this blinkered view is that the aim is simply to deter people from engaging in such activity. Adopting a range of more 'enabling' measures as either a complement or alternative to the raft of punitive measures that it seeks to implement, so as to harness some of its more positive aspects is not considered.

Through what lens, therefore, does this deterrence approach read cash-in-hand work? On the whole, the discourse of the deterrence literature is dominated by two particular negative consequences of cash-in-hand work. On the one hand, there is the fact that this activity is fraudulent behaviour on the part of informal employees and employers that prevents revenue being collected by the state that could be used for social cohesion purposes. On the other hand, there is the view that cash-in-hand work entails the exploitation of labour in a manner deemed totally unacceptable in a modern society. Here, therefore, each of these lens through which cash-in-hand work is read and which lead to the adoption of a deterrence approach, are considered in turn.

Before doing this, however, a brief comment is necessary. The arguments made in this book until now negate neither of these negative consequences of cash-in-hand work that dominates the deterrence literature. Both remain valid. The evidence so far presented, nevertheless, does show that this reading of cash-in-hand work considers only the negative consequences and also only one small segment of such work. The result is little or no reflection on whether deterrence is the most effective way to eradicate such work.

The 'cash-in-hand work as fraudulent' reading

The fact that cash-in-hand work is fraudulent activity dominates the deterrence literature and is the principal rationale underpinning the adoption of stringent regulations and punitive measures. This negative feature of cash-in-hand work is to the fore in the discourses of most national governments (e.g. Grabiner, 2000; Hasseldine and Zhuhong, 1999; MacDonald, 1994; Rowlingson *et al.*, 1997; Wenig, 1990) and supra-national organisations (e.g. European Commission, 1995a,b, 1998; International Labour Office, 1996, 2002; OECD, 1994). For these institutions, the fraudulent nature of cash-in-hand work is unacceptable because it has two major effects. First, it is seen to hinder the achievement of full-employment because it both represents unfair competition and acts as a substitute for formal employment. Second, it is viewed as undermining the advent of comprehensive and universal formal welfare provision by both depriving the state of tax and national insurance income as well as defrauding it when people claim benefits and work on a cash-in-hand basis at the same time. Indeed, it is not only national governments and supra-national agencies whose discourses bring this fraudulent aspect to the fore. Many academic commentators adopt a similar narrative. Exemplifying this is Bajada (2002, p. 6) whose principal rationale for seeking to stamp out cash-in-hand work in the Australian context is that 'an underground economy reduces tax revenue that could otherwise be used to fund community services'. In this reading, therefore, the dominant discourse is that cash-in-hand work is fraudulent activity that disrupts the smooth and efficient running of formal economic and welfare systems.

Indeed, in recent years, such a narrative has become stronger and more entrenched in the mind-sets of national and supranational institutions. Confronted by failure with regard to achieving full- or even fuller-employment along with empty public treasuries and increasing financial pressures with regard to the provision of social protection, many states and supranational bodies have reacted by raising tax rates and trying to reduce social protection expenditure so as to diminish public deficits. The perception is that confronted by such measures, people have increasingly turned to cash-in-hand work, thus thwarting the efforts of government to resolve their fiscal and social crises. As such, a view has arisen that cash-in-hand work is one of the principal reasons for governments being unable to achieve full-employment and/or comprehensive and universal formal welfare provision.

The outcome is that the 'problem' of cash-in-hand work has risen to the top of public policy agendas in many supranational institutions and national governments. At the 2002 International Labour Conference of the International Labour Office for example, the issue of cash-in-hand work received in-depth and prominent attention. The conclusion was that the emergence of this work in every corner of the globe was acting as one of the principal constraints hindering the creation of 'decent work' for all (International Labour Office, 2002). In a similar vein, the European Council in the spring of 2003 decided that the eradication of cash-in-hand work was to be one of its top ten priorities for action in the member states of the European Union. As Anna Diamantopoulou, Commissioner for Employment and Social Affairs, asserted in 2002 in a press release, reflecting the notion that there is a direct cause–effect relationship between the eradication of cash-in-hand work and the achievement of full-employment,

> Member states must increase efforts to quantify undeclared work, to cut it down and to transform it into regular employment. This is vital because of the direct link between combating undeclared work and hitting the Lisbon target of full employment by 2010 within a sound macroeconomic environment (European Commission, 2002, p. 1).

The outcome of this prioritisation of cash-in-hand work by the European Commission has been a whirlwind of activity by policy-makers not only in the European Commission itself but also in national governments in the member states as they struggle to come to terms with how the eradication of this fraudulent work might be achieved.

The result has been an ever more heated discussion of whether stricter enforcement of regulations surrounding labour, taxation and social security (Feige, 1979, 1990; Grabiner, 2000; Gutmann, 1978) needs to be coupled with other policies such as a reduction in marginal tax rates through base broadening so as to encourage compliance (Feige, 1979, 1990; Mingione and Magatti, 1995) or whether a more comprehensible and simplified tax and social security system is needed so that people realise when they are defrauding the state (e.g. Rowlingson *et al.*, 1997). Whatever the measures being discussed, however, the overall thrust is nearly always the same, namely the eradication of cash-in-hand work through deterrence and the replacement of such work with formal sector jobs.

To achieve this, some voice the opinion that both tax and social security fraud should receive the same emphasis since they are equal evils (International Labour Office, 1996; European Commission, 1996a,b; OECD, 1994). Such a view, however, is in the minority since the vast majority of nation-states and commentators put greater emphasis on dealing with benefit fraud, despite tax fraud being more of a problem in terms of the sheer amount of money being lost (Evason and Woods, 1995; Thomas, 2000; Tickamyer and Wood, 1998). In the United States in 1986, for example, only $235 million was fraudulently claimed through unemployment benefit compared with $70 billion not being reported to the tax authorities (Roth *et al.*, 1992). In the United Kingdom, meanwhile, in the tax year ending April 1995, despite £6 billion being recovered in unpaid taxes compared with just £64.56 million recovered from unemployment benefit fraud (1.1 per cent of the total recovered in unpaid taxes), there were 4247 prosecutions for benefit fraud compared with just 357 prosecutions for unpaid taxes (Cooke, 1997; Rowlingson *et al.*, 1997). This emphasis on social security fraud has continued in the United Kingdom in what can be seen as the post-Grabiner era since 2000 when Lord Grabiner prepared a report for HM Treasury on how to deal with cash-in-hand work (Grabiner, 2000). On the whole, therefore, and not just in the United Kingdom, efforts to deter cash-in-hand work have focused largely on what is in effect a relatively small segment of all cash-in-hand work, namely that undertaken by those claiming social security benefits (Home Office, 2003a).

To explain this emphasis, MacDonald (1994, p. 508–9) has argued that one needs to explore the prevailing ideology of work: 'Such ideology holds that the experience of unemployment must remain unpleasant (to deter voluntary unemployment and to energise the search for work) and be seen to be unpleasant (to reassure those in jobs that unemployment must be avoided)', as is epitomised by the workfare system operated in the United States, the United Kingdom and many other nation-states (see Lodemel and Trickey, 2001; OECD, 2000; Peck, 1996b; 1999, 2001). The result is a narrative that constructs social security fraud as more 'criminal' than tax fraud, and even sometimes represents tax avoidance as a semi-legitimate activity whereby tax payers merely try to retain 'their' money, unlike benefit fraudsters who are taking 'other people's' money (see Cook, 1989, 1997).

Whatever measures are adopted to deter this work, and whether or not emphasis is given to benefit or tax fraud, the key issue is that cash-in-hand work is primarily viewed as fraudulent activity that deprives the state of revenue and undermines attempts to achieve both full- or fuller-employment and/or comprehensive and universal formal welfare provision.

The arguments so far detailed in this book have no qualms concerning this view of cash-in-hand work as fraudulent activity. There is no doubt whatsoever that cash-in-hand work is essentially fraudulent activity and it does need to be eradicated. The only issue, given the evidence presented, is whether this negative consequence should be always to the fore in discourses on cash-in-hand work or whether it is also necessary to bring to attention some of the more positive features of this activity. If this were done, then perhaps seeking its deterrence through tougher regulations and punitive measures could start to be complemented by more enabling measures to harness some of the positive aspects of such work. One of the principal reasons why these positive consequences are seldom considered, as will now be seen, is perhaps because of how deterrence advocates narrowly conceptualise the nature of such work.

The 'cash-in-hand work as exploitative' reading

Throughout the deterrence literature, a narrative of cash-in-hand work prevails that reads it as an exploitative form of work situated at the very bottom of a hierarchy of types of employment and a form of work that weakens formal workers' bargaining position (Castells and Portes, 1989; Gallin, 2001; Pfau-Effinger, 2003; Portes, 1994). Read in this manner, cash-in-hand work is criticised alongside all other forms of exploitative work which unscrupulous employers oblige a vulnerable and unprotected workforce to undertake. Indeed, this narrative of cash-in-hand work as a form of exploitative form of employment has been a persistent feature throughout its history.

Take, for example, the evolution of thought on cash-in-hand work in the International Labour Office. More than three decades ago, when the

International Labour Office first used the term 'informal sector', it was ascribed to the activities of the working poor who were working very hard but who were not recognised, recorded, protected or regulated by the public authorities (Hart, 1973; International Labour Office, 1972). From the outset, therefore, the discourse was that such work is the preserve of the poor who are unregulated and unprotected by state regulations. Such a negative view of cash-in-hand work has not changed over time. In 1991 at the 78th Session of the International Labour Conference, the issue was discussed whether this work should be supported as a provider of employment and income. The overwhelming conclusion was that

> there can be no question of the ILO helping to 'promote' or 'develop' an informal sector as a convenient, low-cost way of creating employment unless there is at the same time an equal determination to eliminate progressively the worst aspects of exploitation and inhuman working conditions in the sector (International Labour Office, 1991, p. 58).

By 2002, this reading of cash-in-hand work as characterised by exploitative working conditions had still not weakened. Indeed, it had become stronger. As the International Labour Office (2002, p. 5) asserts, the goal is to

> in the longer term, create enough employment opportunities that are formal, protected and decent for all workers and employers. Already in 1991, the ILO had made it clear that the informal economy should not be developed or promoted as a low-cost way of creating employment. In the twenty-first century, decent work is certainly much more than a job at any price or under any circumstances. Therefore, new job creation should not be in the informal economy. The emphasis has to be on quality jobs.

The central issue, therefore, was now one of 'how to move workers and entrepreneurs currently in the informal economy upwards along the continuum [*sic*] into formal decent jobs and how to ensure that new jobs are created in the formal and not in the informal economy' (International Labour Office, 2002, p. 8).

To more fully comprehend this reading of cash-in-hand work as exploitative activity, it is necessary to understand how such work is being situated in modern economies. Whereas in the past, and as discussed in Chapter 2, cash-in-hand work was sometimes seen as a left-over from the past that would gradually disappear with modernisation, the majority of commentators who view it as a form of exploitative labour do not now see it in such peripheral terms. For them, what is important about cash-in-hand work in the contemporary period is that it is an inherent part of contemporary capitalism and a direct result of the process of globalisation that under neoliberalism is encouraging a race-to-the-bottom (Amin, 1996; Castells and Portes, 1989; Frank, 1996; Gallin, 2001; Ybarra, 1989). In other words, such work is viewed as a 'revenge of the market' against state regulation and working class power in a period of heightened international competition. A strong correlation is thus drawn between the advent of cash-in-hand work under neoliberal globalisation and the impoverishment of workers since firms are believed to turn informal so as to avoid the costs associated with protective labour legislation. Cash-in-hand work, in consequence, is part of the current process of reversing unionisation that is resulting in the disenfranchisement of a large section of the working class (often with the acquiescence of the state) in the name of economic growth and remaining competitive in an era of globalisation (Castells and Portes, 1989; Gallin, 2001; Roberts, 1991). Since cash-in-hand work is an instrument wielded by different participants in the class struggle and the outcome is to alter class structure and privilege, cash-in-hand labourers are seen to share characteristics subsumed under the heading of 'downgraded labour': they receive few benefits, receive low wages and have poor working conditions.

Based on this reading of cash-in-hand work as exploitative work, the only option seen to be available is to bring it within the bounds of the law so that it complies with labour protection rules in order to elim-inate the exploitative labour market conditions inherent in such work. As Portes (1994, p. 433) puts it,

> the way to promote sustained economic development and to avoid the chaos of the uncontrolled market is to implement detailed regu-lations and have them enforced by a competent bureaucracy immune to profit-taking. This course would lead to the absolute hegemony of the formal sector and hence the reduction of illegal and informal activities to a minimum.

However, and as many of these analysts recognise, there is a paradox confronting those wishing to pursue this mode of public action. Extensive regulation, despite being needed, is problematic because it encourages more cash-in-hand work rather than less. As Portes (1994, p. 433) continues, 'state efforts to obliterate it [cash-in-hand work] through the expansion of rules and controls can exacerbate the very conditions that give rise to these activities'. Put another way, 'order creates disorder. The formal economy creates its own informality' (Lomnitz, 1988, p. 54). Consequently, 'while ... the proper realm of long term planning and accumulation is the formal sector, efforts to extend its scope to the entire economy often end up producing the opposite result, namely the expansion of cash-in-hand work' (Portes, 1994, p. 433). How, therefore, is this apparent paradox to be overcome?

For adherents to this perspective, such a problem is no reason for rejecting a deterrence approach based on stricter regulation and more punitive measures. As Portes (1994, p. 433) stresses, 'state regulation creates opportunities for informal activities, but does not give rise *ipso facto* to them'. Instead, for these analysts, it is only when extensive regulation is pursued without providing either sufficient formal employment and/or comprehensive formal welfare provision for these displaced cash-in-hand workers that such work continues to expand. As Lomnitz (1988, p. 54) argues,

> the degree of formality and the inability of the formal system to satisfy societal needs give rise to informal solutions. If the formal system is able to produce and distribute the goods and services required by all members of society, informal solutions would be less needed and thus less pervasive.

For these commentators, in consequence, a policy of tougher regulations and punitive measures with regard to cash-in-hand work will be effective only if it is coupled with complementary policies to create full- or fuller-employment and/or comprehensive formal welfare provision. Without the latter, cash-in-hand work will continue to be not only a stubborn thorn in the side of governments but will grow rather than decline.

In sum, whether a more punitive approach towards cash-in-hand work is desired primarily due to its fraudulent nature or chiefly because of the exploitative work conditions that apparently dominate this sphere, the same common solution is advocated. The goal is to couple stringent regulations and a punitive approach towards such work with the pursuit of full-employment and/or a formal welfare 'safety net' to cushion the circumstances of those 'freed' from this cash-in-hand sphere. To conclude this section, therefore, a case study is here taken of how cash-in-hand work is being treated in policy terms in one nation that has vigorously pursued this deterrence approach, namely the United Kingdom.

The deterrence approach in practice: the case of the United Kingdom

Based on this narrative of cash-in-hand work as fraudulent and exploitative work that needs to be deterred, the UK government has recently made a concerted effort to strengthen both the rate of detection and the punitive measures used for those caught working on a cash-in-hand basis.

To see how this has been implemented, it is first of all necessary to understand that not everybody working on a cash-in-hand basis in the United Kingdom is engaged in fraudulent activity. On the one hand, if they are not claiming any form of benefit and income from paid work is less than the personal tax allowance (£4610 in 2003–04), this work is not fraudulent. However, it is fraudulent if these 'ghosts' in Inland Revenue parlance earn over their personal tax allowance and do not declare their tax liability. On the other hand, if somebody is receiving benefits at the same time as engaging in paid work, this is only fraudulent if their weekly income is over the 'earnings disregard' levels set by the Department of Social Security (DSS) and/or they do not declare these earnings. If the earnings of the registered unemployed from paid work are below these disregard levels and it is declared, this is not unlawful. To understand the UK deterrence approach, therefore, each of these groups – 'ghosts' and those 'working while claiming' – must be considered separately.

Fraud by 'ghosts' and the UK policy response

Starting with 'ghosts' (i.e. those not claiming benefits but earning undeclared income over their personal tax allowance), under section 7 of the Taxes Management Act 1970, they are meant to notify the Inland Revenue of this activity if there is a tax liability so that a self-assessment form can be sent. Once requested, this self-assessment tax return must be returned within six months of the end of the relevant tax year. This means that somebody earning money in mid-April does not have to notify the Revenue until 5 October in the following year (i.e. after 18 months). There is also an additional requirement if turnover exceeds £51 000, to register with Customs and Excise for VAT, although this latter requirement seldom applies given the small sums of money generally involved in cash-in-hand work.

If they fail to comply with section 7 of the 1970 Act and the Inland Revenue identifies that work has been conducted, then the situation has been that wherever possible, the Revenue makes settlements or uses civil proceedings against offenders. It only rarely initiates criminal prosecution. This is simply because the Inland Revenue has the power to recover the tax owed, together with interest under section 86 of the 1970 Taxes Management Act. Under section 93, moreover, it also has the power to impose a civil penalty up to the value of the evaded tax but has discretion to mitigate or remit any penalty applied or, in cases where penalty proceedings would be appropriate, to make a 'contract settlement' with the tax payer. This settlement is an agreement not to take formal proceedings in exchange for an appropriate payment, to reflect the lost tax, interest and abated penalties.

If a 'ghost' comes forward, makes a spontaneous and full disclosure of past profits and co-operates with further enquiries, they have in practice found that the Revenue is prepared to reduce the maximum penalty (100 per cent of the tax evaded) to 10 per cent or even less (Grabiner, 2000). This is because the Inland Revenue has a general responsibility for 'care and management' of taxes which enables it in appropriate circumstances to waive tax which is in law due and payable. Furthermore, where a person has been unable to realistically fund all or part of a settlement, the practice has been to treat the tax in question as irrecoverable. Although the Revenue has been entitled to take proceedings under the criminal law, under section 17 on false accounting of the Theft Act 1968 or for the common law offence of 'cheat', this rarely happens. The relative inefficiency of criminal investigation and prosecution as a method of recovering sums owed means that there are just 50–100 prosecutions per annum and only in the most serious cases (usually involving businesses evading sums far in excess of the tax evaded by the unemployed engaged in cash-in-hand work).

Fraud by those 'working whilst claiming' and the UK policy response

Such an approach to recovering money owed and criminal prosecution stands in stark contrast to how the registered unemployed are dealt with by the DSS. 'Working whilst claiming' is fraudulent because entitlement to some social security benefits depends on the means of the claimant. Claimants have a responsibility to declare any earnings from part-time work. If they work for 16 hours or more per week, they are generally not entitled to benefit. If they declare earnings, their benefit is reduced pound for pound above the 'earnings disregard' thresholds of £5 for any weekly part-time earnings for single people, £10 for a couple or £15 a week for certain other groups such as lone parents and disabled people. These levels have been largely unchanged since their introduction in 1988.

When they first claim, benefit recipients are required to make a signed declaration that they have given accurate information about their circumstances under regulation 4 of the Social Security (Claims and Payments) Regulations 1987 (S.I. 1987/1968). Those receiving Jobseeker's Allowance must re-declare every fortnight, when they 'sign on' at a Jobcentre that they are available for and actively seeking work. Other benefits have no fixed requirement, but claimants paid by order book or girocheque have to sign, whenever they cash an order, confirming that they remain entitled to benefit, while some of those paid direct to their bank accounts sign a declaration from time to time. Estimating the level of 'working whilst claiming', the DSS asserts that it constitutes some 40 per cent of all benefit fraud and effects the means-tested benefits of Income Support, Jobseekers Allowance as well as Housing Benefit. Indeed, the DSS has calculated that at any one time, 120 000 people are fraudulently working and claiming. Table 7.1 indicates the nature and level of the resulting fraud.

Unlike the low prosecution rates that have occurred until now amongst 'ghosts', the DSS policy towards those caught 'working whilst

Table 7.1   Benefit overpayments due to fraudulent failure to declare earnings (£million)

Claimant failed to declare	Income Support	Jobseeker's Allowance[a]	Housing Benefit[b]	Total
Full-time earnings	125	178	n/a	
Part-time earnings	16	5	n/a	
Partner's earnings	10	11	n/a	
Total	151	194	120	465

Notes

[a] This only covers the means-tested part of Jobseeker's Allowance, not the part that is based on NICs.

[b] The figure for Housing Benefit is based on different methodology. And a full breakdown is not available.

Source: DSS Area Benefit Reviews April 1998/99; National Housing Benefit Accuracy Review, 1997/98 (cited in Grabiner, 2000: table 1).

claiming' is to recover all benefit overpaid as a result of fraud and to initiate criminal proceedings. This is done through the civil courts under the Social Security Administration Act 1992, section 112 on false representations for obtaining benefit, or under section 111A covering the dishonest obtaining of benefit. Despite the Social Security Administration (Fraud) Act 1997 introducing an alternative to prosecution by allowing offenders to be given a caution or an administrative penalty of 30 per cent of the overpayment, this has seldom been applied. Indeed, in 1998/99, the DSS prosecuted some 6000 people for failing to declare earnings. Some such as Cook (1989, 1997) have compared these figures to the 50–100 cases prosecuted by the Inland Revenue in order to highlight the inequities in the system. Such comparisons, nevertheless, ignore that the Inland Revenue is entitled to recover money owed whilst the DSS is not. Indeed, it was in part due to these differential powers of the Revenue compared with the DSS, that in 2000, it was decided to commission Lord Grabiner to review the regulations concerning fraudulent cash-in-hand work.

Post-Grabiner modifications to UK deterrence policy

In response to a government concern that the likelihood of detection, prosecution rates and deterrents were woefully inadequate, the Chancellor of the Exchequer in late 1999 asked Lord Grabiner to conduct an investigation into the 'informal economy' and to produce a report in time for the March 2000 Budget. His terms of reference tellingly were to investigate the problem, examine ways to move economic activity from illegitimate to legitimate businesses and to recommend an action plan. In his report, Grabiner (2000) recommended the following policy changes:

- To provide incentives to join the legitimate economy, a confidential phone line should be launched to enable advice to be given on how people can put their affairs in order;
- To prevent identity fraud, procedures should be tightened for issuing National Insurance numbers and better controls introduced on the issue and use of birth certificates, to prevent their use as proof of identity by third parties;
- To improve the rate of detection and the effectiveness of punishment, it recommended that the Government should: consider ways to use information from private sector sources as a cross-check on the details people provide to Departments; give investigators the power to make routine 'reverse searches' of the telephone directory to find

names and addresses of people who advertise businesses giving only a telephone number; build on the inter-Departmental work already begun by setting up a specific government function to detect and investigate informal businesses, and agree to common guidelines for staff about what data sharing is legally permissible and how it should be carried out in practice. In particular, it advocated a central point of contact to co-ordinate the exercise and monitor its effectiveness;

- To increase punishment through:
  - requiring people suspected of working while claiming that they are unemployed to attend the Jobcentre more frequently, and at unpredictable times, as a condition of receiving their benefit;
  - make more use of a warning procedure such as to employers reasonably suspected of colluding with fraudulent benefit claims, that if they do not clean up their act, they will expose themselves to more detailed investigation and possible prosecution;
  - if other measures fail to work, consider the option of punishing persistent fraudsters by removing, or heavily reducing, their right to benefit for a specific period; and
  - carry out research into the sentences imposed for benefit fraud and particularly into variation in the sentencing of persistent offenders.
- To resolve the inequities in prosecution rates between 'ghosts' and those 'working whilst claiming', meanwhile, it advocated the introduction of a new statutory offence of fraudulently evading income tax to be tried in the magistrate's court;
- To use publicity as a deterrent, whereby the incentives available to people to take formal jobs and the costs of being informal should be advertised, and also use advertising as a tool for changing attitudes regarding the social acceptability of cash-in-hand work.

As can be seen, the overarching thrust was both to increase the probability of detection and to increase the punishments for those caught so as to deter people from engaging in such work. For Grabiner (2000, p. 19), therefore,

as long as people can profit by not declaring their work, it will be impossible entirely to eradicate the hidden economy. Therefore, the most effective way of tackling the problem is significantly to improve the likelihood of detecting and penalising offenders. What is needed is a strong environment of deterrence.

In the March 2000 Budget Statement by the Chancellor of the Exchequer, it was announced that this report by Lord Grabiner QC would be implemented in full. Starting in May 2000, a confidential phone line was launched to advise people on how to legitimise their activity followed from January 2001 onwards by the tougher rules and penalties outlined above applied to those who failed to respond (e.g. HM Customs and Excise, 2003; Home Office, 2003a,b; Small Business Service, 2003).

As such, both the narrative of cash-in-hand work adopted by the UK government as well as its resulting policy approach is firmly grounded in this deterrence discourse that views cash-in-hand work in mainly negative terms as fraudulent activity grounded in exploitative work conditions. Here, therefore, the aim is to eradicate such work through a deterrence approach and in doing so, to facilitate the shift towards a full- or fuller-employment society by transferring such activity from the cash-in-hand sphere to the formal realm. Given the dominance of this discourse not just in the United Kingdom but elsewhere too, the rest of this chapter thus evaluates critically the practicality and desirability of this perspective in terms of its vision of both the future of work and welfare as well as its policy prescription for cash-in-hand work.

A critical evaluation of the deterrence approach

Given that this discourse on cash-in-hand work focuses upon its fraudulent and exploitative nature and seeks to deter it using stringent regulations and punitive measures so as to achieve full-employment and/or comprehensive formal welfare provision, the various component parts are here evaluated critically. First, the possibility of creating full-employment is analysed, second, the feasibility of creating universal and comprehensive formal welfare provision should full-employment not be achievable is examined, and third and finally, the practicality and desirability of seeking solely to deter cash-in-hand work without putting in place substitutes beyond full-employment and/or comprehensive welfare provision is evaluated.

Evaluating critically its vision of the future of work

At the heart of this approach is an employment-centred vision of the future of work in which 'progress' is seen to lie in a return to full-employment. Deterring cash-in-hand work is viewed as a necessary step that needs to be taken in order to move closer to this vision. Here, however, consideration is given to whether this vision of the future is achievable and as such, whether deterring cash-in-hand work without putting in place substitutes is a sensible action.

To do this, the first issue that needs to be considered is whether the advanced economies are moving towards the goal of full-employment. Examining their trajectories of economic development, there is in fact little to suggest that this is happening. Instead, quite the opposite is the case. As the International Labour Office (2002) reported, in recent years, the global economy has been creating about 40 million jobs a year, whereas there are 48 million new jobseekers annually. The result is a widening global 'jobs deficit'. It thus appears that the world economy is moving ever further away from, rather than towards, a full-employment scenario.

The problem is perhaps that this approach looks back to the future, rather than forwards (cf. Beck, 2000). Its vision is one embedded in a lust for a return to a previous supposedly 'golden age', which is the era of full-employment that existed for some thirty years or so following the Second World War in a few advanced economies. Returning to such an era, however, is both undesirable and impractical. It is undesirable because this golden age was an era of full-employment for men alone, not women. It is impractical because there has never been an era of full-employment for both men and women, and all of the evidence is that both the advanced economies and nations beyond are moving ever further away from, rather than towards, such a situation.

Take, for example, the size of the 'jobs deficit' in the member states of the European Union. In 1999, just 147 million of the 375 million inhabitants of the EU were in employment (40 per cent of the total population). Some 60 per cent of the population were thus being supported by the remaining 40 per cent and there is widespread agreement that this is due to worsen as the 'baby-boom' generation reach retirement age. Amongst the population of working-age, meanwhile, the employment participation rate in the EU was just 61 per cent (European Commission 2000b). Nearly two in five (39 per cent) of the working-age population in the EU were thus without a job. For full participation to be achieved in the EU, two jobs are thus needed for every three that currently exist. Put another way, a 66 per cent increase in the number of jobs is required. Some EU nations, nevertheless, have a smaller bridge to cross to reach this supposed nirvana than others. In Denmark, the country with the highest employment participation rate in the EU (75.3 per cent), due in no small part to a very high participation rate of women in employment, a mere 33 per cent rise in the number of jobs would suffice. In Spain, the country with the lowest employment participation rate (49.7 per cent), however, the number of jobs would need to double

(European Commission, 2000b). Indeed, if the European Union is to achieve its 'full-employment' target of getting 70 per cent of the working-age population into formal jobs by 2010, more than 15 million new jobs will need to be created in the EU-15 (European Commission, 2003). It might be asserted that presenting employment statistics in this manner is a distortion. For example, it could be suggested that it is far better to investigate the trends over time so that the progress being made towards full-employment can be seen, rather than just provide a snapshot of a particular moment. Here, therefore, this issue is analysed.

Is it the case that despite the size of the current jobs deficit, the long-term trend is nevertheless towards fuller-employment? Examining Table 7.2, little evidence is found that the jobs deficit has narrowed during the last forty years of the twentieth century. Indeed, just three nations appear to have made any progress at all. Denmark managed to raise employment participation rates from 74 to 76 per cent, the Netherlands increased them from 64 to 71 per cent, and Portugal, which starting from the low base level of 58 per cent participation, managed to raise it to 67 per cent. These, however, are the exceptions. The jobs deficit in the majority of nations widened over this forty year time period, often in a quite drastic manner. Employment participation rates

Table 7.2 Labour force participation rates, 1960, 1973 and 1999

Country	Total participation rate			Growth (+) or decline (−) 1960–1999
	1960	1973	1999	
Finland	77	71	67	−
Sweden	75	75	71	−
Denmark	74	75	76	+
UK	72	73	71	−
Austria	71	69	68	−
France	70	68	60	−
Germany	70	69	65	−
Ireland	68	64	63	−
Greece	66	57	55	−
Italy	65	58	53	−
Netherlands	64	61	71	+
Spain	61	60	52	−
Belgium	60	61	59	−
Portugal	58	64	67	+

Sources: ILO (1997: table 2.2) and European Commission (2000a: annexure 1).

in Finland slid from 77 per cent in 1960 to 67 per cent in 1999. In France they fell from 70 per cent to 60 per cent, in Greece from 66 per cent to 55 per cent and in Italy from 65 per cent to 53 per cent. The notion that there is a long-term trend towards full- or fuller-employment, therefore, must be treated with the utmost caution. It is not borne out by the evidence. Is it different anywhere else in the advanced economies? To answer this, let us start with the United States. After all, this is the major competing trading bloc that provides the 'baseline' against which the EU measures its progress on employment participation rates (see European Commission, 2000a). In the United States, there is little doubt that the employment participation rate is higher than in the EU. However, even here it is only 73 per cent, meaning that one job needs to be created for every three that currently exist if full participation is to be achieved (European Commission, 2000b). Put another way, this requires a 37 per cent increase in the number of jobs in the US economy. In Japan, similarly, the employment participation rate is 70 per cent, necessitating a 42.8 per cent growth in the number of jobs to achieve full participation (European Commission, 2000b).

Nor is the trend narrowing over time. Between 1960 and 1995, just 13 of the 22 advanced economies improved their employment participation rates. The outcome was that by 1995, only 9 of the 22 advanced economies had managed to achieve participation rates in employment of over 75 per cent of the working age population and none over 83 per cent (International Labour Office, 1996). Advanced economies, therefore, are far from being in a steady state of full-employment and many are moving ever further away from such a situation.

Given this shift away from full-employment, the only conclusion that can be reached is that it is unrealistic to expect its achievement in the near future or beyond. If the advanced economies are not shifting towards a steady-state of full-employment, then the next question is whether the formal welfare 'safety net' is increasingly being put in place to protect those households and workers that are being encouraged to give up their cash-in-hand work.

Evaluating critically its vision of the future of welfare

Given the evidence that the advanced economies are not moving towards an era of full- or even fuller-employment, is a welfare 'safety net' nevertheless being put in place to protect those excluded from the formal sphere and deterred from working on a cash-in-hand basis? To evaluate this, the social democratic EU rather than neoliberal welfare regimes are here considered. The rationale for this geographical area being examined is that if universal and comprehensive formal welfare provision is in demise even in those nations which proclaim a wish to protect it, then there is little prospect of its protection and/or extension elsewhere.

Examining the EU in terms of its direction of change so far as welfare provision is concerned leaves one with little cause for optimism. The overarching objectives of the 1986 Single European Act, and the Single European Market (SEM) in particular, was to revitalise tired European economies, make industry more productive and promote faster European growth. By opening up vastly differing economies more fully to one another, a concern was raised that there might be a levelling down of social protection. A social dimension to the Single European Act was thus introduced in the form of the Social Charter. At the outset of discussions of a Social Charter in the EU, however, the perfunctory debate about citizens' rights was quickly transformed into a discussion of workers' rights (Culpitt, 1992; Meehan, 1993), reinforcing a trend that already existed in many Member States towards a 'bifurcated welfare model' (Abrahamson, 1992). This offers some basic protection for workers but little if any to the more marginalised populations in that a dual welfare system is fostered whereby company-based or employment-related welfare schemes take care of those in employment but neglect or exclude marginal and less privileged groups. Thus, and as Bennington *et al.* (1992) suggest, many were concerned that a corporatist model of welfare would evolve in the EU in which social rights would be attached primarily to formal employment rather than to citizenship.

In the early years of the EU, little has occurred to dissipate these fears. The Social Charter has continued to focus upon workers' rights and thus exacerbated inequalities between those with and without employment. Even its attempts to introduce workers' rights, however, have met with only limited success. Pressures not only within but also external to the EU have limited progress on this matter. For instance, competition on wage costs from countries outside the EU such as those in south east Asia and central and eastern Europe, has put great pressure on the EU nations to keep down their social costs. Indeed, the evidence suggests that such constraints have resulted in cutbacks in formal welfare provision. Between 1993 and 1998, expenditure on social protection as a percentage of GDP decreased (European Commission, 2000b). This was most pronounced in those countries where spending had been amongst the highest in 1993 such as Sweden (-5.3 percentage points), Finland (-7.4 points) and the Netherlands (-5.0 points). As feared at the advent of the EU, therefore, there has been a levelling down of social protection. Those

Table 7.3 Expenditure on social protection as a percentage of GDP in European Union Nations, 1993 and 1998

	1993	1998	% change
EU-15	28.9	27.7	−1.2
Sweden	38.6	33.3	−5.3
Finland	34.6	27.2	−7.4
Netherlands	33.5	28.5	−5.0
Denmark	31.9	30.0	−1.9
France	30.9	30.5	−0.4
Belgium	29.5	27.5	−2.0
United Kingdom	29.1	26.8	−2.3
Austria	28.9	28.4	−0.5
Germany	28.4	29.3	+0.9
Italy	26.2	25.2	−1.0
Spain	24.7	21.6	−3.1
Luxembourg	24.5	24.1	−0.4
Greece	22.3	24.5	+2.2
Portugal	21.3	23.4	+2.1
Ireland	20.5	16.1	−4.4

Source Eurostat – European System of Integrated Social Protection Statistics (ESSPROS). Cited in European Commission (2000b: 91).

nations whose level of social protection has decreased most sharply are those who had the highest level of social protection in the first place (see Table 7.3). Meanwhile, and with the exceptions of Ireland and Spain, those with the lowest levels of social protection in 1993 have converged towards the norm. The result is that although there is a convergence of social protection between member states, this is happening within the context of an overall levelling down process. The fear today, of course, is that the accession states now joining the EU will cause a further levelling-down of overall social protection measures. Whether this is borne out only the future will tell.

The fact that a levelling-down process has occurred so far, nevertheless, should come as no surprise. Even Keynes and Beveridge, the founders of the welfare state, recognised that the bases of social welfare lie in the formal labour market. For them, full-employment, not welfare states, was the key to well-being. Full-employment meant low demand for social transfers and a large tax base to finance social programmes for the aged, sick and the minority of persons without jobs. Comprehensive formal welfare states were possible only so long as most people found their 'welfare' in the market most of the time (Myles, 1996). The persistently wide 'jobs deficit', not to mention an ageing population, in the advanced economies thus has profound implications for the future of comprehensive formal welfare provision.

If the goal of a full-employment and/or comprehensive formal welfare provision seems beyond reach, the question that arises is whether it is appropriate to deter cash-in-hand work without putting in place substitutes. In this discourse where a blind faith is put in a return to full-employment and comprehensive welfare provision, little consideration is given to the notion that this might not be achievable and that people need to be given alternative modes of work and welfare.

Evaluating critically its approach towards cash-in-hand work

Besides this issue of where those currently engaged in cash-in-hand work are to find their livelihood if this work is deterred and alternative coping practices are not put in place, a further critical issue that needs to be considered is whether it is in fact practical and/or desirable to deter people from engaging in such work. In other words, there are features of cash-in-hand work, independent of the 'work/welfare' vision in which this approach is embedded, that mean that it might be first, impractical to eradicate cash-in-hand work without putting in place substitutes and second, undesirable due to its implications for building social capital. Each issue is here considered in turn.

Is it practical to try to deter cash-in-hand work?

A major problem with this deterrence approach is whether it could ever implement sufficiently stringent regulations and punitive measures to eliminate cash-in-hand work. On the one hand, this is because of 'resistance cultures' to such a policy approach in parts of the advanced economies. For example, many local and regional state authorities do not wish to abolish cash-in-hand work and it will be difficult to persuade them to do otherwise in the context of an increasingly competitive international economic system. On the other hand, even for those authorities that do wish to deter such work, there are some inherent problems involved in attempting to do so. First, there are 'practical barriers' in achieving such an end since this is a form of work that is so deeply entrenched in everyday social life and economic production. Second, one has to take into account the 'unintended impacts' of tougher rules and regulations that may not be those intended.

The first barrier, therefore, is that of 'resistance cultures'. It will be difficult to persuade many local, regional and even state authorities to deter cash-in-hand work since it is currently used as a strategy for promoting economic competitiveness. This is especially the case in southern EU nations. During the 1970s and 1980s, for example, manufacturing industry in many southern EU nations turned towards organised cash-in-hand work as a competitive strategy in order to free businesses from restrictive labour laws and corporatist work practices (Benton, 1990; Cappechi, 1989; Mingione, 1991). Moreover, state authorities in numerous localities, regions and nations became heavily implicated in these cash-in-hand work practices (Cappechi, 1989; Van Geuns *et al.*, 1987; Husband and Jerrard, 2001; Portes and Sassen-Koob, 1987; Warren, 1994). Indeed, this has sometimes been an active economic development strategy. As Vinay (1987) reports, in Italy both the Communist Party in the regional government of the central regions and the Christian Democrats in the north east have collaborated in the cash-in-hand practices of small and medium sized enterprises in their regions through their influence on industrial relations. Such situations have also been reported in Spain (Benton, 1990; Lobo, 1990a; Recio, 1988).

More usually, however, it has simply been a case of lax enforcement rather than active promotion that has been the strategy adopted by state authorities relying on such work. In Greece, for example, Mingione (1990) reports how industrial home-working legislation is not enforced. In 1957, a bill was approved for the Greek clothing industry, compelling employers to pay social insurance contributions for home-workers. This was never implemented. According to another bill, approved in 1986, all home-workers must be considered as waged workers. This also was not enforced due to employer opposition as well as opposition from the self-employed. Lobo (1990a,b) reveals a parallel lax attitude in Spain and Portugal. In Portugal, for example, Lobo (1990b) argues that interviews with unionists and public administrators reveal that the dominant government attitude is one of 'tolerance'. This is for three reasons: first, because it is seen to help the Portuguese economy compete in a world market where regular conditions would make them uncompetitive; second, because the welfare state is weak and this sector gives many households a level of income not possible if they relied on solely formal employment; and third and finally because inspection of employment-places is inefficient and they cannot control such work.

How to overcome such active rejection and/or lax enforcement of employment regulations is a difficult proposition. Most northern EU nations desire stronger regulation, especially since the opening of borders following the SEM means that such work is now directly in competition with that of their own businesses. Ultimately, this is a delicate matter of national sovereignty because in the majority of cases, what is being discussed is enforcement of national legislation and the protagonists in the 'fraud' all want to or must continue with it for their survival. The EU, moreover, cannot police laws when no cases come before the European Court and if it introduces tougher penalties or tries to toughen up on the policing of cash-in-hand work in order to reduce unfair competition, it may find that there is not the 'political will' in the southern EU nations to comply with and implement such policies. The issue, therefore, is essentially one of whether the political will, especially in these southern EU nations, exists to deter cash-in-hand work.

It is not simply the lack of 'political will' in the form of these resistance cultures, however, which remains an obstacle. As discussed throughout this book, there are also other practical barriers that must be taken into account. It has been continuously stressed that cash-in-hand work in the form of the moral economy of favours is deeply embedded in everyday social life. Quite how tougher rules and regulations could put a stop to such 'social' activity is not immediately apparent since in its most autonomous manifestation, cash-in-hand work is merely a monetary form of community exchange which could equally well be undertaken within a relationship of barter or gift.

This practical barrier to its eradication through deterrence is displayed in studies that show how attempts by the state to regulate cash-in-hand work are unacceptable to the populace. In Quebec, for example, Fortin *et al.* (1996) find that 14.7 per cent of the population believe that cash-in-hand work is morally acceptable and 42.7 per cent perceive it as neither moral nor immoral, whilst just 31.0 per cent see it as immoral. With less than a third of the population being opposed to such a form of work, it is thus questionable whether attempts to deter it could ever be successful. This is similarly found to be the case in the United Kingdom. A study by Travers (2002) in the London borough of Newham finds that 64 per cent of respondents would not report someone who works for cash while claiming benefit and how it is widely recognised amongst the population that those working on a cash-in-hand basis are motivated to engage in such work by moral values rather than greed.

In major part, this means that tougher rules and regulations will be problematic to introduce in practice. Much of the theoretical work, for example, displays that there is a trade-off in policy-making between the probability of detection and the penalty imposed. Given the high cost of increasing the probability of detection, the tendency is to increase the cost of the penalty. However, such policies may not be politically viable given public attitudes. Punishments cannot be set in isolation from other crimes and there is likely to be strong public reaction if the penalty for working on a cash-in-hand basis, especially in the moral economy of favours, is thought to be unfair in relation to broader criminal acts. Consequently, there may be limits to the range and degree of the penalties that can be implemented.

The only option, therefore, may be to increase the rate of detection but this involves high administration costs that again may be politically unacceptable both to governments and the populations. Even if money is forthcoming, however, significant problems may be still encountered. Take, for example, Northern Ireland. There is a good deal of evidence that attempts to increase the rate of detection must confront significant barriers due to the lack of co-operation of the population, especially in the Catholic areas of Belfast (Howe, 1990; Leonard, 1994). Indeed, Maguire (1993, p. 278) argues that 'the use of intimidation by terrorist groups on social security inspectors means that their work cannot be of the same level of efficiency and effectiveness as that of their colleagues on the mainland'. Although such oppositional tendencies to state regulations may not be of the same order of magnitude elsewhere, the important point is that regulations cannot be implemented without compliance from the population. As shown above in the context of Quebec and the London borough of Newham, however, the proportion of the population desiring the deterrence of cash-in-hand work is not perhaps sufficient to allow this to happen.

A further practical problem with deterring cash-in-hand work concerns the unintended impacts of such a policy. The principal reason for seeking to deter cash-in-hand work is so that taxes can be raised and fraud/exploitation reduced. In practice, however, this may not occur. Starting with the desire to raise tax revenue, the implicit belief in the deterrence approach is that cash-in-hand work reduces the amount of revenue raised through taxation and that by eliminating it one can raise more revenue and reduce the burden on the honest taxpayer. To display that one cannot simply assume that all cash-in-hand work would become formal employment if such work was eradicated, Mogensen (1985) evaluates the notion that if the 200 million hours of cash-in-hand work provided in 1984 in Denmark was converted into jobs for the unemployed, some 110 000 new full-time jobs could be created, thus lowering the unemployment rate of 10.8 per cent in 1984 to 7.8 per cent. He states that this could only be achieved if the extreme price differentials between the formal and informal labour supply could be abolished. Purchasers of cash-in-hand work in his survey, however, stated that they would rather resort to do-it-yourself activities (34 per cent) or simply not consume the services (30 per cent) than pay the official formal price. Hence, nearly two-thirds of the work currently undertaken through cash-in-hand work would not be converted into formal jobs if it were successfully eradicated. One cannot expect, therefore, cash-in-hand work to be fully replaced by formal jobs.

There is also much evidence to suggest that any attempt to eradicate cash-in-hand work through tougher rules and regulations will have the opposite effect to that which is intended: it will increase, not decrease, the level of cash-in-hand work. To see this, one has only to look at the former Central and East European socialist states. There, state policies aimed at controlling every aspect of economic activity gave rise to a vast range of cash-in-hand work (Bernabe, 2002; Boren, 2003; Burawoy and Lukacs, 1985; Chavdarova, 2002; Ilie, 2002; Neef, 2002; Portes, 1994; Salmi, 2003; Sedleonieks, 2003; Sik, 1994; Smith, 2002; Wallace and Haerpfer, 2002). This is because, as Peck (1996a, p. 41) has stated, '*Pressures* for regulation do not necessarily result in effective regulation'. As Portes (1994, p. 444) thus puts it:

> The more state policies prevent the satisfaction of individual needs and access to inputs by firms, the wider the scope of informalisation that they encourage. The response will vary, of course, with the specific characteristics of each society. Yet recent evidence on the extent of irregular activities suggests that state officials have more often than not underestimated the capacity of people to circumvent unwanted rules.

The universal persistence of such work thus reflects in part the considerable capacity for resistance in most societies to the exercise of state power. Implementing policy towards cash-in-hand work and understanding their consequences thus 'requires a keen sense of the limits of state enforcement and of the ingenuity and reactive capacity of civil society' (Portes, 1994, p. 444).

Indeed, there is a good deal of evidence that cash-in-hand work will grow if civil society rejects the principles of the tax and welfare system. An analysis of the 1987 American Taxpayer Opinion Survey by Smith (1992) for instance, reveals that perceived procedural fairness and responsiveness in providing a service were positive incentives that increased taxpayers' commitment to paying taxes. Kinsey (1992), meanwhile, discovers that while detection and punishment attempt to force people to comply with the law, these processes also alienate taxpayers and reduce willingness to comply voluntarily. An increase in the perceived severity of punishment may therefore increase fraud and reduce respect for the fairness of the system. Consequently, in some nations, a simple deterrence model has started to be superseded. For instance, in New Zealand between 1984 and 1990, tax reforms not only increased the financial penalties but also resorted to media campaigns to persuade taxpayers that their money was being used efficiently on worthwhile projects (Hasseldine and Bebbington, 1991). Unfortunately, no evaluation has been conducted so far as is known of the effectiveness of this strategy.

Raising the level of cash-in-hand work, however, is not the only unintended consequence of pursuing tougher regulations and more punitive measures. A further unintended consequence, as will now be shown, is that it would lead to a decline of social capital.

Implications for social capital

The perception of nearly all governments (see Hasseldine and Zhuhong, 1999) and many academics (e.g. Castells and Portes, 1989; Sassen, 1989) is that deterring cash-in-hand work is a positive move that will have beneficial impacts for all concerned. It is here argued that this is wholly correct with regard to the small proportion of cash-in-hand work undertaken for and by businesses and on a self-employed basis for people that the supplier did not previously know. Such work is nearly always conducted for unadulterated economic reasons and is fraudulent activity that represents unfair competition for formal activity, has a deleterious effect on formal employment and undermines the welfare state by depriving it of income that could be used for social cohesion purposes. It is also work that unscrupulous businesses and individual consumers oblige a weak and unprotected workforce to undertake and a form of work that needs to be brought back within the bounds of the law so as to help eliminate exploitative labour market conditions.

However, is it beneficial to deter the cash-in-hand work conducted by people for relatives, neighbours and friends to help each other out and/or to cement or forge social networks? Indeed, given the current desire of the UK government to develop social support structures, especially in deprived neighbourhoods (e.g. Cabinet Office, 2001; Home Office, 1999; Social Exclusion Unit, 1998), the pursuit of a policy that seeks to eradicate the type of material and social support that government wishes to develop seems, to say the least, paradoxical. If paying for favours were only a minor segment of mutual aid this would not be such a problem. However, of all the non-kinship material help that households receive from other households, 84 per cent in deprived neighbourhoods is provided on a cash-in-hand basis. Unpaid mutual aid is thus relatively minor in comparison. To deter cash-in-hand work, therefore, is to take away from these neighbourhoods one of their principal coping mechanisms and social support structures (Williams and Windebank, 1999d, 2000a). As will be seen later, therefore, it is perhaps not deterrence of such work that is required through tougher regulations and punitive measures but, rather, its conversion into legitimate mutual aid through more positive initiatives.

Conclusions

This chapter has evaluated critically the dominant approach towards cash-in-hand work that seeks to eliminate such work by deterring people from engaging in it through the use of stringent regulations and punitive measures. Here, it has been shown that such a discourse is grounded in a reading of cash-in-hand work that recognises only its negative features, such as its fraudulent and exploitative nature. It does not recognise any of the more positive aspects of cash-in-hand work (e.g. as a seedbed for entrepreneurship: as a moral economy of favours). As shown in Part II, however, only a small proportion of cash-in-hand work is low-paid employment conducted for unadulterated economic reasons.

As such, this chapter has argued that this deterrence approach might be wholly appropriate with regard to the small proportion of the cash-in-hand work undertaken in the underground economy, which is nearly all conducted for unadulterated economic reasons. Such work is fraudulent activity that represents unfair competition for formal activity, has a deleterious effect on formal employment and undermines the welfare state by depriving it of income that could be used for social cohesion purposes. It is also work that unscrupulous businesses and individual consumers oblige a weak and unprotected workforce to undertake that needs to be brought back within the bounds of the law so as to help eliminate exploitative labour market conditions. There is little doubt that deterrence is thus required, although as will be later shown, this perhaps needs to be coupled with more positive measures to transform such work into formal employment.

However, such a deterrence approach is not appropriate in relation to the vast bulk of cash-in-hand work conducted by and for friends, relatives and neighbours to help each other out and/or to cement or forge social networks. Given the current desire of government to develop such support structures, the pursuit of a policy that seeks to deter precisely the material and social support networks that other government policy wishes to develop seems to say the least problematic. If cash-in-hand work constituted only a minor proportion of such material help, this would not be a problem. However, some 84 per cent of all non-kinship community exchange in lower-income urban neighbourhoods in the United Kingdom occurs on a paid basis. In consequence, some other policy option must be sought beyond simply deterring people from engaging in such support networks. In Chapter 8, therefore, one possibility is explored. This is the policy option of adopting a *laissez-faire* approach towards cash-in-hand work.

8
A *Laissez-Faire* Approach

Introduction

If the deterrence approach towards cash-in-hand work is relatively ineffective at preventing engagement in the underground sector and has the unintended consequence of hindering the continuation of those activities that cement and develop social capital, especially in deprived populations, then the question that begs an answer is the following. What alternative approach could be adopted towards cash-in-hand work? In this chapter, one possible answer is explored, namely a *laissez-faire* approach.

On the whole, and in contrast to the deterrence approach outlined in the last chapter, this *laissez-faire* approach towards cash-in-hand work is espoused by analysts politically right-of-the-centre. Evaluating critically the implications of adopting this approach, the argument in this chapter is that the net result of such a *laissez-faire* perspective would be that although this would enable people to freely engage in the hidden economy of favours and thus help cement and forge social capital, it would do little to either stem the current socio-spatial inequalities in the ability of populations to draw upon the resources of this sphere as a coping practice, nor would it do anything about the profit-motivated exploitative work that currently occurs in the underground economy. Instead, the net result of this neoliberal discourse that pursues a *laissez-faire* approach towards cash-in-hand work as well as a deregulatory approach towards formal employment would be a levelling down rather than up of material and social circumstances for the majority of the population in the advanced economies.

Before commencing a critical evaluation of this right-of-centre political discourse towards economic life, it is necessary to briefly consider that the notion of adopting a *laissez-faire* approach towards cash-in-hand work (without adopting the deregulatory approach towards the formal sphere) might be considered an option by some left-of-centre analysts, especially when they recognise that much of this work is conducted not as profit-motivated exploitative employment but as a form of paid mutual aid. Throughout this chapter, however, I wish to argue that this policy option of adopting a *laissez-faire* approach towards cash-in-hand work is not a viable option. If adopted, it would leave intact the underground economy and do little or nothing to facilitate the engagement of that significant minority of people currently excluded from participating in the hidden economy of favours who are perhaps most in need of the benefits that come from such paid mutual aid.

In this chapter, however, it is the neoliberal deregulatory approach that is the focus for investigation. First, therefore, this *laissez-faire* approach towards work, welfare and cash-in-hand work will be outlined and then the implications of pursuing such a policy approach will be evaluated critically.

The *laissez-faire* approach towards work, welfare and cash-in-hand work

In a market economy without state regulation, there would be no distinction between formal employment and cash-in-hand work. In consequence, and in direct contrast to the approach detailed in the last chapter, this discourse argues that the only way to rid the economy of cash-in-hand work is not more stringent regulations but rather, deregulation. This essentially neoliberal narrative is grounded in a view that cash-in-hand work is the result of over-regulation by the state of both the market and welfare provision (De Soto, 1989; Matthews, 1982; Minc, 1982; Sauvy, 1984). The aim, therefore, is not to promote cash-in-hand work as such but to 'formalise' those activities presently undertaken within a relationship of informality by reducing the regulations imposed on formal employment that supposedly force up labour costs and act as a brake on flexibility and thus cause certain businesses and individuals to work on a cash-in-hand basis. The suggestion is that if the unemployed were given more latitude for self-help, unemployment protection could be reduced, thereby eliminating the culture of welfare dependency. Implicit within this approach, moreover, is a view that the negative impacts of such a reduction in unemployment protection on those presently unemployed would be minimal since many are already heavily engaged in cash-in-hand work as a principal means of earning a living (De Soto, 1989; Matthews, 1982; Minc, 1982; Sauvy, 1984). Following the structure of the previous chapter, therefore, first, the view of the future of work and welfare in this approach is outlined and second, the conceptualisation of cash-in-hand work.

Laissez-faire discourses on the future of work and welfare

The key point to emphasise concerning the vision of the future of work adopted by this approach is that its ultimate goal is the return of full 'formal' employment. In this respect, and this respect alone, there are no differences between this approach and the last one. However, as mentioned above, their explanations of and solutions to the problem of unemployment could not be more different. For these analysts, over-regulation of the market is to blame for many of the economic-ills befalling society (Amado and Stoffaes, 1980; De Soto, 1989; Minc, 1982; Sauvy, 1984; Stoleru, 1982). As Peck (1996a, p. 1) so incisively summarises, 'From this viewpoint, failure is seen to have occurred *in* the market, not *because* of the market'. For these neoliberals, therefore, the solution is to give the market free reign such as by liberating the labour market from 'external interference'.

Indeed, for many neoliberal commentators, the growth of unemployment is the result of state regulation frustrating the market (Minc, 1980, 1982; Sauvy, 1984; Stoleru, 1982). Sauvy (1984), for example, blames mass unemployment on the rigidity of the economy, expressed in terms of legal controls on employment (e.g. redundancy laws, health and safety legislation, minimum wages), on the social security system and on the general way in which the state imposes itself on the lives of the population. For him, however, legislation in itself is not the cause of rigidity. In an individualistic fashion typical of this approach, he asserts that this legislation is a product of the general desire of individuals for stability and security, resulting in inflexibility. He contends that workers do not seek work as such but a stable job and those job seekers that also seek such jobs are encouraged to do so by the welfare system. Sauvy (1984) maintains that it is these attitudes that have led to protective legislation and produced a society in which needs go unmet whilst workers claim benefit. Therefore, the way to tackle unemployment is first, to allow wages to fall so that employers will be induced to create jobs and thus absorb surplus labour and second, to cut back on welfare payments so as to give workers an incentive to be less fastidious about the jobs which they accept. Consequently, the future of work is one in which market forces hold sway so as to enable supply and demand to return to equilibrium. If implemented, the goal of full-employment will be achieved.

As witnessed in the United Kingdom and United States over the past decades, the various policies and initiatives that comprise this neoliberal ideology add up to an economic strategy that places low waged labour and deregulated labour markets at the forefront of the solution to resolve the 'jobs deficit'. The implicit and sometimes explicit consequence of such a strategy is to make cash-in-hand work less necessary. By stripping away regulations, the need for employers to turn to operating in the underground sector is reduced. To some extent, therefore, this approach is precisely what the commentators in the last chapter were referring to when they discuss how 'cash-in-hand' work is becoming embedded in the mainstream in late capitalism as the neoliberal project takes hold. As regulations are stripped away in neoliberal regimes, formal employment starts to become akin to cash-in-hand work since employees are left without protection and with minimal safeguards vis-à-vis working conditions.

If the neoliberal project with regard to the sphere of work is to deregulate and give the market free reign, what is its approach towards welfare provision? It is commonly assumed that this *laissez-faire* discourse has a very different outlook towards the future of welfare compared with the approach discussed in the previous chapter. Although this is superficially correct, there are some common threads to their narratives. Both approaches view the welfare state and the economy as adversaries in that one is usually seen as the root cause of problems in the other. The difference between the two approaches is that whilst the commentators in the last chapter largely favour the welfare state and view free market capitalism as destroying social equality, *laissez-faire* theorists support the free market and dislike any structure that constrains it. The former, in consequence, read the welfare state as a necessary institution for the functioning of modern capitalism and indeed, a prerequisite for efficiency and growth as well as individual self-realisation. The latter, in marked contrast, read the nature of the adversarial relationship between the welfare state and economic efficiency in the opposite manner. The welfare state is construed as interfering with individual freedoms and the ability of the market to optimise the efficient allocation of scarce resources.

Given this reading of the relationship between welfare and economy, the major debate within the *laissez-faire* approach is over the extent to which a welfare state is required. This debate in neoliberal thinking is nothing new. As Esping-Anderson (1994) displays, it has been prevalent ever since the English Poor Law reforms in the early part of the nineteenth century. Within the tradition of classical economics and libertarian thought, one extreme, exemplified by Samuel Smiles, held that virtually any socially guaranteed means of livelihood to the able-bodied would pervert work incentives and individual mobility. This, in turn, would stifle the market, freedom and prosperity. This extreme narrative is echoed in modern times when it is argued that welfare provision is the antithesis of social equality. As social rights are essentially claims against the income and resources of others, commentators adopting this stance view the welfare state not as the guarantor of equal status and autonomy for citizens, but as a divisive system under which a class of claimants becomes parasitic upon others' labour and property, with disastrous effects upon their morals (Gray, 1984; Murray, 1984).

Other more liberal thinkers such as Adam Smith, however, and unlike Smiles, understood that society did need some welfare provision, especially in health and education. Today, some liberal thinkers are similarly more willing to accept that the modern economy needs a basic welfare safety net, but stress that due to the conflicting relationship between welfare and economy, this will incur a certain price in terms of economic performance. For these *laissez-faire* theorists, therefore, the principal issue is where to set the trade-off between equality and efficiency (Barr, 1992; Gilder, 1981; Lindbeck, 1981; Okun, 1975).

As such, there is a spectrum of neoliberal thought ranging from those who see no need for a welfare state at one pole to those who regard the need for greater degrees of emphasis on equality rather than efficiency as one moves along the continuum towards the other pole. All positions on this continuum, however, emphasise the efficiency trade-offs of pursuing greater equality, particularly with reference to the possibly negative effect of the welfare state on savings (and hence investment), work incentives (and hence productivity and output) and the institutional rigidities that welfare states introduce (such as in the mobility of labour).

Although such debates over the degree to which a welfare state should be provided are important to adherents of this approach, the fundamental fact should not be masked that *laissez-faire* commentators are largely negative about the welfare state due to its deleterious influence on economic performance. For such *laissez-faire* commentators, competitive self-regulatory markets are far superior as allocation mechanisms from the viewpoint of both efficiency and justice. It follows, therefore, that government interference in allocation processes (aside from marginal cases of imperfections, externalities or market failure) will risk generating crowding-out effects, maldistribution and inefficiency with the inevitable end result that the economy will produce less aggregate wealth than if a *laissez-faire* approach were adopted (Lindbeck, 1981;

Okun, 1975). Some even insist that the current inequalities must be accepted, and perhaps even encouraged, because their combined disciplinary and motivational effects are the backbone of effort, efficiency and productivity (Gilder, 1981).

If this *laissez-faire* reading of work and welfare were but 'academic' theory in the most derogatory sense of the word (i.e. of little or no importance), then perhaps it would not even matter. But it takes only a moment's reflection to realise that this narrative of economic progress and development is so much more than simply an academic theory about work and welfare. This theorisation is not just an abstraction that is seeking to reflect reality but also an economic discourse that is being used to shape the material world. As Carrier (1998, p. 8) puts it, there is a 'conscious attempt to make the real world conform to the virtual image, justified by the claim that the failure of the real to conform to the idea is a consequence not merely of imperfections, but is a failure that itself has undesirable consequences'. In this virtualism, economic theory and practice thus act to shape each other in an ongoing recursive and reflexive loop 'driven by ideas and idealism [and] the desire to make the world conform to the image' (Carrier, 1998, p. 5).

For anybody in doubt that this is the case, one has only to consider the way in which this theorisation of the economy and welfare has been a mirror against which the reality of the economy and welfare has been held and found wanting. Indeed, it is somewhat ironic that despite this theory being heavily opposed to state-led change, it is precisely the states of Anglo-Saxon nations, such as the United Kingdom and United States and to a lesser extent Canada and Australia, that have been the primary vehicle for implementing this vision of the world. Indeed, this recognition is not new. Over half a century ago, Polanyi (1944, p. 140) realised that 'the road to the free market was opened and kept open by an enormous increase in continuous, centrally organised, and controlled interventionism'. The *laissez-faire* approach towards work and welfare, therefore, is not just an attempt to reflect reality but also a narrative used to shape the material world.

From the late 1970s until the change of government in 1997 in the United Kingdom, for example, the state pursued the implementation of such a *laissez-faire* narrative by increasing flexibility in the labour market, eroding employment rights and removing or privatising welfare protection and regulatory institutions (see Beatson, 1995; Crompton *et al.*, 1996; Deakin and Wilkinson, 1991, 1992; Peck, 1996a; Pinch, 1997; Rubery, 1996). The significance of this experiment was that it was an attempt to dissolve any visible social and labour market institutions that might provide a check on the supposed operation of market forces (Rubery, 1996) or what Hutton (1995) terms all 'intermediary institutions between state and individual' so as to construct a reality more reflective of the theory.

In the United States, similarly, the reconstruction of reality by deregulating formal employment and welfare provision to conform to the *laissez-faire* theory is perhaps even more acutely seen (see Esping-Anderson, 1996; Myles, 1996). In the realm of employment legislation, there has been a slow and continual whittling away of labour laws whilst in the welfare sphere, there has been a rolling back of welfare provision as displayed in the 1996 Welfare Act (see Peck, 1996b). Similar to the deterrence approach, therefore, this *laissez-faire* approach is much more than an academic exercise. It has been implemented, sometimes with ardent fervour, across many of the advanced economies.

The *laissez-faire* approach toward cash-in-hand work

For these neoliberals, the growth of cash-in-hand work is interpreted to be a direct consequence of the encumbrance of state regulations and their costs. Contini (1982) reads its growth as the 'revenge of the market' for over-regulation by the state. Confronted by excessive state regulations, cash-in-hand workers are viewed as heroes (rather than 'villains' as in the deterrence approach) who are casting off the shackles of an overburdensome state (e.g. Biggs *et al.*, 1988; De Soto, 1989; Matthews, 1982; Sauvy, 1984). In this narrative, cash-in-hand work is not read as undermining the creation of formal jobs and short-circuiting the macroeconomy but instead, is viewed as responding, as any other economic activity should do, to 'needs expressed by people' (Sauvy, 1984, p. 274). Cash-in-hand workers are meeting material needs that would otherwise go unmet due to state interference in the formal sphere that has had the inevitable consequence of market distortion. In this reading, cash-in-hand work is thus the people's 'spontaneous and creative response to the state's incapacity to satisfy the basic needs of the impoverished masses' (De Soto, 1989, p. xiv-xv). As Sauvy (1984, p. 274) explains, such work represents 'the oil in the wheels, the infinite adjustment mechanism' in the economy. It represents the elasticity that facilitates a snug fit of supply to demand, which is the aim of every economy. Indeed, for *laissez-faire* theorists, it is the only mechanism through which one can guarantee the utopia of full employment.

From the perspective of neoliberals, cash-in-hand workers are only breaking rules and regulations that are inherently unfair. Engagement in such work is thus a form of popular resistance to an unfair and excessively intrusive state and cash-in-hand workers are a political force that can generate both true democracy and a rational competitive market economy. Given this reading of cash-in-hand work as one of the last bastions of untrammelled enterprise in an over-rigid economic system, these *laissez-faire* theorists view in its supposedly recent growth a resurgence of the free market against state regulation and union control. According to them, cash-in-hand work is the 'essence of liberalism' (Sauvy, 1984). The Italian economist, Antonio Martino for example, considers cash-in-hand work 'a masterpiece of my countrymen's [*sic*] ingenuity, a second Italian economic miracle which has saved the country from bankruptcy, and an example for the other "free" countries to follow' (Martino, 1981, p. 89). Milton Friedmann, moreover, asserts that 'the clandestine economy is a real life belt: it effectively limits collective coercion ... allowing individuals to get round the restrictions imposed by government on personal enterprise' (cited in De Grazia, 1982, p. 480).

In this *laissez-faire* perspective, therefore, cash-in-hand work is the locus for the development of pure and perfect competition which is prevented from spreading into the 'modern sector' by the many barriers imposed by the state such as protectionism, legal measures, excessive bureaucracy, wage rigidity and so on (De Soto, 1989). These measures make it possible to maintain barriers to entry that prevent the market from working competitively. In order to throw off these shackles, the (universal) entrepreneurial spirit currently has to operate on the fringes of laws and regulations so as to circumvent the barriers to entry. An example is the set of cash-in-hand activities known as the 'second economy' in the now defunct state socialist regimes of Central and Eastern Europe. Here, cash-in-hand work became associated with the market and individual freedom. Second economy enterprises producing and trading goods unavailable in state-controlled outlets overcame the logic of the socialist economy. Even state firms and managers frequently used informal supply chains to overcome the bottlenecks of the official system (Grossman, 1989; Lomnitz, 1988). Indeed, some Hungarian sociologists assert that the free-market forces unleashed by the second economy were the key solvent that undermined the political legitimacy of state socialist regimes and led to their demise (Borocz, 1989; Gabor, 1988).

Such a positive reading of cash-in-hand work, it should be noted, is not confined to a neoliberal perspective. The modern origins of the 'informal economy' concept lie in the work of Keith Hart in a study of urban labour markets in Africa (Hart, 1973). In his report to the ILO, Hart postulated a dualist model of income opportunities of the urban labour force, or what Hart (1990, p. 158) referred to as 'people taking back in their own hands some of the economic power that centralized agents sought to deny them'. Indeed, *laissez-faire* theorists such as the Peruvian economist, Hernando de Soto, can be seen to have given this original theme, that was lost in subsequent ILO documents, renewed impulse. In *The Other Path* (1989), De Soto recaptures this positive essence by representing cash-in-hand work as the popular response to the rigid 'mercantilist' states in Peru and other Latin American nations that survive by granting privileges of legal participation in the economy to a small elite. Hence, unlike its portrayal in the International Labour Office (2002) as a survival mechanism in response to insufficient modern job creation, the view that such enterprise represents the irruption of real market forces in an economy straitjacketed by state regulation draws upon a relatively long tradition in conceptualisations of cash-in-hand work, not all of which is grounded in wider neoliberal theory.

Until now, it has been shown that *laissez-faire* theorists tend to heap praise on both cash-in-hand work and cash-in-hand workers. This is not to assert, however, that the *laissez-faire* approach wants to promote cash-in-hand work. That is a popular misconception. Instead, their desire is to eradicate cash-in-hand work as much as those in the deterrence approach outlined in the last chapter but their approach is not to adopt more stringent regulations and punitive measures. For them, the way to achieve this is by reducing state regulations in the realms of formal work and welfare so as to both unshackle formal employment from the constraints that force up labour costs and prevent flexibility and remove the welfare constraints that act as a disincentive to the unemployed to seek formal jobs. With fewer regulations, the notion is that the distinction between formal and cash-in-hand work will wither away so that the two become inseparable since all activities would be performed in the manner we now call 'cash-in-hand', although such activity would be 'formal' since it would not be breaking any rules. In this way, and in this way alone, the goal of full-employment is seen to be achievable.

Evaluating the *laissez-faire* approach

Having outlined this *laissez-faire* approach towards work, welfare and cash-in-hand work, the assumptions underlying it as a policy solution are here evaluated critically. To do this, first, its approach towards work and welfare in the contemporary advanced economies is addressed and second, its approach towards cash-in-hand work.

Evaluating critically its vision of the future of work and welfare

The core narrative of this approach is that full-employment can and will return if market forces are allowed to operate unhindered. Here, the validity of this discourse is assessed. Measured purely in terms of whether this *laissez-faire* approach is more effective in achieving the goal of full-employment than more interventionist approaches, there is little doubt that this is the case. It does indeed appear that unemployment is lower in advanced economies such as the United Kingdom and United States that have pursued such a deregulatory strategy with greater fervour than in the more social democratic nations of mainland Western Europe. However, this sound performance in terms of job creation must be seen both in terms of the quality of the jobs created and the degree of social polarisation that this 'success' has entailed (see Conroy, 1996; Esping-Anderson, 1996; European Commission, 1996b, 2000a; Fainstein, 1996; OECD, 1993; Peck, 1996a,b; Rubery, 1996).

In the advanced economies, two distinct approaches to social polarisation have been adopted (see Pinch, 1994; Williams and Windebank, 1995b). First, and most widely used, is the approach that examines inequalities in relation to employees in the employment-place, such as in terms of widening income or earnings differentials. Second, and popular in the United Kingdom, is the approach that takes the household as the unit of analysis and examines the increasing disparities. Whichever approach is adopted towards social polarisation, the finding is the same. The neoliberal nations appear to be witnessing social polarisation to a much greater degree than the more social democratic nations. So far as the former approach is concerned, the OECD (1993) report that during the 1980s in neoliberal nations, the lowest-decile earners lost ground relative to the median, by 11 per cent in the United States, 14 per cent in the United Kingdom, 9 per cent in Canada and 5 per cent in Australia. For example, and as Fainstein (1996) displays in the United States, the percentage of permanent full-time workers with earnings below the official poverty line (about $13 000 in 1992) increased by 50 per cent between 1979 and 1992, from 12.1 per cent of workers in 1979/80 to 18.0 per cent by 1992/93. Such disparities, moreover, are far higher than in social democratic nations. Workers in the lowest earnings decile in *laissez-faire* nations such as Canada and the United States, for example, earn about 40 per cent of median earnings compared with 70 per cent or more in social democratic nations such as Germany and in Scandinavia (OECD, 1993).

Examining the latter approach based on widening household inequalities, moreover, the same distinction between neoliberal and social democratic nations in terms of the degree of social polarisation is identified. As Myles (1996) reports in the United States, between 1973 and 1987, the income of the richest 20 per cent of families increased by 25 per cent whilst that of the poorest 20 per cent fell by 22 per cent. More widely, examining Table 8.1, a clear trend is apparent. The United States and the United Kingdom, as the two nations that have led the race towards deregulation, are also the nations with the highest levels of social polarisation between households. These nations have the highest proportion of households that are either multiple-earner or no-earner households. One can thus only agree with Peck (1996a, p. 2) that, 'Contrary to the nostrums of neoliberal ideology and neo-classical economics, the hidden hand of the market is not an even hand'.

A further problem is that there is little evidence that some of the fundamental tenets of this ideology will have the impact *laissez-faire* theorists desire. Take, for example, the policy of stripping away the welfare state so as to encourage people to find employment. Numerous studies of the effects of reducing welfare benefits on the levels of unemployment conclude that decreasing levels of benefit (or withholding benefit) will not cause an increase in flows off the unemployment register (Atkinson and Micklewright, 1991; Dawes, 1993; Deakin and Wilkinson, 1991, 1992; Dilnot, 1992; Evason and Woods, 1995; McLaughlin, 1994). In an extensive review of the effect of benefits on (un)employment, McLaughlin (1994) concludes that the level of unemployment does have some impact on the duration of individuals' unemployment spells, but the effect is a rather small one. Following Atkinson and Micklewright (1991) and Dilnot (1992), she states that the level of unemployment benefits in the United Kingdom do not contribute to an explanation of unemployment to a degree that is useful when considering policy. Moreover, extremely far-reaching cuts would be required in benefit levels to have any significant impact on the duration and level of unemployment. The effect of such cuts would be to create a regime so different from the present one from which the estimates of elasticities (of unemployment duration with respect to out-of-work benefits) are derived, that their predictive usefulness would be very suspect (Dilnot, 1992).

Neither will taking away the cushion of the welfare state simply allow people to get-by. The so-called 'dependency culture' resulting from the onslaught of formal welfarism has stripped away the institutions of civil society that once allowed people to survive outside the nexus of the welfare state (see, e.g. Mingione, 1991; Williams and Windebank, 2003a). Therefore, the possibility that greater self-help will occur simply by taking away people's safety net appears mistaken. The net result is

Table 8.1 The polarisation of employment between households, OECD Nations, 1983–94

% of all households	Jobless households			Mixed employment status households			Households where all are in employment		
	1983	1990	1994	1983	1990	1994	1983	1990	1994
United Kingdom	16.0	14.3	18.9	30.1	22.0	18.6	53.9	63.7	62.1
United States	13.1	10.0	11.5[d]	32.3	24.9	24.9	54.6	65.1	63.6
Germany	15.0[a]	12.8	15.5	32.5	27.7	25.6	52.5	59.5	58.9
Netherlands	20.6[b]	17.2	17.2	39.1	31.9	27.0	40.3	50.9	55.7
France	12.5	14.4	16.5	30.6	28.3	27.9	56.9	57.4	55.7
Belgium	16.4	18.0	19.6	41.8	33.7	28.8	41.8	48.3	51.6
Australia	11.9[c]	14.5[e]	—	32.6	28.3	—	55.8	57.2	—
Portugal	12.7[c]	10.8	11.0	38.3	32.9	32.6	49.0	56.4	56.4
Canada	15.2	12.5	15.1	35.7	37.0	35.9	49.1	50.6	49.0
Ireland	17.2	20.0	22.3	47.3	40.8	36.9	35.5	39.3	40.9
Greece	16.0	16.9	17.6	46.3	40.1	38.9	37.7	43.0	43.5
Luxembourg	10.9	9.3	10.5	47.3	42.1	39.0	41.8	48.7	50.5
Italy	13.2	14.3	17.2	47.4	43.1	42.8	39.4	42.6	40.0
Spain	19.4[c]	15.2	10.8	54.5	51.6	48.1	26.2	33.2	31.8

Notes
a. Data for 1984
b. Data for 1985
c. Data for 1986
d. Data for 1993
e. Data for 1991

Source: Gregg and Wadsworth (1996: table 1)

more likely to be that people will be simply left bereft of the means of survival. Nevertheless, given the increasingly untenable pressures being put on formal welfare provision in the advanced economies, it remains obvious that something will need to be done about the way in which welfare is provided. The choice, however, is not either to strive to restore full-employment and a comprehensive welfare 'safety net' for the economically excluded as the interventionists advocate or to strip away the welfare safety net and deregulate the formal labour market as a means of encouraging full-employment, as the *laissez-faire* theorists propose. As shown, the former is impractical and flies in the face of the direction of the advanced economies, whilst the latter, even if it were to achieve full-employment, would do so at an extremely high price in terms of the levels of absolute and relative poverty. Instead, some alternative path needs to be sought that enable people to pursue full-engagement (rather than full-employment) in order to meet needs and desires (for an in-depth analysis, see Williams and Windebank, 2003a). In the next chapter, it will be shown how cash-in-hand work enables this to happen. For the moment, however, attention turns towards a critical evaluation of the *laissez-faire* approach towards cash-in-hand work.

Evaluating critically *laissez-faire* discourses on cash-in-hand work

For many *laissez-faire* theorists, cash-in-hand work represents not only an indicator of the way forward for formal employment but a means by which the unemployed and marginalised are currently getting-by in the advanced economies. As such, many assert that there is little need for concern over the dismantling of the welfare 'safety net' (e.g. Matthews, 1983). The problem, however, and as Part II of this book has already displayed, is that this is not the case. The unemployed engage in cash-in-hand work to a lesser extent than the employed. Consequently, there are good reasons to suppose that if the formal labour market and formal welfare provision were further deregulated then the social and spatial inequalities would not be reduced and might even widen.

Reviewing the barriers that prevent people from engaging in cash-in-hand work discussed in Chapter 4, there is no reason to suppose that deregulating formal welfare provision will improve their participation in either formal or cash-in-hand work. For example, the reason why many of the poor and unemployed conduct little cash-in-hand work is not only because of institutional barriers (e.g. the fear of prosecution) but also their lack of money, tools, social networks, skills and opportunities to engage in such work (Pahl, 1984; Williams and Windebank, 1993,

1994, 1995a,b, 2001a, 2003a). Consequently, even if a *laissez-faire* approach eradicates the institutional barriers to engagement, it will do little to help people tackle the other barriers that hinder their participation. For example, it would not enhance their skills or their social networks. Neither would it provide them with access to the tools and money necessary to engage in this form of work. All that such a move would do is to enhance their incentive to work on a cash-in-hand basis in order to survive.

This alone, however, appears to be insufficient to tackle the barriers that prevent those excluded from the formal and/or cash-in-hand labour market from participating in such work. As Gilbert (1994, p. 616) argues, 'The hope that it [cash-in-hand work] can generate economic growth on its own, that the micro-entrepreneurs can go it alone, with a bit of credit and some deregulation, seem to be hopelessly optimistic'. Therefore, by adopting a *laissez-faire* approach which, for example, asserts that the way to solve the problem of poverty and unemployment is to take away formal welfare support, with little if any state assistance to facilitate the transition, the only possible reason that greater economic competitiveness and socio-economic equality would be achieved is because there would be a levelling down, rather than up, of material and social circumstances for the vast majority of the population.

This similarly applies to spatial inequalities. As evidence of how deregulation of formal employment and the welfare system is also insufficient by itself to enable poorer localities and regions to improve their circumstances, there are several lessons to be learned from Emilia-Romagna in Italy. As Amin (1994) makes clear, the success of this region in turning itself into a competitive area is founded not only on the deregulation of the formal sphere but equally, on strong public sector support and co-ordination. The success of Emilia Romagna has been very much dependent upon strong state intervention such as industry-specific services to firms to foster task specialisation and inter-firm co-operation to advertise the products of an area and to secure the long-term reproduction of sector-specific skills. This view that the success of this area is based on 'controlled de-regulation' is reinforced by many other studies (e.g. Cappechi, 1989; Warren, 1994). These all find that the creation of contemporary Marshallian industrial districts in this region are not only the result of a particular 'cocktail' of conditions being present (e.g. in inter-firm co-operation, structure of sociability, local 'industrial atmosphere' and 'institutional thickness') which have allowed this transition to occur but also due to strong state intervention in co-ordinating this transformation. On its own, therefore, deregulation is insufficient to make poorer regions and localities more economically competitive. Systemic support is required for firms along and across value-added chains. It is clear that deregulation on its own will not revitalise deprived regions and localities.

Conclusions

In this chapter, it has been revealed that the *laissez-faire* approach, similar to the deterrence approach in the previous chapter, desires a return to 'full-employment' but the nature of the 'full-employment' society envisaged by the former is very different from that of the latter as is its means of achieving this end. Rather than bolstering what they see as the flagging edifices of 'diluted' or 'welfare' capitalism through state-led work sharing and job creation as well as comprehensive welfare support, supporters of this approach largely advocate 'undiluted' capitalism. The intention, in so doing, is to close the gap between formal employment and cash-in-hand work by eradicating the regulations and constraints that currently hinder the achievement of full-employment. Consequently, although many exponents of this approach see the already de-regulated sphere of cash-in-hand work as an exemplar of economic and social organisation, they do not wish to promote or protect it in its present form. Instead, this approach seeks to replace this dichotomy not by regulating cash-in-hand work out of existence but by deregulating formal employment to a degree that renders cash-in-hand work unnecessary.

Evaluating critically the implications of pursuing this approach, this chapter has revealed that although there is little doubt that deregulation of formal employment would reduce the magnitude of cash-in-hand work which by definition is a product of the regulations imposed on formal employment, it is very doubtful that deregulation of formal employment and the welfare state alone would enable people to improve their circumstances. On the one hand, it has revealed that the impact of such deregulation is to widen inequalities at a quicker rate in those nations that have pursued deregulation than in more social democratic countries. On the other hand, it has revealed that deregulation will not automatically allow marginalised groups and areas to solve their problems regarding their livelihoods.

Taken together, therefore, the last two chapters have reviewed the deterrence and *laissez-faire* approaches to cash-in-hand work that are more widely embedded in views of the future of work and welfare that seek to restore full-employment and/or a comprehensive welfare 'safety net' by controlled interventionism and deregulation respectively. As shown, the former is impractical and flies in the face of the direction of the advanced economies, whilst the latter, even if it were to achieve full-employment, would do so at an extremely high price in terms of the levels of absolute and relative poverty. Instead, and as is becoming increasingly apparent, a middle-path is required that seeks full-engagement (rather than full-employment) by giving people the means to help themselves (see Williams and Windebank, 2003a). This alternative approach is the subject of the next chapter.

9
Harnessing Cash-in-hand Work

Introduction

In the last two chapters, the policy options of deterring and doing nothing about cash-in-hand work have been evaluated critically. Recognising that cash-in-hand work is composed of not only the underground sector but also a moral economy of paid mutual aid, it has been argued that pursuing a deterrence approach is both impractical and undesirable. It is impractical not only because deterrence alone seems incapable of stemming the underground sector but also because the moral economy of paid mutual aid is heavily embedded in everyday life. It is undesirable because eradicating paid mutual aid would destroy one of the principal means through which people now cement and build social capital, especially in deprived populations. A laissez-faire approach towards cash-in-hand work, meanwhile, has been shown to leave intact the underground economy whilst doing little or nothing to facilitate the engagement of that significant minority of people currently excluded from participating in the hidden economy of favours who are perhaps most in need of the benefits that come from such engagement. If these policy options of deterring or doing nothing about cash-in-hand work are inappropriate, then what should be done about this heterogeneous sphere of activity? In this chapter, a third and final possible policy option is considered, namely that of harnessing such work.

Given the heterogeneous character of cash-in-hand work, this chapter will argue that great care needs to be taken over what is meant by 'harnessing' such work and how its meaning varies depending upon whether one is considering the underground sector or the hidden economy of favours. Throughout this chapter, and as will be made clear, 'harnessing' cash-in-hand work does not refer to a strategy of cultivating greater engagement in each of these forms of cash-in-hand work. Instead, and in the case of the underground sector, it refers to transferring such work into the realm of formal employment primarily through the use of positive measures and incentives to help this activity move from the informal to the formal sphere. Unlike the deterrence approach discussed in Chapter 7 that largely seeks to punish those engaged in such cash-in-hand work, the emphasis here is on providing positive help to enable the transfer of such activity into the formal realm. In the case of the hidden economy of favours, meanwhile, 'harnessing' such work refers to enabling its transfer into the realm of legitimate mutual aid through either changes to government regulations or the provision of substitute mechanisms through which paid favours can be legitimately conducted. The intention in so doing is to move towards what Williams and Windebank (2003a) call a full-engagement (rather than full-employment) society in which people are facilitated to engage in both formal and informal work (rather than simply formal employment) in order to meet their needs and desires.

First, therefore, this chapter will review the heterogeneous nature of cash-in-hand work along with the positive and negative features of both the underground sector and the social economy of favours. Arguing that deterrence and laissez-faire approaches need to be replaced by a more positive enabling approach, this chapter then sets out how this should occur. Setting out how there is a need to transfer the underground sector into the formal sphere and the social economy of favours into legitimate paid mutual aid, this chapter then evaluates a number of initiatives that could be used in this more positive approach. The intention, in so doing, is to develop an approach for harnessing cash-in-hand work that not only differentiates between the underground sector and the hidden economy of favours but also does so in a manner that retains the currently beneficial aspects of each sphere whilst reducing their more negative aspects.

The heterogeneous nature of cash-in-hand work

Throughout this book, the focus has been upon the variable nature, rather than the size, of cash-in-hand work. Drawing inspiration from the cultural turn across the social sciences that has resulted in a rethinking of whether monetised exchange is always embedded in profit-motivated behaviour (Byrne *et al.*, 1998; Crang, 1996; Crewe, 2000; Crewe and Gregson, 1998; Davies, 1992; Gudeman, 2001; Lee, 1996, 1997, 2000a,b; Thrift and Olds, 1996; Williams and Windebank, 2001a; Zelizer, 1994), it has shown that this form of work which is often considered the exemplar of unbridled profit-motivated capitalism is far from being universally conducted for profit-motivated rationales under work relations akin to formal employment. Such abstract universal hues have been argued to oversimplify and obscure the heterogeneous contemporary meanings of cash-in-hand work and often result in inappropriate policy responses being adopted. Here, in consequence, a less totalising conceptualisation of cash-in-hand work has been sought that recognises the heterogeneity inherent in this dynamic and complex sphere.

If cash-in-hand work in contemporary advanced economies is to be more fully understood and appropriate policies developed, it has shown that a more socially, culturally and geographically embedded appreciation of monetised exchange is required. Identifying that although some cash-in-hand work is of the profit-motivated variety pictured in conventional discourse, there is also a realm of cash-in-hand work conducted under social relations more akin to mutual aid for friends, neighbours and kin for non-profit reasons. As such, cash-in-hand work has been theorised as composed of not only an 'underground economy' of market-like profit-motivated cash-in-hand work but also a 'hidden' or 'social' economy of favours where such work is conducted under social relations and for purposes more akin to unpaid mutual aid.

Exploring how the nature of cash-in-hand work varies across different populations, Part II then revealed that cash-in-hand work is much more commonly a form of profit-motivated monetised exchange for those in formal employment, men and affluent areas. For the unemployed, women and deprived areas, however, cash-in-hand work is much more embedded in the hidden economy of favours. The implication, therefore, is that the conventional reading cash-in-hand work as composed of an underground sector is a discourse grounded in the meanings of such work to the employed, men and those living in affluent areas. It is not a discourse reflecting the dominant meanings of cash-in-hand work for the unemployed, women and deprived areas.

In order to start to both understand cash-in-hand work and develop appropriate policy, therefore, it is necessary to separate out these two broad spheres and to consider the contrasting consequences of their existence.

Positive and negative features of the underground sector and the hidden economy of favours

Conventionally, discourses on cash-in-hand work have focused upon the underground sector and its negative features. These include:

- It is fraudulent activity that causes a loss of revenue for the state in terms of non-payment of income tax, national insurance and VAT (e.g. Grabiner, 2000; Home Office, 2002, 2003a);

- It leads to 'dumping' of wages and social security payments (e.g. Mateman and Renooy, 2001);
- It weakens trade unions and collective bargaining (e.g. Gallin, 2001);
- It creates unfair competitive advantage for firms who use undeclared labour over those who do not;
- It leads to competition between cash-in-hand and formal workers and businesses and generates circumstances of 'hypercasualisation' (Jordan and Travers, 1998) as more formal workers are forced to 'informalise' to compete effectively;
- It leads to a loss of regulatory control over the quality of jobs and services provided in the economy;
- It erodes compliance with health and safety standards;
- It creates circumstances conducive to the exploitation of workers due to the reduction of wage rates;
- It results in the loss of various employment rights (e.g. annual and other leave, sickness pay, redundancy, training); and
- It leads to the stigmatisation and social exclusion of people undertaking cash-in-hand work, including a shift from a latent stigma to an active one such as from 'scrounger' to 'fraudster' (e.g. Travers, 2002).

Given these negative consequences, it is perhaps unsurprising that there has been a concerted effort to deter such work through tougher regulations and punitive measures. However, once it is realised that there are also some positive features of the underground sector then questions arise over whether eradicating it through deterrence measures is the appropriate policy response (e.g. Vaknin, 2000). These positive features include:

- It enables people to be active instead of being idle and losing motivation, and often becoming depressed and ill, which can be an effect of long-term unemployment (Engbersen *et al.*, 1993);
- It provides a possible route into participation in the formal labour market, particularly for those with negative educational experiences, few skills and little experience (Leonard, 1998b);
- It reduces the burden on the benefit authorities in terms of individuals having to sign off and sign on as a fresh claimant each time they undertake a piece of work;
- It acts as a school for entrepreneurialism for people looking to test out and establish a business but initially uncertain about coming off benefit (Leonard, 1998b); and
- It reduces the possibility that individuals in poverty will resort to more serious crime in order to cope and survive.

When these positive outcomes are recognised, especially the fact that it acts as a seedbed for microenterprise, then the underground sector starts to be seen as a potential asset rather than always as an obstacle, as will be seen below. This in turn leads to changes in relation to the policy approach adopted towards it.

Similarly, and when cash-in-hand work conducted in the social economy of favours is considered, there are again both negative and positive consequences resulting from its existence. Some of the positive features are:

- It enables people to be active instead of being idle and losing motivation, and often becoming depressed and ill, which can be an effect of long-term unemployment (Engberson *et al.*, 1993);
- It extends the range of opportunities available to individuals and families to cope in situations of deprivation (Leonard, 1998b);
- It both relies upon and develops social networks as providers of information about opportunities and, when more developed, sources of further support (e.g. Perri 6, 1997a,b);
- It enhances social cohesion and social inclusion through mutual aid and reciprocity (e.g. Williams and Windebank, 2001a,b,c,f, 2002a); and
- It enables the provision of goods and services at a cheaper rate and frequently for those in most need.

The negative features of this cash economy of favours, meanwhile, include:

- Such work, even if providing a way of helping others, still represents illegal activity that might involve either tax or benefit fraud; and
- The distribution of such work is highly uneven not least in the sense that a significant minority of people are unable to access such support networks at present (Williams, 2001a).

Given this summary of the positive and negative consequences of both the underground sector and the hidden economy of favours, it appears that so far as is possible, policy needs to try to retain the positive features of such work whilst minimising the negative features. How, therefore, is this to be achieved?

Evaluating the policy options

Given these positive and negative consequences of both the underground sector and the hidden economy of favours, it is necessary to consider the implications of pursuing different policy approaches. First, and as discussed in Chapter 7, a deterrence approach is premised on the belief that cash-in-hand work is composed solely of an underground sector that is viewed purely in terms of its negative consequences. Such an approach fails to recognise either the positive features of the underground sector or how cash-in-hand work is also composed of a hidden economy of favours that it is both impractical and undesirable to deter. It is impractical because such work is heavily embedded in everyday life and it is undesirable because such paid mutual aid is one of the principal vehicles through which both redistribution occurs and social capital is forged and cemented in contemporary societies, especially amongst deprived populations where cash for favours is part of the culture of exchange.

Second, therefore, there is the laissez-faire policy option. If pursued, however, not only will all of the negative impacts of the underground sector persist, but little if anything will be done to help those currently excluded from the hidden economy of favours gain access to such aid as an additional coping practice to meet their material and social needs.

Other alternatives include adopting some combination of deterrence and *laissez-faire*. A *laissez-faire* approach towards the underground sector and a deterrence approach towards the hidden economy of favours is perhaps the worst possible option that could be chosen. It would leave intact the profit-motivated work of the underground sector with all of its negative impacts whilst seeking to deter cash-in-hand work conducted as a form of paid mutual aid.

What, however, about the option of deterring the underground sector and adopting a *laissez-faire* approach towards the hidden economy of favours? Although more focused on retaining the more positive hidden economy of favours and preventing the more negative underground sector, several key problems remain. First, it would be very difficult for state actors to identify what cash-in-hand work was being conducted for unadulterated reasons and what was being conducted for reasons akin to mutual aid. Although some forms of cash-in-hand work such as informal or formal businesses working on a cash-in-hand basis are easily categorised as operating in the underground sector, it becomes much more difficult once one starts examining individuals conducting cash-in-hand on an autonomous basis. Whether they are acting as self-employed people working in the underground sector or as individuals engaged in mutual aid to help others would be difficult to decipher. A second problem with this approach is that adopting a *laissez-faire* approach towards the hidden economy of favours leaves intact the inequalities that presently exist in this sphere. A significant minority of the population are currently excluded from drawing upon the resources of this social economy of favours as a coping practice in order to meet their material and social needs. To adopt such a *laissez-faire* approach is thus to leave intact these disparities. Third and finally, it fails to recognise some of the more positive aspects of the underground sector such as its function as a seedbed for entrepreneurship. For these three reasons alone, it is here considered that the policy option of deterring the underground sector and adopting a *laissez-faire* approach towards the social economy of favours is inappropriate.

Towards a 'harnessing' approach

A third policy option is to 'harness' such work. In recent years, there has been much greater recognition of some of the more positive aspects of cash-in-hand work summarised above. The result is that this sphere has started to be seen not as an obstacle to modernisation but, rather, as a potential asset to be harnessed or even a driver of economic development (e.g. Global Employment Forum, 2001; International Labour Office, 2002; Tabak, 2000). The most prominent display of this conceptual shift is that cash-in-hand work is no longer read in a purely negative light by some of the supranational agencies (e.g. International Labour Office, 2002) but, instead, is seen more positively, particularly in terms of its role as a breeding ground for the microenterprise system. The result of this rereading is that it has started to become more common to discuss 'harnessing' cash-in-hand work.

Until now, however, this emergent literature that discusses the notion of 'cultivating' or 'harnessing' cash-in-hand work has viewed such activity purely as something to be transformed into formal employment. Although the ideas propounded in this chapter resonate with this emergent stream of thought, the intention here is to argue that recognition of the heterogeneity of this sphere necessitates some significant modifications to existing views on how to harness such work. The argument here is that what is meant by 'harnessed' markedly varies according to the form of cash-in-hand work being discussed. In the realm of the underground sector, that is, 'harnessing' cash-in-hand work needs to mean transforming such work into formal employment, akin to the contemporary discussions highlighted above. So far as the hidden economy of favours is concerned, however, 'harnessing' cash-in-hand work needs to seen in a very different light. Given the character of this type of cash-in-hand work, the meaning of 'harnessing' such work here has to refer to the very different process of transferring paid mutual aid out of the illegal cash-in-hand realm into a sphere of legitimate paid mutual aid.

In other words, if the problem of cash-in-hand work is to be dealt with, activity conducted in both the underground sector and the hidden economy of favours needs to be converted into legal activity. However, the type of activity into which it should be transformed differs according to which form of work is being considered. The argument here, therefore, is to leave neither as cash-in-hand work due to the difficulties involved in deciphering whether activity conducted by individuals is underground activity or conducted in the social economy of favours. By seeking to harness both, albeit in different ways, one avoids such problems. But a twin-track approach is adopted whereby one seeks to use enabling measures to transform the underground sector into formal employment and the hidden economy of favours into legitimate paid mutual aid. This twin-track policy approach, if it achieves its goals, both retains the positive features of these spheres whilst minimizing the negative features.

How, therefore, can this approach be implemented? To answer this question, the next section addresses the issue of initiatives that can be used to transfer the underground sector into formal employment and this is then followed by initiatives that could be used to transfer the hidden economy of favours into legitimate mutual aid.

Policies for formalising the underground sector

As Chapter 7 highlighted, the dominant policy approach in most advanced economies is one of deterring the underground sector through the use of stringent regulations and punitive measures. However, and despite this overwhelming emphasis on deterrence, many governments recognise that what they actually wish to do is to formalise this activity and that pursuing a policy of 'sticks rather than carrots' is inappropriate to achieving such a goal. Until now, however, little attempt has been made to consider what 'carrots' might be provided to actively encourage such activity to move into the formal sphere rather than merely pursuing policies to punish those caught working on a cash-in-hand basis. Here, therefore, the intention is to review just a few of the more positive measures that could be taken alongside, if not instead of, the current punitive measures so as to encourage the formalisation of cash-in-hand work conducted in the underground sector.

In this regard, there are many possible positive measures that could be taken in theory. On the one hand, an attempt could be made to provide sufficient formal employment and/or comprehensive welfare provision to make working in the underground sector unnecessary. As discussed in Chapter 7 however, this does not appear to be a feasible option. Alternatively, therefore, there is a range of incentives as well as aid that could be given to those working on a cash-in-hand basis in order to enable them to transfer their activity into the formal sphere. These include both introducing changes to state regulations (e.g. shifting the income tax threshold and changing earnings disregard levels) so that their work is no longer classified as cash-in-hand work, and developing initiatives to ease their transition to the formal sphere (e.g. amnesties). Here, five specific initiatives are outlined that all attempt, in different ways, to take positive measures to formalise the underground sector. Although not comprehensive in coverage, and sometimes nationally specific, they at least begin to open up some of the possibilities once this asset-orientated approach towards the underground sector is adopted.

The Street (UK) initiative

Street (UK) was created in 2000 when its current Director, Rosalind Capisarow, recognised that if the self-employed were going to be facilitated to maximise their business potential, then those operating in the cash-in-hand sphere would need to be helped to formalise their businesses. At present, Street UK has around 200 clients and they fall into two main categories. First, people claiming benefits (e.g. disability benefit, carers allowance) and second, those who are not claiming any benefit but who are either under-declaring income from their enterprise activity or are not declaring at all.

On the Street UK web site (www.street-uk.com), one can find case studies of the type of self-employed clients that have been so far helped to formalise their enterprises. For instance, there is a case study of a female client in East London (originally from Ghana) who was able to save enough from working in the cleaning industry to start up as a hairdresser first in the cash-in-hand sphere but now, after intervention by Street (UK), in the formal economy. Her original microenterprise has grown to create 5–6 additional formal jobs that have enabled other Ghanaian migrants to gain entry into the formal labour market. Another case study cites a married couple in Newcastle who for some 20 years had been running a window cleaning enterprise on a cash-in-hand basis but who have now been assisted to move this enterprise into the formal sector. What is so important about this case study, besides the fact that the Street (UK) interventions can shift stalwart cash-in-hand enterprises into the formal sphere, is that it provides a useful example of how cash-in-hand work operates as a 'school for entrepreneurialism'. Over the two decades that this couple had been running their cash-in-hand enterprise, they had helped numerous young people into employment and/or self-employment by starting them up in window-cleaning rounds. What is of more importance here however is the strategy that Street (UK) adopts to help people to formalise their cash-in-hand work. As Table 9.1 displays, this organisation views the transition from cash-in-hand work to formality as involving 12 separate steps. As they recognise, it is highly unlikely that any microenterprise will take all 12 steps in one fell swoop and its intention is to help them take each of these steps individually so that eventually, they can become a formal business. For this organisation, moreover, the objective is to encourage their clients to take at least three new steps in any 12-month period. If they do, then they are classified as being on the road to transforming themselves from a cash-in-hand enterprise to a formal business.

What is perhaps so interesting about this policy initiative is its starting premise. It is based on the recognition that governments can include as many punitive measures as they like to deter cash-in-hand work, but the owners of these microenterprises often do not know how to go about formalising their businesses. If more are to make the transition from the underground sector to the formal sphere, therefore, active intervention is required to enable this transformation to occur.

Table 9.1   The 12 steps to formalisation of cash-in-hand work of Street (UK)

1. Moving from part-time to full-time work.
2. Moving from home to business premises.
3. Keeping basic-level records.
4. Keeping higher-level accounts.
5. Purchasing public liability and employers liability insurance.
6. Hiring employees on a PAYE basis.
7. Using a bank account for their business transactions and opening a separate business bank account.
8. Obtaining the required licences and permits to operate the business (e.g. health and safety inspection certificates, driver instructor licence).
9. Graduating off all non-work state benefits.
10. Graduating from majority cash revenues to majority invoiced revenues.
11. Incurring a formal business tax liability.
12. Becoming VAT registered.

A basic income scheme

A second positive measure that could be used to stop people engaging in cash-in-hand work in the underground sector is one that takes a more macrolevel top-down approach and seeks to facilitate the transfer of activity out of the cash-in-hand sphere in a very different manner to the above initiative. The intention of a basic income scheme is to provide every citizen with a basic 'wage' as a social entitlement without means test or work requirement (e.g. Jordan *et al.*, 2000; van Parijis, 1992, 1996a,b). Eligibility is *automatic* for all citizens and *unconditional*. There would be no tests of willingness to work, or disqualification. The advantage of pursuing this policy option is that by providing all citizens with a guaranteed minimum income, one might well cut off the supply of workers to the underground sector, especially to some of the lowest-paid and most precarious organised work in 'sweatshops' that is in dire need of eradication.

Known variously as a citizens income, social wage, social dividend, social credit, guaranteed income, citizen's wage, citizenship income, existence income or universal grant, this top-down initiative would enable individuals with their guaranteed minimum income in hand, to free themselves from exploitative forms of cash-in-hand employment conducted in the underground sector because nobody would be obliged to engage in such work to augment income to a basic survival level (e.g. Jordan *et al.*, 2000; Mayo, 1996; Williams and Windebank, 1998). As Mayo (1996, p. 158) asserts,

> The approach of a Citizen's Income ... would help to support beneficial changes in working patterns and practices by removing unemployment and poverty traps, eliminating today's black economy of undeclared earnings, raising pay levels for dirty and unsociable jobs, and encouraging work in the [unpaid] informal economy.

Even amongst advocates of a basic income, however, it is now accepted that a fully individualised and unconditional basic income could not be introduced in one operation, if only because of the way in which it would upset the current distribution of incomes and labour supply. Instead, and particularly for the working age population, the growing consensus is that one should not proceed by cohorts or by categories, but start with a very modest (partial) basic income that would not be a full substitute for existing guaranteed minimum income provisions (Jordan *et al.*, 2000; Parker, 1989).

Here, however, and whatever the feasibility of such a scheme, it is simply important to recognise that positive initiatives to eradicate the underground sector do not have to be small-scale bottom-up initiatives. There is also a need to consider the option of creating top-down solutions that eliminate the need or people to engage in such work as a way of eradicating it. Rather than adopt measures to punish people who engage in such work, one can also provide alternative sources of income so as to reduce the need for them to engage in such activity.

Active citizens' credits

Another top-down initiative that operates in a similar vein to the basic income scheme, but is perhaps more in keeping with contemporary political thought on wanting to tie minimum incomes to some form of economic endeavour, is the Active Citizens' Credits (ACC) scheme (see Williams and Windebank, 2003a). Here, the intention is likewise to eliminate the need or people to engage in such work in the underground sector by providing an alternative source of income. However, the intention is to do so by linking such an income to engagement in active citizenship. This notion of a 'participation income' is a long-standing strand of thought in the citizens' income literature and has a wide range of advocates (e.g. Atkinson, 1995; Briscoe, 1995; Gough, 2000; Lipietz, 1992, 1995; McCormick, 1994). One recent development in this field, however, has been to argue that such an income could be paid under the tax credit system that is currently being implemented in many advanced economies as a means of integrating the tax/benefit system (see Liebman, 1998; Meadows, 1997; Millar and Hole, 1998).

   In this tax–credit approach, ACC accredit active citizenship by recording, storing and rewarding participation in caring and other work conducted for the community. Under this non-compulsory scheme, individuals engage in a self-designed portfolio of work of their choosing for which they would be reimbursed. This would be non-compulsory in that individuals could freely choose whether or not to participate. Individuals would also decide what portfolio of work they wish to undertake. The idea that such a scheme should be developed to encourage individuals to engage in freely chosen work to benefit their community is perhaps uncontroversial. The major controversy is how to reward them. Williams and Windebank (2003a) argue that such active citizenship should be embedded within the tax credit framework so as to move towards a fully integrated tax/benefit system. Presently, the unemployed and part-time workers are not included in the tax credits framework. If paid a guaranteed minimum income, they would receive this for engaging in employment for fewer hours or not at all. To give everybody wishing to receive a guaranteed minimum income the opportunity to do so, they suggest that besides employment, pensioner and disability/sickness tax credits, there should be also training tax credits and three types of active citizens credits, namely parents tax credits, carers tax credits and community worker tax credits (see Williams and Windebank, 2003a, for more detail). If implemented, everybody would have access to one tax credit that they could claim so as to receive a guaranteed minimum income. The result would be the creation of a society founded upon the 'working citizen' without a radical policy overhaul, as well as an integrated tax/benefit system.

More importantly so far as the purpose of this chapter is concerned, it would provide a way of introducing a guaranteed minimum income in a way that is in keeping with contemporary thought on the 'working citizen'. If implemented, it would eliminate the need for people to engage in such work in the underground sector by providing an alternative source of income. Not all top-down initiatives to deal with the underground sector, however, have to be quite so wide-ranging in their impacts. There are also a host of policy initiatives that are more targeted in terms of their focus that could go some way towards encouraging people not to engage in the underground sector of cash-in-hand work.

Extending the Back to Work Bonus scheme to self-employment

In the United Kingdom, the Back to Work Bonus was introduced in October 1996 with the aim of encouraging individuals and where relevant their partners to 'keep in touch' with the labour market by undertaking small amounts of work whilst still claiming Income Support (IS) or Jobseekers' Allowance (JSA). The rationale was that it would provide an incentive for claimants to move from unemployment into paid work. It works in a complex way by the accrual of a bonus if the claimant's earnings from part time work reduce the amount of JSA or IS they are paid. They can then claim the bonus (a tax-free lump sum of up to £1000) if and when they move off benefit and into employment proper. The bonus is accumulated from 50 per cent of the declared earnings above the 'earnings disregard' (normally £5) but this can only commence after 91 days of being on IS/JSA. It also has to be claimed within 12 weeks of leaving benefit (otherwise it is lost) and it can only be paid if the claimant starts work within two weeks of leaving benefit. It cannot be accrued by people aged over 60 claiming IS, although men aged 60–64 on JSA can join the scheme. If a claimant is on IS, the earnings of the claimant's partner are taken into account in the calculation of the bonus, but this is not the case if the claimant is on JSA (Department for Work and Pensions, 2003a,b,c; Elam and Thomas, 1997).

A qualitative evaluation of the scheme carried out in 1998 (Thomas *et al.*, 1999) found a real lack of awareness of the scheme amongst those who were eligible and dissatisfaction amongst those who knew about it. A more recent quantitative evaluation (Ashworth and Youngs, 2002) found that increased awareness but little evidence supporting the hypothesis that the Bonus has encouraged recipients of benefits into part-time work. Rather than cease the operation of this scheme, the suggestion here is that it could provide a template for supporting those seeking to move from cash-in-hand work whilst claiming benefit into their own microenterprise, as a lump sum of up to £1000 would have a clearer purpose. For this to occur, however, would require a sea-change in the culture of the benefit authorities and a recognition on the part of claimants that they were not going to be prosecuted for prior working on a cash-in-hand basis whilst claiming. Such a scheme, if implemented, would nevertheless, provide a bridge to help those seeking to use their cash-in-hand work to set up in self-employment.

Formalising domestic service work: the case of France

In France, there has been a good deal of policy emphasis in recent years on how to reduce the amount of cash-in-hand work taking place in the domestic services sphere (e.g. cleaners). The result is that the Cheque Emploi Service (CES) was introduced in 1993 to simplify the process of hiring and paying a domestic worker and making social security contributions. Salary cannot be less than the minimum wage, plus a 10 per cent indemnity for paid leave. This was followed by the creation of the Titre Emploi Service (TES) in 1996. This allows work councils, regional and local authorities and welfare associations to guarantee financial assistance to their own staff members who hire domestic workers in their homes. Modelled on the restaurant ticket system, the TES vouchers are issued by an authorised organisation and are purchased by another organisation that can top up their value before making them available to employees who use them to purchase household services from an approved provider. This and other measures to support demand – such as tax incentives for families, the child home care allowance (allocation de garde d'enfant a domicile, or AGED) and family assistance for the employment of a registered childminder (Aide a la famille pour l'emploi d'une assistante maternelle agree, or AFEAMA) – resulted in an increase of 190000 jobs in family-related services between 1991 and 1997 (Cancedda, 2001, p. 30). It is likely that such initiative would have had a significant impact on the level of cash-in-hand work. For the purchaser of domestic services, there is now a clear reason for employing formal workers rather than paying on a cash-in-hand basis for such services.

Facilitating employment in domestic services: the Melkert initiative in Holland

According to a 1995-survey in the Netherlands, one family in three needs more help at home, especially with cleaning, washing and ironing clothes (Cancedda, 2001). Under the 'Melkert Plan', a programme was implemented to subsidise the wages of declared domestic cleaners so that they could compete with cash-in-hand workers. A subsidy of not more than 19 000 NLG was granted for every long-term unemployed individual hired by a private cleaning company. The government, in effect, was paying the difference between the cost of declared and undeclared domestic cleaners. The government thus paid a subsidy to firms to hire formal domestic cleaners rather than benefits to the unemployed. In 1997, only 250 jobs were created. In 1998, however, changes were made to the scheme and it is claimed to function better now. Cleaning companies however, have more trouble finding workers than they do customers since the potential workers are required to have been registered unemployed for at least a year, which excludes many women who would like such work but have not been registered as unemployed. The Melkert Plan also created subsidised jobs in other spheres of domestic service beyond cleaning, including home help services and childcare. In the realm of home help, the finding was that some of these jobs were replacing regular formal jobs. However, some 1700 Melkert jobs were created in the sphere of childcare by the end of 1998 (Cancedda, 2001).

Obviously, these initiatives are just a few of the more positive approaches that could be undertaken to transfer work from the underground sector into formal employment. There are doubtless many more. The point here, however, is not to provide a comprehensive listing of the various initiatives available in the form of an 'initiatives bank'. It is simply to show that there is currently a range of policy initiatives available that can be used if governments wish to take a more positive approach towards facilitating the transition from cash-in-hand work to formal employment. Adopting negative measures to detect and punish those caught working on a cash-in-hand basis is not the only approach available. Harnessing such work is another feasible option.

Policies for harnessing the hidden economy of favours

If cash-in-hand work is to be effectively dealt with, it is not only necessary to transfer work in the underground sector into formal employment, but it is also necessary to transform the activity that currently takes place in the social economy of favours into the sphere of legitimate mutual aid. How, therefore, can this be achieved? To answer this, a number of initiatives are again presented.

Before doing so, however, it is important to bear in mind two issues. First, and as displayed throughout this book, engaging in this social economy of favours is a key coping practice and way in which material and social needs are met, especially in deprived populations. As such, it is insufficient to simply deter this endeavour. Instead, it needs to be maintained but transferred into legitimate paid mutual aid. This can occur either by developing substitute mechanisms through which such work can be conducted but in a more legitimate manner than at present, or by changing the rules so as to make this activity no longer illegal. Second, there is also a need to consider that a significant minority in deprived populations are presently unable to participate in this social economy of favours as a means of meeting their material and social needs. This is largely because they not only lack the social network, economic and human capital to do so but also due to a range of institutional constraints that lead them to avoid engaging in such activity in case they are caught. Hopefully, initiatives developed to transfer such activity might also facilitate the entry of these citizens into the networks of mutual aid by tackling their current barriers to entry.

Any initiative developed to try to siphon off such activity from the cash-in-hand sphere by providing a more legitimate way of engaging in mutual aid, however, cannot avoid the fact that there is a culture of paying for favours, especially in deprived populations. As such, policy initiatives designed to transfer this activity into legitimate mutual aid will need some form of tally system or monetary payment to be involved if they are to be effective. Here, therefore, a number of initiatives are highlighted that might be capable of transferring paid mutual aid from the sphere of illegitimate cash-in-hand work into the sphere of legitimate mutual aid and resonate with this culture of paying for favours.

Local exchange and trading schemes (LETS)

A LETS is created where a group of people form an association and create a local unit of exchange. Members then list their offers of, and requests for, goods and services in a directory and exchange them priced in a local unit of currency. Individuals decide what they want to trade, who they want to trade with and how much trade they wish to engage in. The price is agreed between the buyer and seller. The association keeps a record of the transactions by means of a system of cheques written in the local LETS units. Every time a transaction is made, a cheque is sent to the treasurer who works in a similar manner to a bank sending out regular statements of account to the members. No actual cash is issued since all transactions are by cheque and no interest is charged or paid. The level of LETS units exchanged thus entirely depends upon the extent of trading undertaken. Neither does one need to earn money before one can spend it. Credit is freely available and interest-free (see Barnes *et al.*, 1996; Williams, 1996a,b,c,d,e,f).

As Williams (1996a) has pointed out, these schemes have the potential to provide a means of formalising paid mutual aid by providing a structure for facilitating multilateral reciprocal exchange. Indeed, a 1999 national survey of 2515 LETS members in the United Kingdom, with a response rate of 34 per cent, reveals that 39.1 per cent of the goods and services bought on LETS would have been purchased on a cash-in-hand basis if the LETS had not been used and that 23.2 per cent of goods and services sold on LETS would have been sold in such a manner (Williams *et al.*, 2001a). LETS, therefore, appear to be useful vehicles for formalising cash-in-hand work.

They are also powerful vehicles for tackling many of the barriers preventing people from engaging in mutual aid discussed in Chapter 4. Take, for example, the fact that many do not engage in acts of paid mutual aid due to their 'thin' social networks, meaning that they have few people to call upon to either give or receive help. The 1999 survey of UK LETS members, for example, reveals that 76 per cent of members asserted that the LETS had helped them to develop a network of people upon whom they could call for help, 56 per cent stated that it had helped them develop a wider network of friends and 31 per cent deeper friendships. LETS, therefore, appears to successfully develop 'bridging' social capital and to a lesser extent, 'bonding' social capital.

LETS also appear to tackle the barrier of economic capital that prevents people from engaging in mutual aid. Some 40 per cent of UK members asserted that LETS had provided them with access to interest-free credit (62 per cent of the registered unemployed). Similarly, there is also evidence that LETS tackles the barrier of human capital. As Williams *et al.* (2001a,b) discuss, they appear to build self-confidence, enable people to recognise the skills that they possess, maintain existing skills and acquire new ones.

Finally, and in relation to institutional barriers, LETS have had relatively less success. Although only 13 per cent of members are worried about tax liabilities and 12 per cent about reductions in welfare payments, some 65 per cent of the registered unemployed members were concerned that their participation in LETS might result in their benefits being reduced. This would occur if their earnings on LETS were treated as earnings and they were considered to have received a sum over the earnings disregard. This fear was also true of non-members interviewed. All non-members interviewed who were registered unemployed expressed grave concerns that their trades would result in a reduction in benefits. The UK government, however, has done little to curtail this fear. A *laissez-faire* approach has been adopted towards the regulation of LETS by government and this has been insufficient to appease members and potential members. Indeed, the report by Williams *et al.* (2001a,b) was used by the UK government to decide whether to more actively intervene by passing a regulation that would allow people working on LETS to do so without fear of prosecution. The finding that the 303 schemes in the United Kingdom in 1999 had a turnover equivalent to just £1.4 million and a total membership of only 21 800 meant that government felt such schemes were too small to warrant such a regulation (Williams *et al.*, 2001a,b). As such, a *laissez-faire* attitude still prevails and the 'favours' provided on LETS have not been officially exempted from being counted as earned income by either the tax or benefit authorities.

Time banks

Unlike LETS, time banks sought guarantees from government at the outset that the 'favours' earned would be exempt from being treated as earnings by the tax and benefit authorities. Having received that guarantee both in the United States and United Kingdom, it is perhaps unsurprising that they are now witnessing more rapid growth than LETS.

Originating in the United States, time banks are the creation of Edgar Cahn, a Washington DC-based lawyer (Cahn, 1994, 2000; Cahn and Rowe, 1992). What in effect they do is to record, store and reward participation mutual aid. Recognising the existence of the desire on the part of people to keep some form of tally of favours given and received, time banks reward reciprocity by converting that contribution into a form of currency that can be used to acquire goods and services that one needs and/or desires. Participants are paid one 'hour' for each hour that they work, which they can at any time 'cash in' by requesting an hour's work in return from the system (see Boyle, 1999; Cahn, 1994; Cahn and Rowe, 1992; Seyfang and Smith, 2002; Williams, 2001c). As such, time dollars are a local tax-exempt currency that one earns by helping others. It records, stores and rewards transactions where neighbours help neighbours. Put another way, time banks reward civic engagement in a way that generates social capital, one hour at a time.

Time currencies thus represent a means by which cash-in-hand work in the moral economy of favours can be transferred into the realm of legitimate paid mutual aid. By 1998, over 200 time banks and service credit programmes were estimated to be operating in 30 states in the United States and these schemes frequently have thousands of members (Boyle, 1999). In the United Kingdom, meanwhile, there were in September 2002 some 36 active time banks with 2196 members who had exchanged a total of 63 756 hours (Seyfang and Smith, 2002).

Again, and similar to LETS, it also appears that time banks are useful vehicles for tackling the barriers that prevent a significant number of people from engaging in acts of paid mutual aid. As Seyfang and Smith (2002) find, time banks are effective mechanisms for not only developing bridging and bonding social capital amongst participants but also tackling the economic and human capital barriers that have previously excluded a significant minority of people from engaging in paid mutual aid. This is also an initiative that appears to appeal to the registered unemployed. In the United Kingdom, for example, some 54 per cent of time bank members received income support or the Job-Seekers Allowance and some 72 per cent of all members are non-employed.

Time banks, in consequence, represent a vehicle for transforming cash-in-hand work conducted in the hidden economy of favours into legitimate paid mutual aid. Indeed, given that time banks are rapidly expanding, it seems to be the case that many people have already recognised this fact for themselves.

Employee mutuals

A third initiative that could transform activity currently conducted in the hidden economy of favours into legitimate paid mutual aid is the 'employee mutual' (Leadbeater and Martin, 1997). Currently on the drawing board, the proposal is that these would be localised bodies that the unemployed, employed and firms can voluntarily join through the payment of a weekly subscription fee. Akin to LETS and time banks, members would earn points on a smartcard from their work for the Mutual, which would enable them to 'buy' goods and services from it. As such, they are seen as a 'new institution for collective self-help' that matches local demand for work with local supply. The major intention behind them is to allow people to undertake the many one-off jobs that need doing but that they are unable to afford to do formally.

Learning from LETS in relation to social security benefit rules, the proponents of Employee Mutuals have again argued from the outset for special benefit rules to be applied to members of the Mutual. These would make it easier for members to combine income from part-time or temporary work on the Mutual with benefits so as to reduce the insecurity that deters people from engaging in such organisations and making the transition from welfare to work. In return for such preferential treatment regarding the earnings disregard, jobless members of a Mutual would make a token contribution of 50 pence per week but would contribute at least fifteen hours per week of services in kind. In return, the mutual would not only provide work but also training and childcare facilities, job searches and a job placement service, as well as job accreditation and even a social life.

An employee mutual, therefore, would not only provide a local 'one-stop shop' for people seeking help to get various tasks completed, and thus tackle the social network barrier that prevents many people from giving and receiving aid, but these new institutions would also tackle the barriers of economic capital, by allowing people to acquire credit/debit on their smartcard, and human capital by providing training. They also tackle the institutional barriers to engaging in paid mutual aid by seeking changes in the regulations regarding the earnings disregard from the outset.

Changing the 'earnings disregard'

When considering how to legitimise paid favours, the focus in this section until now has been on creating and developing institutions through which such work can be conducted in a more legitimate manner. If the cash-in-hand work that exists in the moral economy of favours is to be converted into legitimate paid mutual aid, however, it is insufficient to rely on bottom-up initiatives. In each case so far discussed, for example, the issue has been raised that in the United Kingdom at least, there also need to be changes in the regulations, particularly with regard to the 'earnings disregard', if these initiatives are to succeed. Given this common thread, it is here thought necessary to consider this issue directly rather than on a piecemeal initiative-by-initiative exemption basis.

Just as formal employment creation requires top-down intervention to be effective, it is the same with other forms of work such as legitimate paid mutual aid. Today, few people question the need for tax breaks, subsidies, incentives and high levels of state intervention in the market in order to generate formal jobs. Until now, however, the same has not applied to harnessing paid mutual aid. Instead, it has been perhaps viewed as some organic or natural economy. If so, this is incorrect.

One simple policy change in the UK context to prevent the registered unemployed from being defined as engaging in cash-in-hand work when they take money for favours given to friends, neighbours and kin is to change the 'earnings disregard'. At present, if they earn over

£5 per week, this needs to be declared and their benefits are reduced accordingly. Given that many of the tasks undertaken in this hidden economy of favours are short-term one-off tasks, honesty on their part would result in their benefits being reduced. To legitimise this activity, therefore, the earnings disregard could be converted to a quarterly or annual sum, such as £250 or £1000. If this were implemented, then much of the work conducted in this hidden economy of favours by the registered unemployed would cease to be 'cash-in-hand' work and would become legitimate paid mutual aid. Here, therefore, is one simple change in the regulations that might be implemented in the United Kingdom and elsewhere in order to legitimise the vast majority of work that the registered unemployed conduct in the hidden economy of favours, and to break down the institutional barrier that prevents many unemployed people from doing paid favours for one another.

Conclusions

Reviewing how cash-in-hand is composed of an underground sector and a hidden economy of favours, along with their positive and negative consequences, this chapter has argued that neither the deterrence or *laissez-faire* approach, nor some combination of them, allows the positive features of these forms of work to be retained whilst dealing with their more negative impacts. For this to be achieved, this chapter has argued that a 'harnessing' approach is required. Here, it has been asserted that what is required is a twin-track approach that transfers activity that currently takes place in the underground sector into the sphere of formal employment and activity presently undertaken in the social economy of favours into legitimate paid mutual aid. In both cases, moreover, the argument has been that the most effective way of doing this is to adopt positive measures that facilitate this transformation rather than simply seeking to deter and punish those caught engaging in cash-in-hand work. Here, therefore, a number of possible policy initiatives have been outlined to encourage the transfer of cash-in-hand work into these two spheres. Obviously, the initiatives reviewed here are just a few of the more positive approaches that could be employed. There are doubtless many more. The point here, however, has not been to provide a comprehensive listing of the various initiatives available. It has been simply to show that there is currently a range of policy initiatives available that can be utilised by governments wishing to take a more positive approach to legitimising cash-in-hand work.

10
Conclusions

This book has sought to answer three key sets of questions about cash-in-hand work. What types of cash-in-hand work exist and why do people engage in these activities? Who undertakes these different types of cash-in-hand work, where is such work to be found and how does the character of cash-in-hand work vary across different populations? And what should governments do about cash-in-hand work? Part I sought theoretically-informed empirically-grounded answers to the first set of questions regarding the varieties of cash-in-hand work and the motives underpinning such activity, Part II sought answers to who undertakes cash-in-hand work, where it takes place and how the character of cash-in-hand work varies socially and spatially while Part III addressed the issue of what governments should do about the cash-in-hand sphere. In this concluding chapter, therefore, the findings are synthesised so as to summarise the contributions of this book to knowledge.

Examining cash-in-hand work: theory and methods

Reviewing the vast literature on cash-in-hand work, it was shown that the traditional focus of inquiry when studying this sphere has been upon investigating its magnitude and how this varies geographically and across socio-economic groups (e.g. Feige, 1990; Fortin *et al.*, 1996; Leonard, 1998a,b; Renooy, 1990; Thomas, 1999; Williams and Windebank, 2001a). Using the marginality thesis as the referent that asserts how cash-in-hand work is concentrated amongst marginalised groups and areas (e.g. Castells and Portes, 1989; De Soto, 1989; Lagos, 1995; Maldonado, 1995; Rosanvallon, 1980), a Popperian-like approach to knowledge advancement has gripped the subject whereby most studies have done little more than affirm or falsify this thesis, with the majority showing that such work is not concentrated amongst marginalised groups and/or areas but is instead a means of accumulating advantage for more affluent groups and areas.

In this book, however, to cast-off the shackles of this incremental approach to knowledge advancement, attention has been turned to the relatively unexplored but nevertheless important issues of the relations within which these monetised exchanges are embedded and the motives of the purchasers and suppliers of such work. Until now, it has been simply assumed that the relations and motives underpinning cash-in-hand work exemplify unbridled profit-motivated capitalist exchange practices. For adherents to the marginality thesis, such work is characterised as a low-paid form of work conducted under exploitative employment-like relations by some of the most marginalised groups in society (e.g. Castells and Portes, 1989; De Soto, 1989; Lagos, 1995; Maldonado, 1995; Rosanvallon, 1980). Although the recognition that affluent groups also conduct such work has led some to show that such work does not always have to be low paid or conducted under exploitative working conditions (e.g. Van Eck and Kazemeier, 1985; Fortin *et al.*, 1996; Renooy, 1990; Williams and Windebank, 1998), nobody has so far stopped to question whether cash-in-hand work is always conducted under work relations akin to employment or whether the profit motive universally prevails.

Here, however, drawing theoretical inspiration from cultural analysts who have questioned whether monetised exchange is always and everywhere embedded in profit-motivated behaviour (e.g. Crang, 1996; Crewe, 2000; Davies, 1992; Crewe and Gregson, 1998; Gudeman, 2001; Lee, 1996, 1997, 2000a,b; Thrift and Olds, 1996; Zelizer, 1994), by which is meant the desire to 'achieve maximum money gains' (Polanyi, 1944, p. 68), an empirically grounded rereading of cash-in-hand has been sought.

In order to move beyond the totalising economic discourse that portrays monetary exchange in general, and cash-in-hand work in particular, as universally market-like and profit-motivated, this book has sought a more socially, culturally and geographically embedded appreciation of monetised exchange. To do this, it has argued that as societies become more commodified in the sense that goods and services are increasingly produced for monetised exchange, cash payments seem to have become more common in circumstances where previously they would have had no place. Research has been reported, for example, which shows that when people conduct favours for friends, neighbours and kin, it is now common for cash to change hands. The result of this broadening of the circumstances in which monetary exchange takes place is that the constitution of cash-in-hand work has begun to change. Although there persists a sphere of cash-in-hand work conducted under work relations akin to formal employment for profit-motivated purposes (or what I have here called an 'underground sector'), there is also emerging a realm of cash-in-hand work composed of activity carried out under relations more akin to mutual aid for non-profit purposes for friends, neighbours and kin (or what I have here called a 'hidden economy of favours').

This identification of heterogeneous forms of work under the umbrella of cash-in-hand work, it has been argued, necessitates a fundamental rethinking of its anatomy as well as how it is dealt with in policy. Such a retheorisation of cash-in-hand work also brings two fields of enquiry and policy-making together that have so far been treated as wholly separate from each other. Once it is recognised that the on-going march of commodification has led to mutual aid being penetrated by monetised exchange, the result is that changes are required in both how social capital is conceptualised and how policy approaches its development. It appears that the literature on social capital now needs to further expand its scope to incorporate the 'hidden economy of favours' and that policy-making needs to more fully appreciate the contemporary cultural desire for some form of tally system or money to be involved when favours are given and received. For the first time, therefore, this book argues that the issues of cash-in-hand work and social capital overlap in significant ways that display the need for 'joined up' thinking and policy with regard to these two spheres that until now have been treated as separate realms.

Such a retheorisation of the nature of cash-in-hand work, as Chapter 3 displayed, also shows the need for a reconsideration of the methods used to study such activity. Evaluating critically the various methods that have been previously employed, ranging from the indirect monetary and non-monetary methods to the more direct survey methods, this chapter revealed that the indirect methods are not only incapable of providing any indication of the heterogeneous nature of cash-in-hand work but also that most are premised on assumptions about its character that at best, apply only to the underground sector. If a fuller understanding of this heterogeneous sphere is to be achieved, therefore, then this chapter has argued that it is only the direct methods that appear to be 'fit for purpose'. Chapter 3 thus reviewed the various direct survey methods available and reported the direct survey technique used by the author to conduct a survey of the nature of cash-in-hand work in English localities, the results of which have been used throughout this book to explain the contemporary anatomy of cash-in-hand work.

Socio-spatial variations in the nature of cash-in-hand work

Having both retheorised the character of cash-in-hand work and evaluated the available methodologies, Part II of the book then turned its attention to providing an analysis of how the nature of cash-in-hand work varies socially and spatially. Drawing upon empirical evidence from the advanced economies in general, and detailed evidence from the United Kingdom in particular, Chapter 4 commenced this evaluation by examining how cash-in-hand work varies according to the employment status of the participant. This revealed that the formally employed not only conduct more cash-in-hand work than the unemployed but also that the work that they undertake on a cash-in-hand basis is more frequently market-like and profit-motivated than amongst the unemployed where such work is more often embedded in social relations and motives akin to mutual aid. In other words, this chapter found that the cash-in-hand work of the employed is skewed towards the 'underground sector' and that of the unemployed towards the hidden economy of favours. Exploring the implications of this finding for comprehending social capital, it was asserted that although cash-in-hand work plays a relatively minor role in understanding social capital amongst employed populations, this is not the case amongst the unemployed. For this latter group, the hidden economy of favours represents a principal vehicle used to build bridging and bonding social capital and as such, to ignore it is to misunderstand the uneven contours of social capital in contemporary society as well as what needs to be done to bolster social capital amongst the unemployed.

Turning to the gender dimension, Chapter 5 then revealed that although men conduct slightly more cash-in-hand work than women, there are again some significant differences in the nature of the cash-in-hand work that they conduct. It found that when men engage in cash-in-hand work, it is much more likely to be of the market-orientated variety in the 'underground sector'. Women's cash-in-hand work, in contrast, is significantly more likely to be conducted for friends, neighbours and kin for rationales other than profit or, put another way, embedded in a social economy of favours. The implication, therefore, is that the low pay often identified amongst women when engaged in cash-in-hand work, although sometimes a result of their participation in exploitative organised forms of informal employment in the underground sector, is also due to their engagement in the social economy of favours where market rates seldom apply.

This finding again has implications for the study of social capital. Somewhat surprisingly for those who have assumed that it is women who hold together communities through their community participation, the social capital literature has so far failed to reveal that this is the case. Focusing upon involvement in unpaid community-based groups and the propensity of women and men to provide unpaid favours to neighbours, the majority of surveys have found little difference in participation rates between men and women. From this, it might be concluded that the view of women as providing the social glue that holds communities together is a myth. Here, however, it has been argued that one reason why this might not have been found is because this social capital literature has so far not considered the participation of women in the social economy of paid favours. The argument of this chapter has been that as monetised exchange has penetrated deeper into every corner of social life, it appears to have been the case that mutual aid that might have been previously conducted on an unpaid basis may well have been transferred into a paid realm of mutual aid. When such paid mutual aid is weaved into the equation, the assumption that women play a more significant role than men in building social capital has been shown to be more prevalent for it is women who conduct the majority of acts of paid mutual aid.

Chapter 6 then dealt with the geographical variations in the nature of cash-in-hand work. Until now, literature on the geographies of cash-in-hand work has concentrated on how its magnitude varies mostly on a cross-national level but also regionally and locally. Here, however, the focus was on identifying the geographical variations in the nature of cash-in-hand work. In the few instances where this has been previously considered, the conclusion has been that cash-in-hand work in deprived areas is characterised by low-paid exploitative forms of 'organised' cash-in-hand work conducted for informal or formal businesses, whilst cash-in-hand work in affluent areas tends to be composed of more 'autonomous' better paid forms of cash-in-hand work conducted on a self-employed basis. However, this chapter has shown that such a view of cash-in-hand work as being always embedded in market-like work relations akin to formal employment misrepresents not only the nature of cash-in-hand work but also the spatial heterogeneity of such work. Reporting evidence from a large-scale survey of English localities, Chapter 6 revealed that although cash-in-hand work in affluent areas is more likely to be conducted under work relations akin to employment and motivated by economic gain, in deprived areas the majority is undertaken for and by close social relations for redistributive and social reasons. In consequence, it was argued that there is a need to move towards a geographically embedded appreciation of the meanings of cash-in-hand work. Again, this has been shown to have implications for understanding social capital. Until now, the assumption has been that deprived areas have lower levels of social capital. Given that the culture of doing favours in deprived areas is deeply engrained with payment and that the provision of favours on an unpaid basis is often seen as a last resort, the chapter finds that the contours of social capital might be slightly more even than previously thought and importantly, argues that policy-making will need to much more fully take into account the culture of paying for favours in deprived neighbourhoods if it is to build social capital in such areas in a more effective manner than has so far been the case.

Synthesising these findings about the variable nature of cash-in-hand work across social groups and areas, Part II thus revealed that to conceptualise cash-in-hand work as profit-motivated market-like exchange is to read such work through the lens of, and to reflect the meanings of cash-in-hand work to, the employed, men and those living in affluent areas. It is not the meaning of such work for the unemployed, women and people living in deprived areas. To break out of the grip of such a narrow reading of cash-in-hand work, therefore, the message of Part II was that there is a need to recognise the existence of both an underground sector and a hidden economy of favours, and for appropriate policy approaches to be developed that recognise this heterogeneity.

Evaluating the implications of the policy options

Having provided this empirically grounded theorisation of the diverse and variable nature of cash-in-hand work, Part III turned its attention to evaluating the implications of pursuing various policy options with regard to cash-in-hand work. Showing how there exists both an underground economy and a hidden economy of favours, the key issue raised here was how this work could be dealt with in a way that retained the positive benefits of each form of work whilst eradicating the negative consequences. For example, although the underground sector possesses many negative consequences (e.g. loss of state revenue, dumping of wages, weakening of collective bargaining and trade unions, unfair competitive advantage, hypercasualisation, loss of regulatory control, lack of health and safety, low wages, exploitation, loss of employment rights), there are some positive aspects (e.g. it is a seedbed for microenterprise, a route to participation in the formal labour market). Similarly, the hidden economy of favours although having many positive features (e.g. enabling people to be active citizens, providing a coping practice, source of social capital and social cohesion and vehicle for meeting material and social needs) also possesses a number of negative aspects (e.g. it is illegitimate activity that involves tax and social security fraud, and its distribution is highly uneven with a significant minority unable to access such support).

Given these positive and negative features, three policy options have been here reviewed in terms of their implications. These are the policy options of deterrence through increasing detection and punishment, laissez-faire and harnessing such work. Starting with the option of deterring cash-in-hand work, Chapter 7 argued that this not only fails to recognise the positive assets of the underground sector but also is both impractical and undesirable. It is impractical because the work in the hidden economy of favours is heavily embedded in everyday life and it is undesirable because such paid mutual aid is one of the principal vehicles through which both redistribution occurs and social capital is forged and cemented in contemporary societies, especially amongst deprived populations where cash for favours is part of the culture of exchange.

Second, therefore, a laissez-faire approach towards cash-in-hand work was reviewed in Chapter 8. If this is pursued, however, it was shown that not only would the underground sector persist, which possesses exploitative work conditions and defrauds the state of revenue that could be used for social cohesion purposes, but such an approach would also fail to help those currently excluded from the hidden economy of favours gain access to such aid as an additional coping practice to meet their material and social needs. Neither would a combining of deterrence with *laissez-faire* maximise the positive consequences of these spheres whilst minimizing the negative impacts. A *laissez-faire* approach towards the underground sector and a deterrence approach towards the hidden economy of favours is perhaps the worst possible option. It would leave intact the host of negative consequences resulting from the underground sector whilst attempting to obliterate the numerous positive impacts that result from paid mutual aid.

A deterrence approach towards the underground sector and *laissez-faire* approach towards the hidden economy of favours, meanwhile, was seen as being hindered by three key problems. First, it would be very difficult for state actors to identify what cash-in-hand work was being conducted in which sphere. Although some forms of cash-in-hand work such as informal or formal businesses working on a cash-in-hand basis are easily categorised as operating in the underground sector, it becomes much more difficult once one starts examining individuals conducting cash-in-hand on an autonomous basis. Whether they are acting as self-employed people working in the underground sector or as individuals engaged in mutual aid to help others would be difficult to decipher. A second problem with this approach is that adopting a *laissez-faire* approach towards the hidden economy of favours leaves intact the inequalities that presently exist in this sphere. A significant minority of the population are currently excluded from drawing upon the resources of this social economy of favours as a coping practice in order to meet their material and social needs. To adopt such a *laissez-faire* approach is thus to leave intact these disparities. Third and finally, deterrence has been shown to be not only an ineffective way of preventing engagement in the underground sector but also an approach that fails to recognise and harness some of the more positive aspects of engagement in this sphere. For these reasons alone, it was thus argued that the policy option of a deterrence approach towards the underground sector and a *laissez-faire* approach towards the social economy of favours is inappropriate.

In Chapter 9, therefore, a third policy option was introduced, namely that of 'harnessing' such work. Arguing that the emerging literature is quite correct to view such work not as an obstacle to modernisation but, rather, as a driver for economic development (e.g. Global Employment Forum, 2001; International Labour Office, 2002; Tabak, 2000), it nevertheless takes issue with the notion in this literature that 'cultivating' or 'harnessing' cash-in-hand work means transforming it into formal employment. The realisation that cash-in-hand work is composed of both an underground sector and a hidden economy of favours is here argued to necessitate some significant modifications to this emergent literature on how to harness such work.

It has been argued that although it is appropriate to argue that both forms of cash-in-hand work need to be harnessed, what is meant by 'harnessed' markedly varies according to the form of cash-in-hand work being discussed. In the realm of the underground sector, that is, 'harnessing' indeed needs to refer to transforming such work into formal employment but this is not the case with the hidden economy of favours. Here, and given the character of this type of cash-in-hand work, the meaning of 'harnessing' such work refers to the very different process of transferring paid mutual aid out of the illegal cash-in-hand realm into a sphere of legitimate paid mutual aid.

The argument is that by seeking to harness both, albeit in different ways, one avoids the problems of deciphering whether activity conducted by individuals is underground activity or conducted in the social economy of favours. The chapter then set out a number of possible policy initiatives that could be used to transfer the underground sector into formal employment and the hidden economy of favours into legitimate mutual aid and that might retain the positive aspects of these spheres whilst minimizing or resolving their negative implications.

Conclusions

In sum, by rereading cash-in-hand work through the lens of the contemporary cultural literature on monetised exchange that has shown how not all monetised exchange is market-like and profit-motivated, this book has significantly contributed to understandings of cash-in-hand work. With the on-going penetration of monetised exchange into every crevice of daily life, this book has uncovered that one result is that alongside the conventional cash-in-hand work that is market-like and profit-motivated (the underground sector) has emerged a realm where cash payments are starting to become more common in situations where previously they would have had no place. In this moral economy of paid favours, cash is changing hands amongst friends, kin and neighbours. These contrasting types of cash-in-hand work, however, are variably distributed. Amongst the employed, men and affluent areas, cash-in-hand work is more likely to be conducted in the underground sector while amongst the unemployed, women and deprived areas, such work is more oriented towards the hidden economy of favours.

Given this finding about the diverse and variable nature of cash-in-hand work, a variegated or twin-track policy approach has been advocated. Resonating with the emergent approaches that view cash-in-hand work as an asset to be harnessed rather than an obstacle to be eradicated, this book has called for a more positive approach that seeks to facilitate the transfer of the underground sector and hidden economy of favours into formal employment and legitimate forms of paid mutual aid respectively. Indeed, such a shift in policy towards cash-in-hand work has been argued to be a necessity. At present, governments intent on deterring what is viewed as profit-motivated informal employment have been shown here to be unintentionally destroying social capital in deprived populations. Unless 'joined up' thinking is now pursued in relation to what has been previously considered separate policy spheres, then governments will with each new initiative to deter cash-in-hand work in deprived populations in equal measure destroy the social capital that they wish to develop.

References

Abrahamson, P. (1992) 'Welfare pluralism: towards a new consensus for a European social policy?', in L. Hantrais, M. O'Brien and S. Mangen (eds), *The Mixed Economy of Welfare*, Cross-National Research Paper no. 6, Loughborough: European Research Centre, Loughborough University.

Ahn, N. and Rica, S.D.L. (1997) 'The underground economy in Spain: an alternative to unemployment?', *Applied Economics*, 29, 6: 733–43.

Aitken, S. and Bonneville, E. (1980) *A General Taxpayer Opinion Survey*, Washington, DC: CSR Inc.

Alden, J. (1982) 'A comparative analysis of moonlighting in Great Britain and the USA', *Industrial Relations Journal*, 13: 21–31.

Allingham, M. and Sandmo, A. (1972) 'Income tax evasion: a theoretical analysis', *Journal of Public Economics*, 1: 323–38.

Amado, J. and Stoffaes, C. (1980) 'Vers une socio-economie duale', in A. Danzin, A. Boublil and J. Lagarde (eds), *La Societe Francaise et la Technologie*, Paris: Documentation Francaise.

Amin, A. (1994) 'The difficult transition from informal economy to Marshallian industrial district', *Area*, 26, 1: 13–24.

Amin, A. and Thrift, N. (2000) 'What kind of economic theory for what kind of economic geography?', *Antipode*, 32, 1: 4–9.

Amin, S. (1996) 'On development: for Gunder Frank', in S.C. Chew and R.A. Denmark (eds), *The Underdevelopment of Development*, London: Sage.

Anderson, B. (2001a) 'Why madam has so many bathrobes: demand for migrant domestic workers in the EU', *Tijdschrift voor Economische en Sociale Geografie*, 92, 1: 18–26.

Anderson, B. (2001b) 'Different roots in common ground: trans-nationalism and migrant domestic workers in London', *Journal of Ethnic and Migration Studies*, 27, 4: 673–83.

Arnstein, S. (1969) 'A ladder of citizen participation', *Journal of the American Institute of Planners*, 35: 216–24.

Ashworth, K. and Youngs, R. (2002) *Prospects of Part-time Work: the impact of the back-to-work bonus*, Research Report No. 115, London: Department of Work and Pensions.

Atkins, F.J. (1999) 'Macroeconomic time series and the monetary aggregates approach to estimating the underground economy', *Applied Economics Letters*, 6, 9: 609–11.

Atkinson, A. and Micklewright, J. (1991) 'Unemployment compensation and labour market transitions: a critical review', *Journal of Economic Literature*, 29: 1679–727.

Atkinson, A.B. (1995) *Public Economics in Action: the basic income/flat tax proposal*, Oxford: Oxford University Press.

Bajada, C. (2002) *Australia's Cash Economy: a troubling issue for policymakers*, Aldershot: Ashgate.

Barnes, H., North, P. and Walker, P. (1996) *LETS on Low Income*, London: New Economics Foundation.

Barr, N. (1992) 'Economic theory and the welfare state: a survey and interpretation', *Journal of Economic Literature*, 30: 741–803.

Barthe, M.A. (1985) 'Chomage, travail au noir et entraide familial', *Consommation*, 3: 23–42.

Barthe, M.A. (1988) *L'Economie Cachee*, Paris: Syros Alternatives.

Barthelemy, P. (1991) 'La croissance de l'economie souterraine dans les pays occidentaux: un essai d'interpretation', in J-L. Lespes (ed.), *Les Pratiques Juridiques, Economiques et Sociales Informelles*, Paris: PUF.

Beatson, M. (1995) *Memories of Class*, London: Routledge.

Beck, U. (2000) *The Brave New World of Work*, Cambridge: Polity.

Bennington, J., Baine, S. and Russell, J. (1992) 'The impact of the Single European Market on regional and local economic development and the voluntary and community sectors', in L. Hantrais, M. O'Brien and S. Mangen (eds), *The Mixed Economy of Welfare*, Cross-National Research Paper no. 6, Loughborough: European Research Centre, University of Loughborough.

Benton, L. (1990) *Invisible Factories: the informal economy and industrial development in Spain*, New York: State University of New York Press.

Berking, H. (1999) *Sociology of Giving*, London: Sage.

Bernabe, S. (2002) *Informal Employment in Countries in Transition: a conceptual framework*, CASE paper no. 56, London: Centre for Analysis of Social Exclusion.

Bhattacharyya, D.K. (1990) 'An econometric method of estimating the hidden economy, United Kingdom (1960–1984): estimates and tests', *The Economic Journal*, 100: 703–17.

Bhattacharyya, D.K. (1999) 'On the economic rationale of estimating the hidden economy', *The Economic Journal*, 109, 456: 348–59.

Biggs, T., Grindle, M.D. and Snodgrass, D.R. (1988) *The Informal Sector, Policy Reform and Structural Transformation*, EEPA Discussion Paper no. 14, Cambridge, MA: Harvard Institute for International Development.

Blair, J.P. and Endres, C.R. (1994) 'Hidden economic development assets', *Economic Development Quarterly*, 8, 3: 286–91.

Blau, P.M. (1994) *Structural Contexts of Opportunities*, Chicago: University of Chicago Press.

Boren, T. (2003) 'What are friends for? Rationales of informal exchange in Russian everyday life', in K. Arnstberg and T. Boren (eds), *Everyday Economy in Russia, Poland and Latvia*, Stockholm: Almqvist and Wiksell International.

Boris, E. and Prugl, E. (1996) 'Introduction', in E. Boris and E. Prugl (eds), *Homeworkers in Global Perspective: invisible no more*, London: Routledge.

Borocz, J. (1989) 'Mapping the class structures of state socialism in East-Central Europe', *Research in Social Stratification and Mobility*, 8: 279–309.

Bourdieu, P. (2001) 'The forms of capital', in N. Woolsey Biggart (ed.), *Readings in Economic Sociology*, Oxford: Blackwell.

Boyle, D. (1999) *Funny Money: in search of alternative cash*, London: Harper Collins.

Briscoe, I. (1995) *In Whose Service? Making community service work for the unemployed*, London: Demos.

Bunker, N. and Dewberry, C. (1984) 'Unemployment behind closed doors', *Journal of Community Education*, 2, 4: 31–3.

Burawoy, M. and Lukacs, J. (1985) 'Mythologies of work: a comparison of firms in state socialism and advanced capitalism', *American Sociological Review*, 50: 723–37.

Burns, D. and Taylor, M. (1998) *Mutual Aid and Self-Help: coping strategies for excluded communities*, Bristol: The Policy Press.

Burns, D., Williams, C.C. and Windebank, J. (2004) *Community Self-Help*, Basingstoke: Palgrave.

Button, K. (1984) 'Regional variations in the irregular economy: a study of possible trends', *Regional Studies*, 18: 385–92.

Byrne, K., Forest, R., Gibson-Graham, J.K., Healy, S. and Horvath, G. (1998) *Imagining and Enacting Non-Capitalist Futures*, Rethinking Economy Project Working Paper no. 1, http//:www.arts.monash.edu.au/projects/cep/knowledges/byrne.html

Cabinet Office (2001) *A New Commitment to Neighbourhood Renewal: National Strategy Action Plan*, report by the Social Exclusion Unit, London: Cabinet Office.

Cahn, E. (1994) 'Reinventing poverty law', *Yale Law Journal*, 103, 8: 2133–55.

Cahn, E. (2000) *No More Throw-Away People: the co-production imperative*, Washington, DC: Essential Books.

Cahn, E. and Rowe, J. (1992) *Time Dollars: the new currency that enables Americans to turn their hidden resource – time – into personal security and community renewal*, Chicago: Family Resource Coalition of America.

Cancedda, A. (2001) *Employment in Household Services*, Dublin: European Foundation for the Improvement of Living and Working Conditions.

Cappechi, V. (1989) 'The informal economy and the development of flexible specialisation in Emilia Romagna', in A. Portes, M. Castells and L.A. Benton (eds), *The Informal Economy: studies in advanced and less developing countries*, Baltimore: John Hopkins University Press.

Caridi, P. and Passerini, P. (2001) 'The underground economy, the demand for currency approach and the analysis of discrepancies: some recent European experience', *The Review of Income and Wealth*, 47, 2: 239–50.

Carrier, J.G. (1997) (ed.) *Meanings of the Market: the free market in western culture*, Oxford: Berg.

Carrier, J.G. (1998) 'Introduction', in J.G. Carrier and D. Miller (eds), *Virtualism: a new political economy*, Oxford: Berg.

Carruthers, B.G. and Babb, S.L. (2000) *Economy/Society: markets, meanings and social structure*, Thousand Oaks, CA: Pine Oaks.

Carter, M. (1984) 'Issues in the hidden economy: a survey', *Economic Record*, 60, 170: 209–21.

Castells, M. and Portes, A. (1989) 'World underneath: the origins, dynamics and effects of the informal economy', in A. Portes, M. Castells and L.A. Benton (eds), *The Informal Economy: studies in advanced and less developing countries*, Baltimore: John Hopkins University Press.

Cattell, V. and Evans, M. (1999) *Neighbourhood Images in East London: social capital and social networks on two East London estates*, York: York Publishing Services.

CENSIS (1976) 'L'occupazione occulta-carratteristiche della partecipazione al lavoro in Italia', cited in Frey, B.S. and Pommerehne, W.W. (eds) (1984) 'The Hidden economy: state and prospects for measurement', *Review of Income and Wealth*, 30, 1: 1–23.

Chavdarova, T. (2002) 'The informal economy in Bulgaria: historical background and present situation', in R. Neef and M. Stanuclescu (eds), *The Social Impact of Informal Economies in Eastern Europe*, Aldershot: Ashgate.

Ciscel, D.H. and Heath, J.A. (2001) 'To market, to market: imperial capitalism's destruction of social capital and the family', *Review of Radical Political Economics*, 33: 401–14.

Cocco, M.R. and Santos, E. (1984) 'A economia subterranea: contributos para a sua analisee quanticacao no caso Portugues', *Buletin Trimestral do Banco de Portugal*, 6,1: 5–15.

Coffield, F., Borrill, C. and Marshall, S. (1983) 'How young people try to survive being unemployed', *New Society*, 2 June: 332–4.

Coleman, J. (1988) 'Social capital in the creation of human capital', *American Journal of Sociology*, (Supp.) 94: S95–120.

Collard, S., Kempson, E. and Whyley, C. (2001) *Tackling Financial Exclusion: an area-based approach*, Bristol: Policy Press.

Comelieau, C. (2002) *The Impasse of Modernity*, London: Zed.

Community Economies Collective (2001) 'Imagining and enacting noncapitalist futures', *Socialist Review*, 28: 93–135.

Conroy, P. (1996) *Equal Opportunities for All*, European Social Policy Forum Working Paper I, DG V, Brussels: European Commission.

Contini, B. (1982) 'The second economy in Italy', in V.V. Tanzi (ed.), *The Underground Economy in the United States and Abroad*, Lexington, MA: Lexington Books.

Cook, D. (1989) *Rich Law, Poor Law: different responses to tax and supplementary benefit fraud*, Milton Keynes: Open University Press.

Cook, D. (1997) *Poverty, Crime and Punishment*, London: Child Poverty Action Group.

Cornelius, W.A. (1992) 'From sojourners to settlers: the changing profile of Mexican immigration to the United States', in J.A. Bustamante, C.W. Reynolds and R.A. Hinojosa Oseda (eds), *US-Mexico Relations: labour market interdependence*, Stanford, CA: Stanford University Press.

Cornuel, D. and Duriez, B. (1985) 'Local exchange and state intervention', in N. Redclift and E. Mingione (eds), *Beyond Employment: household, gender and subsistence*, Oxford: Basil Blackwell.

Coulthard, M., Walker, A. and Morgan, A. (2002) *People's Perceptions of their Neighbourhood and Community Involvement: results from the social capital module of the General Household Survey 2000*, London: Home Office.

Crang, P. (1996) 'Displacement, consumption and identity', *Environment and Planning A*, 28: 47–67.

Crang, P. (1997) 'Cultural turns and the (re)constitution of economic geography', in R. Lee and J. Wills (eds), *Geographies of Economies*, London: Arnold.

Crewe, L. (2000) 'Geographies of retailing and consumption', *Progress in Human Geography*, 24, 2: 275–90.

Crewe, L. and Gregson, N. (1998) 'Tales of the unexpected: exploring car boot sales as marginal spaces of contemporary consumption', *Transactions*, 23, 1: 39–54.

Crnkovic-Pozaic, S. (1999) 'Measuring employment in the unofficial economy by using labor market data', in E.L. Feige and K. Ott (eds), *Underground Economies in Transition: unrecorded activity, tax evasion, corruption and organized crime*, Aldershot: Ashgate.

Crompton, R., Gallie, D. and Purcell, K. (1996) 'Work, economic restructuring and social regulation', in R. Crompton, D. Gallie and K. Purcell (eds), *Changing Forms of Employment: organisation, skills and gender*, London: Routledge.

Culpitt, I. (1992) *Welfare and Citizenship*, London: Sage.

Dagg, A. (1996) 'Organizing homeworkers into unions: the Homeworkers Association of Toronto, Canada', in E. Boris and E. Prugl (eds), *Homeworkers in Global Perspective: invisible no more*, London: Routledge.

Dallago, B. (1991) *The Irregular Economy: the 'underground' and the 'black' labour market*, Aldershot: Dartmouth.

Davies, J. (1992) *Exchange*, Milton Keynes: Open University Press.

Davies, R.B., Elias, P. and Penn, R. (1992) 'The relationship between a husband's unemployment and his wife's participation in the labour force', *Oxford Bulletin of Economics and Statistics*, 54,2: 145–71.

Davis Smith, J. (1998) *The 1997 National Survey of Volunteering*, London: Institute for Volunteering Research.

Dawes, L. (1993) *Long-Term Unemployment and Labour Market Flexibility*, Leicester: Centre for Labour Market Studies, University of Leicester.

De Grazia, R. (1982) 'Clandestine employment: a problem for our time' in V. Tanzi (ed.), *The Underground Economy in the United States and Abroad*, Lexington, MA: Lexington Books.

De Soto, H. (1989) *The Other Path*, London: Harper and Row.

Deakin, S. and Wilkinson, F. (1991/2) 'Social policy and economic efficiency: the deregulation of labour markets in Britain', *Critical Social Policy*, 33: 40–51.

Dean, H. and Melrose, M. (1996) 'Unravelling citizenship: the significance of social security benefit fraud', *Critical Social Policy*, 16: 3–31.

Dekker, P. and Van Den Broek, A. (1998) 'Civil society in comparative perspective: involvement in voluntary associations in North America and Western Europe', *Voluntas*, 9, 1: 11–38.

Del Boca, D. and Forte, F. (1982) 'Recent empirical surveys and theoretical interpretations of the parallel economy', in V. Tanzi (ed.), *The Underground Economy in the United States and Abroad*, Lexington, MA: Lexington Books.

Denison, E. (1982) 'Is US growth understated because of the underground economy? employment ratios suggest not', *Review of Income and Wealth*, 28, 1: 1–16.

Department for Work and Pensions (2003a) *Stepping Stones to Employment*, Research Report No. 71, London: Department for Work and Pensions.

Department for Work and Pensions (2003b) *Keeping in Touch with the Labour Market: qualitative evaluation of the back to work bonus*, Research Report No. 96, London: Department for Work and Pensions.

Department for Work and Pensions (2003c) *Prospects of Part-Time Work: the impact of the back to work bonus*, Research Report No. 115, London: Department for Work and Pensions.

Department of Local Government, Transport and the Regions (2000) *Index of Multiple Deprivation*, London: Department of Local Government, Transport and the Regions.

Dilnot, A. (1992) 'Social security and labour market policy', in I.E. McLaughlin (ed.), *Understanding Employment*, London: Routledge.

Dilnot, A. and Morris, C.N. (1981) 'What do we know about the black economy?', *Fiscal Studies*, 2: 58–73.

Dixon, H. (1999) 'Controversy: on the use of the "hidden economy" estimates', *The Economic Journal*, 109, 456: 335–7.

Dorling, D. and Woodward, R. (1996) 'Social polarisation 1971–1991: a micro-geographical analysis of Britain', *Progress in Planning*, 45, 2: 67–122.

Economist Intelligence Unit (1982) *Coping with Unemployment: the effects on the unemployed themselves*, London: Economist Intelligence Unit.

Elam, E. and Thomas, A. (1997) *Stepping Stones to Employment*, Department of Social Security Research Report no. 71, London: Department of Social Security.

Elkin, T. and McLaren, D. (1991) *Reviving the City: towards sustainable urban development*, London: Friends of the Earth.

Engbersen, G., Schuyt, K., Timmer, J. and Van Waarden, F. (1993) *Cultures of Unemployment: a comparative look at long-term unemployment and urban poverty*, San Francisco: Westview Press.

Esping-Andersen, G. (1994) 'Welfare states and the economy', in N.J. Smelser and R. Swedberg (eds), *The Handbook of Economic Sociology*, Princeton: Princeton University Press.

Esping-Andersen, G. (1996) 'After the golden age? Welfare state dilemmas in a global economy', in G. Esping-Anderson (ed.), *Welfare States in Transition: national adaptations in global economies*, London: Sage.

European Commission (1990) *Underground Economy and Irregular Forms of Employment*, Luxembourg: Office for Official Publications of the European Communities.

European Commission (1991) *Employment in Europe*, Luxembourg: Office for Official Publications of the European Communities.

European Commission (1995a) *The European Employment Strategy: recent progress and prospects for the future*, Luxembourg: Office for Official Publications of the European Communities.

European Commission (1995b) *Social Protection in Europe 1995*, Luxembourg: Office for Official Publications of the European Communities.

European Commission (1996a) *Employment in Europe 1996*, Luxembourg: European Commission DG for Employment, Industrial Relations and Social Affairs.

European Commission (1996b) *For a Europe of Civic and Social Rights: report by the Comite des Sages*, Luxembourg: European Commission DG for Employment, Industrial Relations and Social Affairs.

European Commission (1998) *On Undeclared Work*, COM (1998) 219, Brussels: Commission of the European Communities.

European Commission (2000a) *The Social Situation in the European Union 2000*, Brussels: European Commission.

European Commission (2000b) *Employment in Europe 2000*, Brussels: European Commission.

European Commission (2002) *Commission calls on governments to do more to fight the shadow economy*, Press release IP/02/339, Brussels: European Commission.

European Commission (2003) *European Commission proposes 10 priorities for employment reform*, Press release 0311, Brussels: European Commission.

Evason, E. and Woods, R. (1995) 'Poverty, deregulation of the labour market and benefit fraud', *Social Policy and Administration*, 29, 1: 40–55.

Fainstein, N. (1996) 'A note on interpreting American poverty', in E. Mingione (ed.), *Urban Poverty and the Underclass*, Oxford: Basil Blackwell.

Falkinger, J. (1988) 'Tax evasion and equity: a theoretical analysis', *Public Finance*, 43: 388–95.

Feige, E.L. (1979) 'How big is the irregular economy?', *Challenge*, November/December: 5–13.

Feige, E.L. (1990) 'Defining and estimating underground and informal economies', *World Development*, 18, 7: 989–1002.

Feige, E.L. (1999) 'Underground economies in transition: non-compliance and institutional change', in E.L. Feige and K. Ott (eds), *Underground Economies in Transition: unrecorded activity, tax evasion, corruption and organized crime*, Aldershot: Ashgate.

Feige, E.L. and Ott, K. (1999) 'Introduction', in E.L. Feige and K. Ott (eds), *Underground Economies in Transition: unrecorded activity, tax evasion, corruption and organized crime*, Aldershot: Ashgate.

Felt, L.F. and Sinclair, P.R. (1992) ' "Everyone does it": unpaid work in a rural peripheral region', *Work Employment and Society*, 6, 1: 43–64.

Ferman, L., Berndt, L. and Selo, E. (1978) *Analysis of the Irregular Economy: cash flow in the informal sector*, Detroit: University of Michigan-Wayne State University, Institute of Labour and Industrial Relations.

Fernandez-Kelly, M.P. and Garcia, A.M. (1989) 'Informalisation at the core: Hispanic women, homework, and the advanced capitalist state', *Environment and Planning D*, 8: 459–83.

Forrest, R. and Kearns, A. (1999) *Joined-up Places? Social cohesion and neighbourhood regeneration*, York: York Publishing Services.

Fortin, B., Garneau, G., Lacroix, G., Lemieux, T. and Montmarquette, C. (1996) *L'Economie Souterraine au Quebec: mythes et realites*, Laval: Presses de l'Universite Laval.

Foudi, R., Stankiewicz, F. and Vanecloo, N. (1982) *Chomeurs et Economie Informelle*, Cahiers de l'observation du changement social et culturel, no. 17, Paris: CNRS.

Frank, A.G. (1996) 'The underdevelopment of development', in S.C. Chew and R.A. Denemark (eds), *The Underdevelopment of Development*, London: Sage.

Freud, D. (1979) 'A guide to underground economics', *Financial Times*, 9 April: 16.

Frey, B.S. and Pommerhne, W.W. (1984) 'The hidden economy: state and prospects for measurement', *Review of Income and Wealth*, 30,1: 1–23.

Frey, B.S. and Weck, H. (1983) 'What produces a hidden economy? An international cross-section analysis', *Southern Economic Journal*, 49: 822–32.

Frey, B.S., Weck, H. and Pommerhne, W.W. (1982) 'Has the shadow economy grown in Germany? An exploratory study', *Weltwirtschaftliches Archiv*, 118: 499–524.

Friedman, E., Johnson, S., Kaufmann, D. and Zoido, P. (2000) 'Dodging the grabbing hand: the determinants of unofficial activity in 69 countries', *Journal of Public Economics*, 76, 3: 459–93.

Gabor, I.R. (1988) 'Second economy and socialism: the Hungarian experience', in E.L. Feige (ed.), *The Underground Economies*, Cambridge: Cambridge University Press.

Gadea, M.D. and Serrano-Sanz, J.M. (2002) 'The hidden economy in Spain: a monetary estimation, 1964–1998', *Empirical Economics*, 27, 3: 499–527.

Gallin, D. (2001) 'Propositions on trade unions and informal employment in time of globalisation', *Antipode*, 19: 531–49.

Gardiner, J. (1997) *Gender, Care and Economics*, Basingstoke: Macmillan.

Gershuny, J. (1985) 'Economic development and change in the mode of provision of services', in N. Redclift and E. Mingione (eds), *Beyond Employment: household, gender and subsistence*, Oxford: Basil Blackwell.

Gershuny, J., Godwin, M. and Jones, S. (1994) 'The domestic labour revolution: a process of lagged adaptation', in M. Anderson, F. Bechhofer and J. Gershuny (eds),

The Social and Political Economy of the Household, Oxford: Oxford University Press.

Gibson-Graham, J.K. (1996) *The End of Capitalism as We Knew It? A feminist critique of political economy*, Oxford: Blackwell.

Gibson-Graham, J.K. and Ruccio, D. (2001) ' "After" development: re-imagining economy and class', in J.K. Gibson-Graham, S. Resnick and R. Wolff (eds), *Re/presenting Class: essays in post-modern Marxism*, London: Duke University Press.

Gilbert, A. (1994) 'Third world cities: poverty, unemployment, gender roles and the environment during a time of restructuring', *Urban Studies*, 31, 4/5: 605–33.

Gilder, G. (1981) *Wealth and Poverty*, New York: Basic Books.

Giles, D.E.A. (1999) 'Measuring the hidden economy: implications for econometric modelling', *The Economic Journal*, 109, 456: 370–80.

Giles, D.E.A. and Caragata, P.J. (2001) 'The learning path of the hidden economy: the tax burden and tax evasion in New Zealand', *Applied Economics*, 33, 14: 1857–67.

Giles, D.E.A. and Johnson, B.J. (2002) 'Taxes, risk aversion, and the size of the underground economy', *Pacific Economic Review*, 7, 1: 97–113.

Gittell, R. and Vidal, A. (1998) *Community Organizing: building social capital as a development strategy*, London: Sage.

Glatzer, W. and Berger, R. (1988) 'Household composition, social networks and household production in Germany', in R.E. Pahl (ed.), *On Work: historical, comparative and theoretical approaches*, Oxford: Basil Blackwell.

Global Employment Forum (2001) *Informal Economy: formalizing the hidden potential and raising standards*, Session III-C, Global Employment Forum 1–3 November 2001, Geneva: ILO (last accessed 23 October 2003, http://oracle02.ilo.org/public/english/employment/geforum/informal.htm).

Gough, I. (2000) *Global Capital, Human Needs and Social Policies*, Basingstoke: Palgrave.

Grabiner, Lord (2000) *The Informal Economy*, London: HM Treasury.

Granovetter, M. (1973) 'The strength of weak ties', *American Journal of Sociology*, 78, 6: 1360–80.

Gray, J. (1984) *Hayek on Liberty*, Oxford: Blackwell.

Green, A.E. and Owen, D. (1998) *Where are the Jobless? Changing unemployment and non-employment in cities and regions*, York: The Policy Press.

Gregg, P. and Wadsworth, J. (1996) *It Takes Two: employment polarisation in the OECD*, Discussion Paper no. 304, London: Centre for Economic Performance, London School of Economics.

Gregory, A. and Windebank, J. (2000) *Women and Work in France and Britain: theory, practice and policy*, Basingstoke: Macmillan.

Gregson, N. and Lowe, M. (1994) *Servicing the Middle Classes*, London: Routledge.

Grossman, G. (1989) 'Informal personal incomes and outlays of the Soviet urban population', in A. Portes, M. Castells and L.A. Benton (eds), *The Informal Economy: studies in advanced and less developing countries*, Baltimore: John Hopkins University Press.

Gudeman, S. (2001) *The Anthropology of Economy*, Oxford: Blackwell.

Gutmann, P.M. (1977) 'The subterranean economy', *Financial Analysts Journal*, 34, 11: 26–7.

Gutmann, P.M. (1978) 'Are the unemployed, unemployed?', *Financial Analysts Journal*, 34, 1: 26–9.

Hadjimichalis, C. and Vaiou, D. (1989) 'Whose flexibility?: The politics of informalisation in Southern Europe', Paper presented to the IAAD/SCG Study Groups of the IBG Conference on *Industrial Restructuring and Social Change: the dawning of a new era of flexible accumulation?*, Durham.

Hakim, C. (1995) 'Five feminist myths about women's employment,' *British Journal of Sociology*, 46: 429–55.

Hansson, I. (1982) 'The underground economy in Sweden', in Tanzi, V. (ed.), *The Underground Economy in the United States and Abroad*, Massachusetts: Lexington Books.

Harding, P. and Jenkins, R. (1989) *The Myth of the Hidden Economy: towards a new understanding of informal economic activity*, Milton Keynes: Open University Press.

Hart, K. (1973) 'Informal income opportunities and urban employment in Ghana', *Journal of Modern African Studies*, 11: 61–89.

Hart, K. (1990) 'The idea of economy: six modern dissenters', in R. Friedland and A.F. Robertson (eds), *Beyond the Marketplace: rethinking economy and society*, New York: Aldine de Gruyter.

Harvey, D. (1982) *The Limits to Capital*, Oxford: Blackwell.

Harvey, D. (1989) *The Condition of Post-Modernity: an enquiry into the origins of cultural change*, Oxford: Blackwell.

Hasseldine, D. and Bebbington, K. (1991) 'Blending economic deterrence and fiscal psychology models in the design of response to tax evasion: the New Zealand experience', *Journal of Economic Psychology*, 12, 2: 2–19.

Hasseldine, J. and Zhuhong, L. (1999) 'More tax evasion research required in new millennium', *Crime, Law and Social Change*, 31: 91–104.

Haughton, G., Johnson, S., Murphy, L. and Thomas, K. (1993) *Local Geographies of Unemployment: long-term unemployment in areas of local deprivation*, Aldershot: Avebury.

Hellberger, C. and Schwarze, J. (1986) *Umfang und struktur der nebenerwerbstatigkeit in der Bundesrepublik Deutschland*, Berlin: Mitteilungen aus der Arbeitsmarket-und Berufsforschung.

Hellberger, C. and Schwarze, J. (1987) 'Nebenerwerbstatigkeit: ein indikator fur arbeitsmarkt-flexibilitat oder schattenwirtschaft', *Wirtschaftsdienst*, 2: 83–90.

Henry, J. (1976) 'Calling in the big bills', *Washington Monthly*, 5: 6.

Henry, S. (1978) *The Hidden Economy*, London: Martin Robertson.

Henry, S. (1982) 'The working unemployed: perspectives on the informal economy and unemployment', *Sociological Review*, 30, 3: 460–77.

Hessing, D., Elffers, H., Robben, H. and Webley, P. (1993) 'Needy or greedy? The social pyschology of individuals who fraudulently claim unemployment benefits', *Journal of Applied Social Psychology*, 23, 3: 226–43.

Hill, R. (2002) The underground economy in Canada: boom or bust?, *Canadian Tax Journal*, 50, 5: 1641–54.

Himmelweit, S. (2000) (ed.) *Inside the Household: from labour to care*, Basingstoke: Macmillan.

HM Customs and Excise (2003) *Our fight against smuggling, tax fraud and crime* (last accessed 23 October 2003 http://www.hmce.gov.uk).

Home Office (1999) *Community Self-Help – Policy Action Team no. 9*, London: Home Office.

Home Office (2002) *Income Tax Self-Assessment*, Report no. 33, London: HMSO.

Home Office (2003a) *Tackling Benefit Fraud*, Report no. 31, London: HMSO.

Home Office (2003b) *Prevention of Illegal Working: proposed changes to document list under section 8 of the Asylum and Immigration Act 1996, Consultation from the Immigration and Nationality Directorate of the Home Office*, London: Home Office.

Houghton, D. (1979) 'The futility of taxation menaces', in A. Seldon (ed.), *Tax Avoision*, London: Institute of Economic Affairs.

Howe, L. (1988) 'Unemployment, doing the double and local labour markets in Belfast', in C. Cartin and T. Wilson (eds), *Ireland from Below: social change and local communities in modern Ireland*, Dublin: Gill and Macmillan.

Howe, L. (1990) *Being Unemployed in Northern Ireland: an ethnographic study*, Cambridge: Cambridge University Press.

Hoyman, M. (1987) 'Female participation in the informal economy: a neglected issue', *Annals of the American Academy of Political and Social Science*, 493: 64–82.

Husband, J. and Jerrard, B. (2001) 'Formal aid in an informal sector: institutional support for ethnic minority enterprise in local clothing and textiles industries', *Journal of Ethnic and Migration Studies*, 27,1: 115–131.

Hutton, W. (1995) *The State We're In*, London: Vintage.

Illie, S. (2002) 'Formal and informal incomes of the Romanian households', in R. Neef and M. Stanuclescu (eds), *The Social Impact of Informal Economies in Eastern Europe*, Aldershot: Ashgate.

International Labour Office (1972) *Employment, Incomes and Equality: a strategy for increasing productive employment in Kenya*, Geneva: International Labour Office.

International Labour Office (1991) *The Dilemma of the Informal Sector*, report of the Director-General, International Labour Conference 78th Session, Geneva: International Labour Office.

International Labour Office (1996) *World Employment 1996–97: national policies in a global context*, Geneva: International Labour Office.

International Labour Office (2002) *Decent Work and the Informal Economy*, Geneva: International Labour Office.

Isachsen, A.J. and Strom, S. (1985) 'The size and growth of the hidden economy in Norway', *Review of Income and Wealth*, 31,1: 21–38.

Isachsen, A.J., Klovland, J.T. and Strom, S. (1982) 'The hidden economy in Norway', in V. Tanzi (ed.), *The Underground Economy in the United Sates and Abroad*, Lexington, KY: D.C. Heath.

Izquierdo, M.J., Miguelez, F. and Subirats, M. (1987) *Enquesta Metropolitana, vol. I Informe general*, Barcelona: Instituto de Estudios Metropolitanos de Barcelona.

Jensen, L., Cornwell, G.T. and Findeis, J.L. (1995) 'Informal work in nonmetropolitan Pennsylvania', *Rural Sociology*, 60,1: 91–107.

Jessop, B. (2002) *The Future of the Capitalist State*, Cambridge: Polity.

Jordan, B. (1998) *The New Politics of Welfare: social justice in a global context*, London: Sage.

Jordan, B. and Redley, M. (1994) 'Polarisation, underclass and the welfare state', *Work, Employment and Society*, 8, 2: 153–76.

Jordan, B. and Travers, A. (1998) 'The informal economy: a case study in unrestrained competition', *Social Policy and Administration*, 32, 3: 292–306.

Jordan, B., Agulnik, P., Burbridge, D. and Duffin, S. (2000) *Stumbling Towards Basic Income: the prospects for tax-benefit integration*, London: Citizen's Income Study Centre.

Jordan, B., James, S., Kay, H. and Redley, M. (1992) *Trapped in Poverty? Labour-market decision in low-income households*, London: Routledge.

Keenan, A. and Dean, P.N. (1980) 'Moral evaluation of tax evasion', *Social Policy and Administration*, 14: 209–20.

Kempson, E. (1996) *Life on a Low Income*, York: York Publishing Services.

Kempson, E. and Whyley, C. (1999) *Kept Out or Opted Out: understanding and combating financial exclusion*, Bristol: Policy Press.

Kesteloot, C. and Meert, H. (1994) 'Les fonctions socio-economiques de l'economie informelle et son implantation spatiale dans les villes belges', Paper presented to International Conference on *Cities, Enterprises and Society at the Eve of the XXIst Century*, Lille.

Kesteloot, C. and Meert, H. (1999) 'Informal spaces: the geography of informal economic activities in Brussels', *International Journal of Urban and Regional Research*, 23: 232–51.

Kinsey, K. (1992) 'Deterrence and alienation effects of IRS enforcement: an analysis of survey data', in J. Slemrod (ed.), *Why People Pay Taxes*, Michigan: University of Michigan Press.

Kirchgaessner, G. (1981) 'Verfahren zur Erfassung der grobe und Entwicklung des schattensektors, eidenossische technische hochschule Zurich', cited in Frey BS *et al.* (ed.), (1982) 'Has the shadow economy grown in Germany? An exploratory study', *Weltwirtschaftliches Archiv*, 118: 499–524.

Kitchen, R. and Tate, N. (2001) *Conducting Research in Human Geography: theory, practice and methodology*, London: Prentice-Hall.

Komter, A.E. (1996) 'Reciprocity as a principle of exclusion: gift giving in the Netherlands', *Sociology*, 30,2: 299–316.

Koopmans, C.C. (1989) *Informele Arbeid: vraag, aanbod, participanten, prijzen*, Amsterdam: Proefschrift Universitiet van Amsterdam.

Kovel, J. (2002) *The Enemy of Nature: the end of capitalism or the end of the world?* London: Zed.

Krishnamurthy, A., Prime, D. and Zimmeck, M. (2001) *Voluntary and Community Activities: findings from the 2000 British Crime Survey*, London: Home Office.

Lacko, M. (1999) 'Electricity intensity and the unrecorded economy in post-socialist countries', in E.L. Feige and K. Ott (eds), *Underground Economies in Transition: unrecorded activity, tax evasion, corruption and organized crime*, Aldershot: Ashgate.

Lagos, R.A. (1995) 'Formalising the informal sector: barriers and costs', *Development and Change*, 26: 110–31.

Laguerre, M.S. (1994) *The Informal City*, London: Macmillan.

Langfelt, E. (1989) 'The underground economy in the Federal republic of Germany: a preliminary assessment', in E.L. Feige (ed.), *The Underground Economies: tax evasion and information distortion*, Cambridge: Cambridge University Press.

Leadbeater, C. and Martin, S. (1997) *The Employee Mutual: combining flexibility with security in the new world of work*, London: Demos.

Lee, R. (1996) 'Moral money? LETS and the social construction of local economic geographies in Southeast England', *Environment and Planning A*, 28: 1377–94.

Lee, R. (1997) 'Economic geographies: representations and interpretations', in R. Lee and J. Wills (eds), *Geographies of Economies*, London: Edward Arnold.

Lee, R. (2000a) 'Informal sector', in R.J. Johnston, D. Gregory, G. Pratt and M. Watts (eds), *The Dictionary of Human Geography*, Oxford: Blackwell.

Lee, R. (2000b) 'Shelter from the storm? Geographies of regard in the worlds of horticultural consumption and production', *Geoforum*, 31: 137–57.

Lemieux, T., Fortin, B. and Frechette, P. (1994) 'The effect of taxes on labor supply in the underground economy', *American Economic Review*, 84, 1: 231–54.

Leonard, M. (1994) *Informal Economic Activity in Belfast*, Aldershot: Avebury.

Leonard, M. (1998a) 'The long-term unemployed, informal economic activity and the underclass in Belfast: rejecting or reinstating the work ethic', *International Journal of Urban and Regional Research*, 22, 1: 42–59.

Leonard, M. (1998b) *Invisible Work, Invisible Workers: the informal economy in Europe and the US*, London: Macmillan.

Leonard, M. (2000) 'Coping Strategies in developed and developing Societies: the workings of the informal economy', *Journal of International Development*, 12, 8: 1069–85.

Leontidou, L. (1993) 'Informal strategies of unemployment relief in Greek cities: the relevance of family, locality and housing', *European Planning Studies*, 1, 1: 43–68.

Leyshon, A. and Thrift, N.J. (1994) 'Geographies of financial exclusion: financial abandonment in Britain and the United States', *Transactions of the Institute of British Geographers*, 20: 312–41.

Leyshon, A., Lee, R. and Williams, C.C. (2003) (eds), *Alternative Economic Spaces*, London: Sage.

Liebman, J. (1998) *Lessons about Tax-Benefit Integration from the US Earned Income Tax Credit experience*, York: York Publishing Services.

Lin, J. (1995) 'Polarized development and urban change in New York's Chinatown', *Urban Affairs Review*, 30, 3: 332–54.

Lindbeck, A. (1981) *Work Disincentives in the Welfare State*, Stockholm: Institute for International Economic Studies, University of Stockholm.

Lipietz, A. (1992) *Towards a New Economic Order: post-fordism, ecology and democracy*, Cambridge: Polity.

Lipietz, A. (1995) *Green Hopes: the future of political ecology*, Cambridge: Polity.

Lobo, F.M. (1990a) 'Irregular work in Spain', in *Underground Economy and Irregular Forms of Employment*, Final Synthesis Report, Brussels: Office for Official Publications of the European Communities.

Lobo, F.M. (1990b) 'Irregular work in Portugal', in *Underground Economy and Irregular Forms of Employment, Final Synthesis Report*, Brussels: Office for Official Publications of the European Communities.

Lodemel, I. and Trickey, H. (2001) *An Offer You Can't Refuse: workfare in international perspective*, Bristol: The Policy Press.

Lomnitz, L.A. (1988) 'Informal exchange networks in formal systems: a theoretical model', *American Anthropologist*, 90: 42–55.

Lopez, C. (1986) *El Textil Irregulkar en Terrassa 1975–1985*, Terrassa: Ajuntament de Terrassa.

Lozano, B. (1989) *The Invisible Workforce: transforming American business with outside and home-based workers*, New York: The Free Press.

Lysestol, P.M. (1995) ' "The other economy" and its influences on job-seeking behaviour for the long term unemployed', Paper presented at the Euroconference on *Social Policy in an environment of insecurity*, Lisbon, November.

Macafee, K. (1980) 'A glimpse of the hidden economy in the national accounts' *Economic Trends*, 2: 81–7.

MacDonald, R. (1994) 'Fiddly jobs, undeclared working and the something for nothing society', *Work, Employment and Society*, 8,4: 507–30.

MacGillivray, A., Conaty, P. and Wadhams, C. (2001) *Low Flying Heroes: micro-social enterprise below the radar screen*, London: New Economics Foundation.

Maguire, K. (1993) 'Fraud, extortion and racketeering: the black economy in Northern Ireland', *Crime, Law and Social Change*, 20: 273–92.

Maldonado, C. (1995) 'The informal sector: legalization or laissez-faire?' *International Labour Review*, 134,6: 705–28.

Maloney, W.F. (1999) 'Does informality imply segmentation in urban labor markets? Evidence from sectoral transitions in Mexico', *The World Bank Economic Review* 13,2: 275–302.

Marcelli, E.A., Pastor, M. and Joassart, P.M. (1999) 'Estimating the effects of informal economic activity: evidence from Los Angeles County', *Journal of Economic Issues*, 33: 579–607.

Marie, C-V. (1999) 'Emploi des etrangers sans titre, travail illegal, regularisations: des debates en trompe-l'oeil', in P. Dewitte (ed.), *Immigration et Integration l'Etat des Savoirs*, Paris: Harmattan.

Marie, C-V. (2000) 'Measures taken to combat the employment of undocumented foreign workers in France: their place in the campaign against illegal employment and their results', in OECD (ed.), *Combating the illegal employment of foreign workers*, Paris: OECD.

Martino, A. (1981) 'Measuring Italy's underground economy', *Policy Review*, Spring: 87–106.

Matemen, S. and Renooy, P.H (2001) *Undeclared Labour in Europe: towards an integrated approach of combatting undeclared labour*, Amsterdam: Regioplan.

Mattera, P. (1980) 'Small is not beautiful: decentralised production and the underground economy in Italy', *Radical America*, 14, 5: 67–76.

Mattera, P. (1985) *Off the Books: the rise of the underground economy*, New York: St Martin's Press.

Matthews, K. (1982) 'The demand for currency and the black economy in the UK', *Journal of Economic Studies*, 9, 2: 3–22.

Matthews, K. (1983) 'National income and the black economy', *Journal of Economic Affairs*, 3, 4: 261–7.

Matthews, K. and Rastogi, A. (1985) 'Little mo and the moonlighters: another look at the black economy', *Quarterly Economic Bulletin*, 6: 21–4.

Mauss, M. (1966) *The Gift*, London: Cohen and West.

Mayo, E. (1996) 'Dreaming of work', in P. Meadows (ed.), *Work Out or Work In? Contributions to the debate on the future of work*, York: Joseph Rowntree Foundation.

McCormick, J. (1994) *Citizens' Service*, London: Institute for Public Policy Research.

McCrohan, K., Smith, J.D. and Adams, T.K. (1991) 'Consumer purchases in informal markets: estimates for the 1980s, prospects for the 1990s', *Journal of Retailing*, 67: 22–50.

McGlone, F., Park, A. and Smith, K. (1998) *Families and Kinship*, London: Family Policy Studies Centre.

McInnis-Dittrich, K. (1995) 'Women of the shadows: Appalachian women's participation in the informal economy', *Affilia: Journal of Women and Social Work*, 10, 4: 398–412.

McLaughlin, E. (1994) *Flexibility in Work and Benefits*, London: Institute of Public Policy Research.

Meadows, P. (1997) *The Integration of Taxes and Benefits for Working Families with Children: issues raised to date*, York: York Publishing Services.

Meadows, T.C. and Pihera, J.A. (1981) 'A regional perspective on the underground economy', *Review of Regional Studies*, 11: 83–91.

Meehan, E. (1993) *Citizenship and the European Community*, London: Sage.

Merrett, V. (2001) 'Declining social capital and non-profit organizations: consequences for small towns after welfare reform', *Urban Geography*, 22: 407–23.

Miles, I. (1983) *Adaptation to unemployment?* Occasional Paper no. 20, Brighton: Science Policy Research Unit, University of Sussex.

Millar, J. and Hole, D. (1998) *Integrated Family Benefits in Australia and Options for the UK Tax Return System*, York: York Publishing Services.

Milliron, V. and Toy, D. (1988) 'Tax compliance: an investigation of key features', *The Journal of the American Taxation Association*, 9: 84–104.

Minc, A. (1980) 'Le chomage et l'economie souterraine', *Le Debat*, 2: 3–14.

Minc, A. (1982) *L'Apres-Crise a Commence*, Paris: Gallimard.

Mingione, E. (1990) 'The case of Greece', in *Underground Economy and Irregular Forms of Employment, Final Synthesis Report*, Brussels: Office for Official Publications of the European Communities.

Mingione, E. (1991) *Fragmented Societies: a sociology of economic life beyond the market paradigm*, Oxford: Basil Blackwell.

Mingione, E. (1994) 'Socio-economic restructuring and social exclusion', Paper presented to the IFRESI Conference on *Cities, Enterprises and Society at the Eve of the XXIst Century*, Lille, March.

Mingione, E. and Magatti, M. (1995) *Social Europe Follow up to the White Paper: the informal sector*, DGV Supplement 3/95, Brussels: European Commission.

Mingione, E. and Morlicchio, E. (1993) 'New forms of urban poverty in Italy: risk path models in the North and South', *International Journal of Urban and Regional Research*, 17,3: 413–27.

Mirus, R. and Smith, R.S. (1989) 'Canada's underground economy', in E.L. Feige (ed.), *The Underground Economies: tax evasion and information distortion*, Cambridge: Cambridge University Press.

Mogensen, G.V. (1985) *Sort Arbejde i Danmark*, Copenhagen: Institut for Nationalokonomi.

Mogensen, G.V. (1990) 'Black markets and welfare in Scandinavia: some methodological and empirical issues', in M. Estellie Smith (ed.), *Perspectives on the Informal Economy*, New York: University Press of America.

Morris, L. (1987) 'Constraints on gender: the family wage, social security and the labour market; reflections on research in Hartlepool', *Work, Employment and Society*, 1,1: 85–106.

Morris, L. (1993) 'Is there a British underclass?', *International Journal of Urban and Regional Research*, 17,3: 404–12.

Morris, L. (1994) 'Informal aspects of social divisions', *International Journal of Urban and Regional Research*, 18: 112–26.

Morris, L. (1995) *Social Divisions: economic decline and social structural change*, London: UCL Press.

Murray, C. (1984) *Losing Ground: American social policy, 1950–1980*, New York: Basic Books.

Myles, J. (1996) 'When markets fail: social welfare in Canada and the US', in G. Esping-Anderson (ed.), *Welfare States in Transition: national adaptations in global economies*, London: Sage.

Neef, R. (2002) 'Observations on the concept and forms of the informal economy in Eastern Europe', in R. Neef and M. Stanuclescu (eds), *The Social Impact of Informal Economies in Eastern Europe*, Aldershot: Ashgate.

Nelson, M.K. and Smith, J. (1999) *Working Hard and Making Do: surviving in small town America*, Los Angeles: University of California Press.

North, P. (1999) 'Explorations in heterotopia: local exchange trading schemes (LETS) and the micropolitics of money and livelihood', *Environment and Planning D*, 17: 69–86.

O'Higgins, M. (1981) 'Tax evasion and the self-employed', *British Tax Review*, 26: 367–78.

OECD (1993) *Employment Outlook*, Paris: OECD.

OECD (1994) *Jobs Study: Part 2*, Paris: OECD.

OECD (1997) *Framework for the Measurement of Unrecorded Economic Activities in Transition Economies* (OCDE/GDE (97), 177), Paris: OECD.

OECD (2000) *Tax Avoidance and Evasion*, Paris: OECD.

OECD (2002) *Measuring the Non-Observed Economy*, Paris: OECD.

Offe, C. and Heinze, R.G. (1992) *Beyond Employment: time, work and the informal economy*, Cambridge: Polity.

Offer, A. (1997) 'Between the gift and the market: the economy of regard', *Economic History Review*, L2: 450–76.

Office of the Deputy Prime Minister (2003) *Employment and Enterprise Project*, London: Office of the Deputy Prime Minister.

Okun, A.M. (1975) *Equality and Efficiency: the big trade-off*, Washington, DC: Brookings Institute.

Ott, K. (1999) 'Economic policy and the underground economy in transition', in E.L. Feige and K. Ott (eds), *Underground Economies in Transition: unrecorded activity, tax evasion, corruption and organized crime*, Aldershot: Ashgate.

Paglin, M. (1994) 'The underground economy: new estimates from household income and expenditure surveys', *The Yale Law Journal*, 103, 8: 2239–57.

Pahl, R.E. (1984) *Divisions of Labour*, Oxford: Blackwell.

Pahl, R.E. (1988) 'Some remarks on informal work, social polarization and the social structure', *International Journal of Urban and Regional Research*, 12, 2: 247–67.

Park, T. (1979) *Reconciliation between Personal Income and Taxable Income (1947–1977)*, Washington, DC: Bureau of Economic Analysis.

Parker, H. (1982) 'Social security foments the black economy', *Economic Affairs*, 3: 32–5.

Parker, H. (1989) *Instead of the Dole: an enquiry into integration of the tax and benefit systems*, London: Routledge.

Peck, J. (1996a) *Work-Place: the social regulation of labour markets*, London: Guildford Press.

Peck, J. (1996b) *The Geo-Politics of the Workfare State*, Paper presented at CUDEM Seminar, Leeds Metropolitan University, October.

Peck, J. (1999) 'New Labourers? Making a New Deal for the "Workless Class"', *Environment and Planning C*, 17: 345–72.

Peck, J. (2001) *Workfare States*, London: Guildford Press.

Pedersen, S. (1998) *The Shadow Economy in Western Europe: measurement and results for selected countries*. Study no. 5. Copenhagen: Rockwool Foundation Research Unit.

Perri 6 (1997a) *Escaping Poverty: from safety nets to networks of opportunity*, London: Demos.

Perri 6 (1997b) *The Power to Bind and Loose: tackling network poverty*, London: Demos.

Pestieau, P. (1983) 'Belgium's irregular economy', Paper presented to the *International Conference on the Economics of the Shadow Economy*, University of Bielefeld, West Germany, October 10–14.

Pestieau, P. (1985) 'Belgium's irregular economy', in W. Gaeartner and A. Wenig (eds), *The Economics of the Shadow Economy*, Berlin: Springer Verlag.

Petersen, H.G. (1982) 'Size of the public sector, economic growth and the informal economy: development trends in the Federal Republic of Germany', *Review of Income and Wealth*, 28: 191–215.

Pfau-Effinger, B. (2003) 'Development of Informal Work in Europe', Paper presented to the EU Workshop *Informal/Undeclared Work: research on its changing nature and policy strategies in an enlarged Europe*; DG Research / DG Employment and Social Affairs, Brussels, 21 May 2003 (http://www.cordis.lu/improving/socio-economic/conf_work.htm).

Phizacklea, A. and Wolkowitz, C. (1995) *Homeworking Women: gender, racism and class at work*, London: Sage.

Pinch, S. (1994) 'Social polarization: a comparison of evidence from Britain and the United States', *Environment and Planning A*, 25, 6: 779–95.

Pinch, S. (1997) *Worlds of Welfare: understanding the changing geographies of social welfare provision*, London: Routledge.

Polanyi, K. (1944) *The Great Transformation*, Boston: Beacon Press.

Porter, R.D. and Bayer, A.S. (1989) 'Monetary perspective on underground economic activity in the United States', in E.L. Feige (ed.), *The Underground Economies: tax evasion and information distortion*, Cambridge: Cambridge University Press.

Portes, A. (1994) 'The informal economy and its paradoxes', in N.J. Smelser and R. Swedberg (eds), *The Handbook of Economic Sociology*, Princeton, NJ: Princeton University Press.

Portes, A. (1998) 'Social capital: its origins and applications in modern sociology', *Annual Review of Sociology*, 24, 1: 1–24.

Portes, A. and Sassen-Koob, S. (1987) 'Making it underground: comparative material on the informal sector in Western market economies', *American Journal of Sociology*, 93, 1: 30–61.

Priest, G.L. (1994) 'The ambiguous moral foundations of the underground economy', *The Yale Law Journal*, 103, 8: 2259–88.

Prime, D., Zimmeck, M. and Zurawan, A. (2002) *Active Communities: initial findings from the 2001 Home Office Citizenship Survey*, London: Home Office.

Putnam, R. (1993) *Making Democracy Work: civic traditions in modern Italy*, Princeton: University of Princeton.

Putnam, R. (1995a) 'Tuning in, Tuning out: the strange disappearance of social capital in America', *Political Science and Politics*, 28: 664–83.

Putnam, R. (1995b) 'Bowling alone: America's declining social capital', *Journal of Democracy*, 6, 1: 65–78.

Putnam, R. (2000) *Bowling Alone: the collapse and revival of American community*, London: Simon and Schuster.

Ray, L. and Sayer, A. (1999) 'Introduction', in L. Ray and A. Sayer (eds), *Culture and Economy after the Culutral Turn*, London: Sage.

Recio, A. (1988) *El Trabajo Precario en Catalunya: la industria textilanera des valles Occidental*, Barcelona: Commission Obrera Nacional de Catalunya.

Reissert, B. (1994) 'Unemployment compensation and the labour market: a European perspective', in S. Mangen and L. Hantrais (eds), *Unemployment, the Informal Economy and Entitlement to Benefit*, Loughborough: European Research Centre, University of Loughborough.

Renooy, P.H. (1990) *The Informal Economy: meaning, measurement and social significance*, Amsterdam: Netherlands Geographical Studies.

Roberts, B. (1991) 'Household coping strategies and urban poverty in a comparative perspective', in M. Gottdiener and C.G. Pickvance (eds), *Urban Life In Transition*, London: Sage.

Robson, B.T. (1988) *Those Inner Cities: reconciling the social and economic aims of urban policy*, Oxford: Clarendon.

Rosanvallon, P. (1980) 'Le developpement de l'economie souterraine et l'avenir des societe industrielles', *Le Debat*, 2: 8–23.

Ross, I. (1978) 'Why the underground economy is booming', *Fortune*, October: 92–8.

Ross, R. (2001) 'The new sweatshops in the United States: how new, how real, how many and why?', in G. Gereffi, D. Spener and J. Bair (eds), *Globalisation and Regionalism: NAFTA and the new geography of the North American apparel industry*, Philadelphia: Temple University Press.

Roth, J., Scholz, J. and Witte, A. (1992) *Tax-Payer Compliance, Volume 1: an agenda for research*, Pennsylvania: University of Pennsylvania Press.

Rowlingson, K., Whyley, C., Newburn, T. and Berthoud, R. (1997) *Social Security Fraud*, DSS Research Report no. 64, London: HMSO.

Rubery, J. (1996) 'The labour market outlook and the outlook for labour market analysis', in R. Crompton, D. Gallie and K. Purcell (eds), *Changing Forms of Employment: organisation, skills and gender*, London: Routledge.

Rusega, S. and De Blas, A. (1985) *Mercado de Trabajo y Economia Oculta en Andalucia*, Sevilla: Cuadernos IAR no.3.

Salamon, L.M., Anheier, H.K., List, R., Toepler, S. and Wojcieck Sokolowoski, S. (1999) *Global Civil Society: dimensions of the nonprofit sector*, Baltimore: Center for Civil Society Studies.

Salmi, A-M. (1996) 'Finland is another world: the gendered time of homework', in E. Boris and E. Prugl (eds), *Homeworkers in Global Perspective: invisible no more*, London: Routledge.

Salmi, A-M. (2003) 'Neighbours and the everyday economy', in K. Arnstberg and T. Boren (eds) *Everyday Economy in Russia, Poland and Latvia*, Stockholm: Almqvist and Wiksell International.

Sandford, C. (1999) 'Policies dealing with tax evasion', in E.L. Feige and K. Ott (eds), *Underground Economies in Transition: unrecorded activity, tax evasion, corruption and organized crime*, Aldershot: Ashgate.

Santos, J.A. (1983) *A Economia Subterranea*, Lisboa: Minietrio do trabalho e seguranca social, Coleccao estudos, serie A, no.4.

Sassen, S. (1989) 'New York city's informal economy', in A. Portes, M. Castells and L. Benton (eds), *The Informal Economy: studies in advanced and less developed countries*, Baltimore: John Hopkins University Press.

Sassen, S. (1991) *The Global City: New York, London, Tokyo*, Princeton: Princeton University Press.

Sassen, S. (1994a) *Cities in a World Economy*, California, Thousand Oaks, CA: Pine Forge/Sage.

Sassen, S. (1994b) 'The informal economy: between new developments and old regulations', *Yale Law Journal*, 103,8: 2289–304.

Sassen, S. (1996) 'Service employment regimes and the new inequality', in E. Mingione (ed.), *Urban Poverty and the Underclass*, Oxford: Basil Blackwell.

Sassen, S. (1997) 'Informalisation in advanced market economies', Issues in Development Discussion Paper 20, Geneva: International Labour Office.

Sassen, S. and Smith, R.C. (1992) 'Post-industrial growth and economic reorganisation: their impact on immigrant employment', in J. Bustamante, C.W. Reynolds and R.A. Hinojosa (eds), *US–Mexico Relations: labour markets interdependence*, Stanford, CA: Stanford University Press.

Sauvy, A. (1984) *Le Travail Noir et l'Economie de Demain*, Paris: Calmann-Levy.

Sayer, A. (1997) 'The dialectic of culture and economy', in R. Lee and J. Wills (eds), *Geographies of Economies*, London: Arnold.

Schneider, F. (2000) 'Dimensions of the shadow economy', *Independent Review*, 5, 1: 81–91.

Schneider, F. (2001) 'What do we know about the shadow economy? Evidence from 21 OECD countries', *World Economics*, 2,4: 19–32.

Schneider, F. and Enste, D.H. (2000) 'Shadow economies: size, causes, and consequences', *Journal of Economic Literature*, 38,1: 77–114.

Sedlenieks, K. (2003) 'Cash in an envelope: corruption and tax avoidance as an economic strategy in contemporary Riga', in K. Arnstberg and T. Boren (eds), *Everyday Economy in Russia, Poland and Latvia*, Stockholm: Almqvist and Wiksell International.

Seyfang, G. and Smith, K. (2002) *The Time of Our Lives: using time banking for neighbourhood renewal and community capacity building*, London: New Economics Foundation.

Sik, E. (1993) 'From the second economy to the informal economy', *Journal of Public Policy*, 12: 153–75.

Sik, E. (1994) 'From the multicoloured to the black and white economy: the Hungarian second economy and the transformation', *Urban Studies*, 31, 1: 47–70.

Silburn, R., Lucas, D., Page, R. and Hanna, L. (1999) *Neighbourhood Images in Nottingham: social cohesion and neighbourhood change*, York: York Publishing Services.

Slater, D. and Tonkiss, F. (2001) *Market Society: markets and modern social theory*, Cambridge: Polity.

Small Business Service (2003) *New Drive for Better Enforcement of Regulations Launched*, London: Small Business Service.

Smith, A. (2002) 'Culture/economy and spaces of economic practice: positioning households in post-communism', *Transactions of the Institute of British Geographers*, 27: 232–50.

Smith, J.D. (1985) 'Market motives in the informal economy', in W. Gaertner and A. Wenig (eds), *The Economics of the Shadow Economy*, Berlin: Springer-Verlag.

Smith, K. (1992) 'Reciprocity and fairness: positive incentives for tax compliance', in J. Slemrod (ed.), *Why People Pay Taxes*, Michigan: University of Michigan Press.

Smith, R.S. (2002) 'The Underground Economy: Guidance for Policy Makers?' *Canadian Tax Journal*, 50, 5: 1655–61.

Smith, S. (1986) *Britain's Shadow Economy*, Oxford: Clarendon.

Smithies, E. (1984) *The Black Economy in England Since 1914*, Dublin: Gill and Macmillan.

Snyder, K. (2003) 'Working "Off the Books": patterns of informal market participation within New York's East Village', *Sociological Inquiry*, 73, 2: 284–308.

Social Exclusion Unit (1998) *Bringing Britain Together: a national strategy for neighbourhood renewal*, Cm4045, London: HMSO.

Social Exclusion Unit (2000) *National Strategy for Neighbourhood Renewal: a framework for consultation*, London: The Stationery Office.

Soiffer, S.S. and Herrmann, G.M. (1987) 'Visions of power: ideology and practice in the American garage sale', *Sociological Review*, 35, 1: 48–83.

Sole, C. (1998) 'Irregular employment amongst immigrants in Spanish cities', *Journal of Ethnic and Migration Studies*, 24, 2: 333–46.

Stack, R. (1974) *All Our Kin: strategies for survival in a black community*, New York: Harper and Row.

Staudt, K. (1998) *Free Trade? Informal economies at the US–Mexico Border*, Philadelphia: Temple, University Press.

Stauffer, B. (1995) 'Regulation and reality: streetvending in Washington DC', Paper presented at the *91st Annual Meeting of the Association of American Geographers*, Chicago.

Stoleru, L. (1982) *La France a Deux Vitesses*, Paris: Flammarion.

Stoll, M.A. (2001) 'Race, neighbourhood poverty and participation in voluntary associations', *Sociological Forum*, 16: 529–62.

Tabak, F. (2000) 'Introduction: informalization and the long term', in F. Tabak and M.A. Crichlow (eds), *Informalization: process and structure*, Baltimore: John Hopkins University.

Tanzi, V. (1980) 'The underground economy in the United States: estimates and implications', *Banco Nazionale del Lavoro*, 135: 427–53.

Tanzi, V. (1982) (ed.) *The Underground Economy in the United States and Abroad*, Massachusetts: Lexington Books.

Tanzi, V. (1999) 'Uses and abuses of estimates of the underground economy', *The Economic Journal*, 109, 456: 338–47.

Thomas, J.J. (1988) 'The politics of the black economy', *Work, Employment and Society* 2, 2: 169–90.

Thomas, J.J. (1992) *Informal Economic Activity*, Hemel Hempstead: Harvester Wheatsheaf.

Thomas, J.J. (1999) 'Quantifying the black economy: "measurement with theory" yet again', *Economic Journal*, 109: 381–9.

Thomas, J.J. (2000) 'The black economy: benefit frauds or tax evaders?', *World Economics*, 1, 1: 167–75.

Thomas, R., Pettigrew, N., Cotton, D. and Tovey, P. (1999) *Keeping in Touch with the Labour Market: a qualitative evaluation of the back to work bonus*, Department of Social Security Research Report no.96, London: Department of Social Security.

Thrift, N.J. (2000) 'Commodities', in R.J. Johnston, D. Gregory, G. Pratt and M. Watts (eds), *The Dictionary of Human Geography*, Oxford: Blackwell.

Thrift, N. and Olds, K. (1996) 'Refiguring the economic in economic geography', *Progress in Human Geography*, 20: 311–37.

Tickamyer, A.R. and Wood, T.A. (1998) 'Identifying participation in the informal economy using survey research methods', *Rural Sociology*, 63, 2: 323–39.

Tievant, S. (1982) 'Vivre autrement: echanges et sociabilite en ville nouvelle', *Cahiers de l'OCS*, vol. 6, CNRS, Paris.

Townsend, A.R. (1997) *Making a Living in Europe: human geographies of economic change*, London: Routledge.

Travers, A. (2002) *Prospects for Enterprise: an investigation into the motivations of workers in the informal economy*, Evidence paper no.2, London: Community Links.

Trundle, J.M. (1982) 'Recent changes in the use of cash', *Bank of England Quarterly Bulletin*, 22: 519–29.

US Congress Joint Economic Committee (1983) *Growth of the Underground Economy 1950–81*, Washington, DC: Government Printing Office.

US General Accounting Office (1989) *Sweatshops in New York City: a local example of a nationwide problem*, Washington, DC: US General Accounting Office.

Vaknin, S. (2000) 'The blessings of the informal economy', *Central Europe Review*, 2, 40, 20 November.

Van Eck, R. and Kazemeier, B. (1985) *Swarte Inkomsten uit Arbeid: resultaten van in 1983 gehouden experimentele*, CBS-Statistische Katernen nr 3, Den Haag: Central Bureau of Statistics.

Van Geuns, R., Mevissen, J. and Renooy, P.H. (1987) 'The spatial and sectoral diversity of the informal economy', *Tijdschrift voor Economische en Sociale Geografie*, 78, 5: 389–98.

Van Parijis, P. (1992) (ed.), *Arguing for Basic Incomes*, London: Verso.

Van Parijis, P. (1996a) 'Basic income and the two dilemmas of the welfare state', *The Political Quarterly*, 67, 1: 57–8.

Van Parijis, P. (1996b) 'L'allocation universelle contre le chomage: de la trappe au socle', *Revue Francaise des Affaires Sociales*, 50, 1: 111–25.

Vinay, P. (1987) 'Women, family and work: symptoms of crisis in the informal economy of Central Italy', *Sames 3rd International Seminar Proceedings*, University of Thessaloniki, Thessaloniki.

Vogler, C. (1994) 'Money in the household', in M. Anderson, F. Bechhofer and J. Gershuny (eds), *The Social and Political Economy of the Household*, Oxford: Oxford University Press.

Walby, S. (1997) *Gender Transformations*, London: Routledge.

Waldinger, R. and Lapp, M. (1993) 'Back to the sweatshop or ahead to the informal sector', *International Journal of Urban and Regional Research*, 17, 1: 6–29.

Wallace, C. (2002) 'Household strategies: their conceptual relevance and analytical scope in social research', *Sociology*, 36: 275–92.

Wallace, C. and Haerpfer, C. (2002) 'Patterns of participation in the informal economy in East-central Europe, 1991–1998', in R. Neef and M. Stanuclescu (eds), *The Social Impact of Informal Economies in Eastern Europe*, Aldershot: Ashgate.

Warde, A. (1990) 'Household work strategies and forms of labour: conceptual and empirical issues', *Work, Employment and Society*, 4, 4: 495–515.

Warde, A. and Hetherington, K. (1993) 'A changing domestic division of labour? issues of measurement and interpretation', *Work, Employment and Society*, 7,1: 23–45.

Warren, M.R. (1994) 'Exploitation or co-operation? the political basis of regional variation in the Italian informal economy', *Politics and Society*, 22, 1: 89–115.

Weatherley, R. (1993) 'Doing the right thing: how social security claimants view compliance', *Australian and New Zealand Journal of Sociology*, 29, 1: 21–39.

Weck-Hanneman, H. and Frey, B.S. (1985) 'Measuring the shadow economy: the case of Switzerland', in W. Gaertner and A. Wenig (eds), *The Economics of the Shadow Economy*, Berlin: Springer-Verlag.

Wenig, A. (1990) 'The shadow economy in the Federal Republic of Germany', in *Underground Economy and Irregular Forms of Employment, Final Synthesis Report*, Brussels: Office for Official Publications of the European Communities.

Williams, C.C. (1996a) 'An appraisal of Local Exchange and Trading Systems (LETS) in the United Kingdom', *Local Economy*, 11, 3: 275–82.

Williams, C.C. (1996b) 'Informal sector responses to unemployment: an evaluation of the potential of Local Exchange and Trading Systems (LETS)', *Work, Employment and Society*, 10, 2: 341–59.

Williams, C.C. (1996c) 'Local currencies and community development: an evaluation of green dollar exchanges in New Zealand', *Community Development Journal*, 31, 4: 319–29.

Williams, C.C. (1996d) 'Local Exchange and Trading Systems (LETS): a new source of work and credit for the poor and unemployed?', *Environment and Planning A*, 28, 8: 1395–415.

Williams, C.C. (1996e) 'Local purchasing and rural development: an evaluation of Local Exchange and Trading Systems (LETS)', *Journal of Rural Studies*, 12, 3: 231–44.

Williams, C.C. (1996f) 'The new barter economy: an appraisal of Local Exchange and Trading Systems (LETS)', *Journal of Public Policy*, 16, 1: 55–71.

Williams, C.C. (2001a) 'Does work pay? Spatial variations in the benefits of employment and coping abilities of the unemployed', *Geoforum*, 32, 2: 199–214.

Williams, C.C. (2001b) 'Tackling the participation of the unemployed in paid informal work: a critical evaluation of the deterrence approach', *Environment and Planning C*, 19, 5: 729–49.

Williams, C.C. (2001c) 'Time to give credit to active citizens', *Local Governance*, 27, 2: 67–75.

Williams, C.C. (2002a) 'A critical evaluation of the commodification thesis', *The Sociological Review*, 50, 4: 525–42.

Williams, C.C. (2002b) 'Beyond the commodity economy: the persistence of informal economic activity in rural England', *Geografiska Annaler B*, 83, 4: 221–33.

Williams, C.C. (2002c) 'Cultures of community engagement: some policy lessons from the 2000 General Household Survey', *Local Governance*, 28, 4: 263–71.

Williams, C.C. (2002d) 'Harnessing community self-help: some lessons from rural England', *Local Economy*, 17, 2: 136–46.

Williams, C.C. (2002e) 'Harnessing voluntary work: a fourth sector approach', *Policy Studies*, 23, 3/4: 247–60.

Williams, C.C. (2003a) 'Developing community involvement: contrasting local and regional participatory cultures in Britain and their implications for policy', *Regional Studies*, 37, 5: 531–41.

Williams, C.C. (2003b) 'Developing community participation in deprived neighbourhoods: a critical evaluation of the third sector approach', *Space and Polity*, 7, 1: 65–73.

Williams, C.C. (2003c) 'Developing social capital: some lessons from rural England', *Local Government Studies*, 29, 1: 75–90.

Williams, C.C. (2003d) 'Evaluating the penetration of the commodity economy', *Futures*, 35: 857–68.

Williams, C.C. (2003e) 'Developing voluntary activity: some policy lessons from the 2001 Home Office Citizenship Survey', *Social Policy and Society*, 2, 4: 285–94.

Williams, C.C. and Windebank, J. (1993) 'Social and spatial inequalities in informal economic activity: some evidence from the European Community', *Area*, 25, 4: 358–64.

Williams, C.C. and Windebank, J. (1994) 'Spatial variations in the informal sector: a review of evidence from the European Union', *Regional Studies*, 28, 8: 819–25.

Williams, C.C. and Windebank, J. (1995a) 'Black market work in the European Community: peripheral work for peripheral localities?', *International Journal of Urban and Regional Research*, 19, 1: 22–39.

Williams, C.C. and Windebank, J. (1995b) 'Social polarisation of households in contemporary Britain: a "whole economy" perspective', *Regional Studies*, 29, 8: 727–32.

Williams, C.C. and Windebank, J. (1998) *Informal Employment in the Advanced Economies: implications for work and welfare*, London: Routledge.

Williams, C.C. and Windebank, J. (1999a) 'Unshackling the future of work from the ideology of full-employment', *Foresight*, 1, 4: 309–22.

Williams, C.C. and Windebank, J. (1999b) 'Reconceptualising paid informal work and its implications for policy: some lessons from a case study of Southampton', *Policy Studies*, 20, 4: 221–33.

Williams, C.C. and Windebank, J. (1999c) 'The formalisation of work thesis: a critical evaluation', *Futures*, 31, 6: 547–58.

Williams, C.C. and Windebank, J. (1999d) *A Helping Hand: harnessing self-help to combat social exclusion*, York: York Publishing Services.

Williams, C.C. and Windebank, J. (2000a) 'A helping hand: harnessing mutual aid to tackle social exclusion in deprived urban neighbourhoods', *Local Governance*, 26, 4: 237–45.

Williams, C.C. and Windebank, J. (2000b) 'Paid informal work in deprived neighborhoods', *Cities*, 17, 4: 285–91.

Williams, C.C. and Windebank, J. (2000c) 'Helping each other out? Community exchange in deprived neighbourhoods', *Community Development Journal*, 35, 2: 146–56.

Williams, C.C. and Windebank, J. (2000d) 'Helping people to help themselves: some policy lessons from deprived urban neighbourhoods in Southampton', *Journal of Social Policy*, 29, 3: 355–73.

Williams, C.C. and Windebank, J. (2001a) *Revitalising Deprived Urban Neighbourhoods: an assisted self-help approach*, Aldershot: Ashgate.

Williams, C.C. and Windebank, J. (2001b) 'A critical evaluation of the formalisation of work thesis: some evidence from France', *SAIS Review*, XXI, 1: 117–22.

Williams, C.C. and Windebank, J. (2001c) 'Beyond profit-motivated exchange: some lessons from the study of paid informal work', *European Urban and Regional Studies*, 8, 1: 49–61.

Williams, C.C. and Windebank, J. (2001d) 'Beyond social inclusion through employment: harnessing mutual aid as a complementary social inclusion policy', *Policy and Politics*, 29, 1: 15–28.

Williams, C.C. and Windebank, J. (2001e) 'Paid informal work in deprived urban neighbourhoods: exploitative employment or co-operative self-help?', *Growth and Change*, 32,4: 562–71.

Williams, C.C. and Windebank, J. (2001f) 'Paid informal work: a barrier to social inclusion?', *Transfer: Journal of the European Trade Union Institute*, 7, 1: 25–40.

Williams, C.C. and Windebank, J. (2001g) 'Reconceptualising paid informal exchange: some lessons from English cities', *Environment and Planning A*, 33, 1: 121–40.

Williams, C.C. and Windebank, J. (2002a) 'The uneven geographies of informal economic activities: a case study of two British cities', *Work, Employment and Society*, 16, 2: 231–50.

Williams, C.C. and Windebank, J. (2002b) 'Why do people engage in paid informal work? A comparison of affluent suburbs and deprived urban neighbourhoods in Britain', *Community, Work and Family*, 5, 1: 67–83.

Williams, C.C. and Windebank, J. (2003a) *Poverty and the Third Way*, London: Routledge.

Williams, C.C. and Windebank, J. (2003b) 'The slow advance and uneven penetration of commodification', *International Journal of Urban and Regional Research*, 27, 2: 250–64.

Williams, C.C., Aldridge, T., Lee, R., Leyshon, A., Thrift, N. and Tooke, J. (2001a) *Bridges into Work? An evaluation of local exchange and trading schemes (LETS)*, Bristol: Policy Press.

Williams, C.C., Aldridge, T., Lee, R., Leyshon, A., Thrift, N. and Tooke, J. (2001b) 'Local Exchange and Trading Schemes (LETS): a tool for community renewal?', *Community, Work and Family*, 4, 3: 355–61.

Windebank, J. (1999) 'Political Motherhood and the Everyday Experience of Mothering: a comparison of childcare strategies of French and British working mothers', *Journal of Social Policy*, 28, 1–25.

Windebank, J. and Williams, C.C. (1997) 'What is to be done about the paid informal sector in the European Union? A review of policy options', *International Planning Studies*, 2, 3: 315–27.

Wood, M. and Vamplew, C. (1999) *Neighbourhood Images in Teeside: regeneration or decline?*, York: York Publishing Services.

Ybarra, J-A. (1989) 'Informalisation in the Valencian economy: a model for underdevelopment', in A. Portes, M. Castells and L.A. Benton (eds), *The Informal Economy: studies in advanced and less developing countries*, Baltimore: John Hopkins University Press.

Young, M. and Wilmott, P. (1975) *The Symmetrical Family: a study of work and leisure in the London region*, Harmondsworth: Penguin.

Zelizer, V.A. (1994) *The Social Meaning of Money*, New York: Basic Books.

Index

active citizenship, 188–9
Ahn, N., 5, 65
Aitken, S., 71
Alden, J., 42
Allingham, M., 134
alternative economic spaces, 24–5
Amin, A., 16, 24, 174
Appalachia, 92
Arnstein, S., 124
Atkins F. J., 5
Atkinson, A., 171
Atkinson, A.B., 188
Australia, 108, 135, 172
Austria, 108, 149, 152
autonomous cash-in-hand work
    existence of, 21–2, 32
    employment status of workers,
        66–70, 73–7
    gender variations in, 95–6
    geographical variations in, 114–17

Babb, S.L., 23
baby–sitting, 58
back–to–work bonus, 189–90
Bajada, C., 5, 43, 49, 135
Barnes, H., 193
Barnsley, 50
barriers to cash-in-hand work for
    unemployed, 70–3, 173–4;
    193–4
Barthe, M.A., 20, 55
Barthelemy, P., 108
basic income, 187–8
Bassett, 60
Bayer, A.S., 46
Beatson, M., 166
Beck, U., 148
Belfast, 34, 56, 72, 92, 156
Belgium, 54, 108, 149, 152, 172
benefit fraud, 2, 71, 135–8, 143–5
benefit recipient quotas, 69
Bennington, J., 151
Benton, L., 5, 20, 68

Berking, H., 37
Biggs, T., 5, 167
Birkenhead, 50
Blair, J.P., 19, 20, 26, 66, 69, 109
Blau, P.M., 79
Bonneville, E., 71
Boren, T., 157
Boris, E., 85
Bourdieu, P., 7, 24
Boyle, D., 194
breadwinner wage, 43
Brighton, 50
Briscoe, I., 188
builders, see construction industry
Bunker, N., 20, 110
Burawoy, M., 157
Button, K., 20, 26, 109
Byrne, K., 24

Cahn, E., 25, 194
Canada
    Bas-du-Fleuve, 87
    gender, 86–7, 93–4
    income disparities, 170
    measurement methods 54, 56, 57,
        108
    Montreal, 87
    social polarisation, 172
    see also Quebec
Cappechi, V., 21, 154, 174
car boot sales, 25
Caridi, P., 5, 48
carpentry, 58
car repairs, 58, 91
Carrier, J.G., 7, 23, 166
Carruthers, B.G., 23
cash–deposit ratio approach, 47–50
Castells, M., 8, 15, 16, 18, 26, 28
Cattell, V., 35
Chalford, 60
character of cash-in-hand work
    heterogeneity of, 20–35
    and employment status, 73–7, 201

character of cash-in-hand
  work – *continued*
  and gender, 88–101, 201
  and geography, 114–17, 202
charity, 30, 37
Chavdarova, T., 157
cheques, use of, 50, 56
child-care, 91, 94, 191
child labour, 1
Chilworth, 60
citizen's income, 187–8
Cleveland, 31
Cocco, M.R., 48
Coleman, J., 79
Comelieau, C., 7
commodification, 7, 16–17
community–building, *see* social capital
Community Economies Collective, 24
Conroy, P., 170
construction industry, 1, 29
consumers of cash-in-hand, *see*
  purchasers
Contini, B., 168
Cook, D., 71, 138, 145
Cornelius, W.A., 18
Cornuel, D., 19, 27, 46, 67, 71, 78
Coulthard, M., 127
Crang, P., 7
credit cards, 47, 48
Crewe, L., 7, 15, 23, 24, 25, 178
criminal activity, 2–3
Crnkovic–Pozaic, S., 5, 42
Crompton, R., 166
cross–national variations, 18, 19,
  107–9
cultivating cash-in-hand work, 177–97
cultural turn, 15, 22–5, 38, 178–9

Dagg, A., 85
Dallago, B., 19, 107, 108
De Soto, H., 8, 15, 19, 26, 163, 167
Deakin, S., 166
Dean, H., 31, 71
Dean, P.N., 71
debit cards, 47, 48
decorating, 32, 58, 90, 101
defining cash-in-hand work, 2–7
Dekker, P., 124
Del Boca, D., 42

Denison, E., 43, 44
Denmark
  formalising cash-in-hand work, 156
  jobs deficit, 148, 149
  magnitude, 108
  social protection, 152
  women's participation, 86
de–regulation of labour market, 16,
  18, 161–73, 180
detection, 11, 145
Detroit, 50
Dilnot, A., 52, 53, 171
direct survey methods, 54–62
domestic cleaners, 29, 90, 94, 191
domestic service, 85, 190–1
Dorling, D., 72
drug trafficking, 3
dual economy, 5
Duriez, B., 19, 27, 46, 67, 71, 78

earnings disregard, 143–4, 196–7
economic globalisation, 18
Economic and Social Research
  Council, xi
economic rationales, *see* profit motive
Elam, E., 189
electrical work, 58
electricians, 1, 29, 32
electricity demand, as measure of
  cash-in-hand, 45
Elkin, T., 20, 26, 110
embeddedness, 16, 22–6, 39, 178–9
  199–200
Emilia Romagna, 174
employee mutuals, 195–6
employers of cash-in-hand workers,
  see purchasers
employment status, 69–81
Endres, C.R., 19, 20, 26, 66, 69, 109
English Localities Survey
  methods, 57–62
  gender and cash-in-hand work,
    87–101
  geography and cash-in-hand work
    110–23
Enste, D.H., 19, 107
entrepreneurs, 26, 139, 168, 180–1,
  183, 185–6
Esping-Andersen, G., 164, 167, 170

ethnic enclaves, 18
European Commission: on deterrence, 136
Evans, M., 35
Evason, E., 46, 171
exploitative work conditions, 138–42, 180

Fainstein, N., 170
Falkinger, J., 134
Family Expenditure Survey, 52–4
Feige, E.L., 2, 18, 19, 50–1, 108
Felt, L.F., 5
Ferman, L., 5
Fernandez–Kelly, M.P., 18, 44
fiddling, 31, 56
financial exclusion, 47, 49
Finland, 149, 151, 152
firm size and cash-in-hand, 44–5
Forte, F., 42
Fortin
  attitudes towards cash-in-hand, 30–1
  gender and cash-in-hand, 86, 93–4
  on methods, 54
  on morality, 154
  on unemployed, 69, 74–5
Foudi, R., 19, 20, 67
France
  cheque emploi service, 190–1
  employment status and cash-in-hand, 19
  geography and cash-in-hand, 20, 110
  jobs deficit, 149
  magnitude of cash-in-hand, 108
  new towns, 27
  Orly-Choisy, 110
  reciprocity, 27
  social networks, 71
  social polarisation, 172
  social protection, 152
  titre emploi service, 190–1
  unemployed and cash-in-hand, 67, 71
fraudulent behaviour, 31, 135–8, 179
Frey, B.S., 53, 54
Friedman, E., 18, 45, 107
Fulbourn, 60
full-employment, critique of, 147–50
Fulwood, 60

Gabor, I.R., 168
Gadea, M.D., 17, 51
Gallin, D., 138, 140, 180
gang-masters, 1
garage sales, 25, 92
Garcia, A.M., 18, 44
gardeners, 29, 91, 92
garment industries, 55
General Household Survey, 101, 124
Germany
  attitudes toward cash-in-hand, 72
  gender and cash-in-hand, 88, 94, 95
  jobs deficit, 149
  measuring cash-in-hand, 51, 54, 108
  social protection, 152
  social polarisation, 172
  unemployment and cash-in-hand, 19, 67, 69
Gershuny, J., 5
'ghosts', 142–3
Gibson–Graham, J.K., 23
Gilder, G., 165
Giles, D.E.A., 51
Gittell, R., 79
global cities, 18
Global Employment Forum, 183, 205
globalisation thesis, 17–18, 140
Gough, I., 188
Grabiner, Lord, 129, 135, 137, 142–7
Granovetter, M., 36
Greece
  employment and cash-in-hand, 20, 68
  geography, 114
  jobs deficit, 149
  magnitude, 108
  resistance to formalisation, 154
  social protection, 152, 172
Green, A.E., 72
Gregson, N., 19, 27, 46, 67, 71, 178
Grimethorpe, 60
Grindle, M.D., 5, 167
Gudeman, S., 15, 178, 199
Gutmann, P.M., 48

Hadjimichalis, C., 20, 68, 110, 114
Haerpfer, C., 157
hairdressing 185
Hakim, C., 84
harnessing cash-in-hand, 11, 177–97

Harding, P., 4, 5
Hart, K., 168
Hartlepool, 96
Harvey, D., 22
Hasseldine, J., 129, 134, 135, 158
Haughton, G. 110
Heinze, R.G., 25
Hellberger, C., 8, 20, 42, 67, 69, 72
Henry, S., 31
hidden economy of favours,
    definition, 2–7, 16, 65
Hightown, 60
Himmelweit, S., 84
Hole, D., 188
home repairs, 90, 93
home-workers, 154
household work practices, 27, 57–9
Howe, L., 72
Hoyman, M., 18
Hungary, 168
Husband, J., 5, 154

identity fraud, 145
immigrants, 18
income/expenditure discrepancies,
    51–4
indirect survey methods, 41–54
    cash-deposit ratio approach, 47–50
    income/expenditure discrepancies,
        51–4
    labour force estimates, 42–4
    large denomination notes approach,
        46–7
    monetary transactions approach,
        50–1
    very small enterprise approach,
        44–5
indirect non-monetary measurement
    methods, 42–5
Inland revenue, 142–3
inner cities, 20
International Labour Office
    jobs deficit, 148
    measuring cash-in-hand, 45, 108
    gender and wage rates, 94
    view of cash-in-hand, 136, 138–9
Ireland, 108, 149, 152, 172
ironing, 90
Isachsen, A.J., 50, 54, 66
Isle of Sheppey, 56, 57, 93

Italy
    de–regulation, 168
    Emilia Romagna, 174
    gender and cash-in-hand, 86, 94
    geography and cash-in-hand, 20,
        110, 114
    jobs deficit, 149
    measuring cash-in-hand, 54, 108
    resistance to formalisation, 154
    social protection, 152
    social polarisation, 172
    unemployed and cash-in-hand
        work, 20, 68

Jenkins, R., 4, 5
Jensen, L., 18, 20, 21, 27, 54, 59, 68–9
Jerrard, B., 5, 154
Jessop, B., 23
jobseekers allowance, 189
jobs deficit, 147–50
Jordan, B., 26, 31, 71, 85, 96, 180

Kazemeier, B., 8, 20, 55, 67, 74, 76
Keenan, A., 71
Kempson, E., 30
Kesteloot, C., 26, 54, 59, 72
Kinsey, K., 157
Kitchen, R., 61
Komter, A.E., 71, 78, 115
Krishnamurthy, A., 82

labour force measurement methods,
    42–4
Lacko, M., 45
Lagos, R.A., 5, 8, 15, 19, 26, 66
Laguerre, M.S., 21, 73, 114
Langfelt, E., 51
Lapp, M., 18, 21, 73, 114
large denomination notes method,
    46–7
Lee, R., 15, 23, 24, 25, 178
leisure: definition of, 6
Leonard, M., 34, 56, 72, 156
Leontidou, L., 114
level of cash-in-hand, *see* magnitude
Lipietz, A., 188
Lobo, F.M., 74
local currencies, 25, 192–5
local exchange trading schemes, 25,
    192–4

Lodemel, I., 138
Lomnitz, L.A., 141
London, 31, 50, 185
Lozano, B., 20, 68
Lukacs, J., 157
Luton, 31
Luxembourg, 152, 172
Lysestol, P.M., 71, 72

MacDonald, R., 31, 56, 137
magnitude of cash-in-hand
  employment status variations,
    66–70, 201
  estimates, 17–20, 25, 40–57
  gender disparities, 86–8, 201
  geographical disparities, 106–14, 202
  measurement methods, 40–62
  temporal variations, 17–18
Maguire, K., 156
Maldonado, C., 8, 15, 19, 66, 198
Manor, 60
Marcelli, E., 2
marginality thesis, 7–8, 19–20, 38, 67,
  114
market-centredness, 20–35, 33–4, 166,
  178–9
Mattera, P., 8, 20, 43, 49, 53, 74
Mauss, M., 24
Mayo, E., 187
McGlone, F., 37
McInnis-Dittrich, K., 18, 20, 84, 85,
  92, 93
McLaren, D., 20, 26, 110
measuring cash-in-hand work, 41–62
Meadows, T.C., 48
Meert, H., 26, 54, 59, 72
Melkert initiative, 191
Melrose, M., 31, 71
Micklewright, J., 171
Millar, J., 188
Milliron, V., 134
Minc, A., 162, 163
Mingione, E., 20, 21, 26, 68, 71, 84, 88
Mirus, R., 47
modernisation thesis, 17
monetary measures of cash-in-hand,
  46–54
  large denomination notes approach,
    46–7
  cash–deposit ratio approach, 47–50

monetary transactions approach, 50–1
  income/expenditure discrepancies,
    51–4
monetary transactions approach 50–1
monetised exchange, 15, 22–6, 102,
  178–9, 199–200
morality, of cash-in-hand work, 31
  155
Morris, C.N., 52, 53
motivations for cash-in-hand
  employment status variations,
    77–81, 201
  gender variations, 88–101, 201
  geographical variations, 117–23, 202
Myles, J., 167, 171

nature of cash-in-hand, *see* character
Nelson, M.K., 54, 57, 68
neo-liberalism, 16, 26, 140, 161–73
Netherlands
  attitudes towards benefit fraud, 72
  gender, 86
  geography of cash-in-hand, 20, 110
  jobs deficit, 149
  measuring cash-in-hand, 54
  Melkert Plan, 191
  social networks, 71
  social polarisation, 172
  social protection, 151–2
  unemployed and cash-in-hand, 20,
    67, 69, 76
Newcastle, 185
Newham, 154
New Zealand 158
non–monetary measurement
  methods, 42–5
  labour force estimates, 42–4
  very small enterprise approach,
    44–5
North, P., 19, 25

Offe, C., 25
Offer, A., 34
Okun, A.M., 165, 166
organised cash-in-hand
  existence of, 21–2, 31, 32
  and employment status, 66–70, 73–7
  and gender, 95–6
  and geography, 114–17
Orly–Choisy, 110

Ott, K., 18, 19, 108
Owen, D., 72

Paglin, M., 52
Pahl, R.E., 3, 18, 20, 26, 54, 56, 72
participation in cash-in-hand, reasons,
  see motivations
participation income, 188–9
Passerini, P., 5, 48
pay rates
  by type of cash-in-hand, 21, 32–4
  gender disparities, 85–6, 93–5, 98–9
  geographical disparities, 111–12
  variations by employment status,
    74–5, 79
Peck, J. 157, 171
Pedersen, S., 19
Pennsylvania, 27, 68–9
peripheral regions, 20
Peru, 169
Pestieau, P., 72, 108
Pfau–Effinger, B., 17
Phizacklea, A., 55
Pihera, J.A., 48
Pitsmoor, 60
plastering, 58, 90
plumbers, 1, 29, 32
Polanyi, K., 15, 166
Porter, R.D., 46
Portes
  defining cash-in-hand, 2
  regulating cash-in-hand work, 140,
    141, 157
  social regulators, 42
Portugal
  employment status and cash-in-
    hand, 20, 74
  jobs deficit, 149
  lax enforcement, 154
  social protection, 152
profit-motive
  critique of, 15–16, 22–6, 31–2,
    199–200
  employment status and, 78, 80
  gender and, 95–7, 99–100
  geography and, 117–18, 121–3
Prugl, E., 85
punishments, 133–46
purchasers of cash-in-hand
  motives 28–30, 201–2

variations by employment status,
    80–1
gender variations, 99–101
geographical variations, 117–21
Putnam, R., 30, 35

Quebec
  employment status, 69, 74–5
  gender, 86–7, 93–4
  magnitude of cash-in-hand, 30–1
  morality of cash-in-hand, 154

rational economic actors, *see* profit
    motive
Ray, L., 22
redistributive motives
  prevalence of, 30
  employment status variations,
    80, 81
  gender variations, 98–9, 100–1
  geographical variations, 120–1, 123
Redley, M., 31
Reissert, B., 69
Renooy, P.H., 84, 114, 115, 180, 198
resistance cultures, 153–4
restaurants, 32
Rica S.D.L., 5, 65
Robson, B.T., 19, 20, 67, 110
Rosanvallon, P., 8,15, 19, 26, 66, 67
Rowlingson, K., 31
Rubery, J., 166, 170
Ruccio, D., 23

Salamon, L.M., 124
Salmi, A–M., 85
Sandmo, A., 134
San Francisco, 68
Santos, E, 48
Sassen, S., 8, 16, 18, 27, 85, 115
Sayer, A., 22, 23, 33
Schneider, F., 19, 107
Schwarze, J., 8, 20, 42, 67, 69, 72
second–job holding, 42–4
segmented informal labour market,
    22, 73, 76
self–employment
  prevalence, 21–2, 26, 32
  measure of cash-in-hand, 42–4, 52
Serrano–Sanz, J.M., 17, 51
Seyfang, G., 194, 195

Sheffield, 60–1
Sik, E., 28
Sinclair, P.R., 5
size of cash-in-hand, *see* magnitude
skills, 71
Slater, D., 7, 24
Smith, J., 54, 57, 68
Smith, R.S., 47
Snodgrass, D.R., 5, 167
social capital
  definitions, 29–30, 35–8
  development of, 191–7
  employment status, influences on,
    79, 80–3
  eradication of, 158–9, 206
  gender and social capital, 98–9,
    100–1, 101–3
  geography and social capital,
    119–20, 123–9
Social Charter, 151
  credit, 187–8
  dividend, 187–8
  networks, 27, 70–1
  polarisation of households, 170–3
  protection, 150–3
  relations, *see* character of
  wage, 187–8
Social Security Administration (Fraud)
    Act 1997, 145
social security fraud, *see* benefit fraud
Sole, C., 18
Soto, de, H., 169
Southampton, 60–1
South East Asia, 151
South Wales, 96
South-west England, 31
Spain
  Geography, 114
  jobs deficit, 148, 149
  resistance to formalisation, 154
  social polarisation, 172
  unemployed and cash-in-hand,
    20, 68
St. Blazey, 60
St. Mary's, 60
Stack, R., 124
Standard Industrial Classification
    (SIC) index, 5
Stauffer, B., 19, 67
Stoll, M.A., 124

store cards, 47
Street UK, 185–6
sub–contracting, 42
suppliers' motives
  nature, 28, 30–5, 201–2
  employment status variations,
    77–80
  gender variations, 96–9
  geographical variations, 121–3
survey methods, 41–62
sweatshops, 1
Sweden, 51, 108, 149, 151
Switzerland, 53

Tabak, F., 11, 183, 205
Tanzi, V., 46, 48, 49, 51
Tate, N., 61
tax credits, 188–9
Taxes Management Act 1970, 142
tax evasion, 2, 71, 135–8, 142–3, 179
third sector, 36–7
Thomas, A., 189
Thrift, N., 15, 24, 47, 102, 178, 199
Tievant, S., 19, 67, 110
time banks, 194–5
Tonkiss, F., 7, 24
Toy, D., 134
trade unions, 180
Travers, A., 27, 154
Trickey, H., 138
Trundle, J.M., 47
trust, *see* social capital

underground sector, definition, 2–7,
    16, 65
United Kingdom
  attitudes toward fraud, 71–2
  benefit fraud, 137
  employment status and cash-in-
    hand, 67
  income disparities, 170
  jobs deficit, 149
  magnitude of cash-in-hand, 49, 52,
    108
  measuring, 49, 54, 56
  policy approach, 142–7
  social polarisation, 172
  tax fraud, 137
unemployed and cash-in-hand, 20,
    68, 69

USA
   attitudes toward fraud, 157
   benefit fraud, 137
   Detroit, 50
   income disparities, 170
   measurements, 48, 50, 52, 54, 108
   Pennsylvania, 27, 68–9
   San Francisco, 68
   social polarisation, 172
   tax fraud, 137

Vaiou, D., 20, 68, 110, 114
Vaknin, S., 180
Van Den Broek, A., 124
Van Eck, R., 8, 20, 55, 67, 74, 76
Van Parijis, P., 187
very small enterprises, 44–5
Vidal, A., 79
Vinay, P., 20, 84, 86, 94, 154
voluntary sector, 36–7

Waldinger, R., 18, 21, 73, 114
Wales, 96

Wallace, C., 57, 157
wallpapering, 58, 90
Walsall, 50
Warde, A., 20, 54, 55, 68, 84
Warren, M.R., 20, 21, 68, 154, 174
Weck, H., 53, 54
welfare state, critique of, 150–3
Wenig, A., 72, 135
Wigston, 60
Wilkinson, F., 166
Wilmott, P., 35, 36, 38, 124
window cleaners, 185
Wolkowitz, C., 55
Woods, R., 46, 171
Woodward, R., 72
work: definition of, 6
working citizen, 189

Ybarra, J-A., 16, 26, 140
Young, M., 35, 36, 38, 124

Zelizer, V.A., 15, 23, 34, 178, 199
Zhuhong, L., 129, 134, 135, 158